The American Historical Association

JAMES KENT

A Study in Conservatism

1763-1847

BY

John Theodore Horton
UNIVERSITY OF BUFFALO

THE LAWBOOK EXCHANGE, LTD.
UNION, NEW JERSEY
2000

ISBN-13: 978-1-58477-069-5
ISBN-10: 1-58477-069-4

Second printing 2007

The Lawbook Exchange, Ltd.
33 Terminal Avenue
Clark, New Jersey 07066-1321

Please see our website for a selection of our other publications and fine facsimile reprints of classic works of legal history:
www.lawbookexchange.com

Library of Congress Cataloging-in-Publication Data

Horton, John Theodore.
James Kent : a study in conservatism, 1763-1847 / by John Theodore Horton.
p. cm.
Originally published: New York : D. Appleton-Century Co., c1939.
Includes bibliographical references and index.
ISBN 1-58477-069-4 (cloth : alk. paper)
1. Kent, James, 1763-1847. 2. Lawyers—United States—Biography. 3. Jurisprudence—United States—History. I. Title.

KF368. K4 H6 2000
340.092—dc21
[B] 99-056927

Printed in the United States of America on acid-free paper

JAMES KENT

A STUDY IN CONSERVATISM

James Kent

From an engraving of the portrait by Rembrandt Peale, Law Library of the Eighth Judicial District of New York. Courtesy of George D. Crofts

The American Historical Association

JAMES KENT

A Study in Conservatism

1763-1847

BY

John Theodore Horton
UNIVERSITY OF BUFFALO

D. APPLETON–CENTURY COMPANY
INCORPORATED
New York *London*

This volume is published from a fund contributed to The American Historical Association by The Carnegie Corporation of New York

A contribution from the American Council of Learned Societies has assisted in the publication of this volume.

PRINTED IN THE UNITED STATES OF AMERICA

TO

EVELYN BLANCHE

PRAETEREA animadvertant iuvenes, quatenus leges Anglicanae adoptive inter nos, sive usu diuturno et consuetudine sive senatus nostralium consultis, stabilitate, statuum foederatorum leges iniverunt. Quinetiam iuris Anglicani communis atque statuti grandia nobilissimaque principia, et ratiocinia iudicum reverendorum doctissima perspicere utile foret; narratas item causas sive actiones tum candide litigatas tum iustissime in tribunalibus dijudicatas Westmonasteriensibus; —Hac ratione studiorum cognitio legum nostrarum nunc elicienda est; donec postea genius magnus quidam juralis extiterit, quidam sive *Bractonus,* sive *Fleta, Baconus, Cokeus Seldenusve* e nobismet exoriturus sit, qui mentis *Trebonianae* acumine doctissimo, acerrimique ingenii vi et cognitionis vastissimae autoritate, omnia digestis perstrinxerit; extiteruntque ii sive i.' consulti, sive iudices caeterive eruditi iuris atque periti, qui narratas actiones forenses dictaque iudicia, libris commentariisve mandata tradiderint.

EZRA STILES *Oratio Inauguralis*
Yale College, July 8, 1778

Acknowledgment

THE author of the following biography of James Kent owes much to many persons for aid and counsel generously given; and among the first, to his mother, Jeanette Hatch Horton, who made possible his residence at Harvard University where this work was undertaken as a doctoral dissertation.

Of the scholars in that University, the author is especially indebted to Professor Frederick Merk and Professor Henry Hart for their constructive criticism. He is obliged also to scholars elsewhere, particularly to President Dixon Ryan Fox who has graciously interested himself in this enterprise and made many helpful suggestions concerning it. The shrewd comments of his colleague, Professor Wilfred B. Kerr, the author acknowledges with an equal gratitude. To none, however, in a greater variety of ways, is he more beholden than to the head of the Department of History and Government at the University of Buffalo, Professor Julius W. Pratt, whose interest in this venture has been unflagging, whose help in setting it forward decisive. His criticism, and that of the scholars above named, have born fruit in a work which, how far soever short of that finished scholarship which is their standard, yet errs from it less notoriously than it would otherwise have done.

There are others whose assistance it is also a pleasure to acknowledge. Mr. Wallace P. Rusterholtz has obligingly discharged the tiresome task of reading proof. In that same task the author's wife has had a part. She has, moreover, heard these pages read and read again and has made many constructive, if not always favorable observations upon them.

Not less to institutions than to individuals does the writer find himself in debt. In Cambridge, the Harvard College

Library has proved indispensable; in Buffalo, the Law Library of the Eighth Judicial District; and in the same city, the Public Library, the Lockwood and the Grosvenor Libraries have been most useful. It is with pleasure that he takes this opportunity to express his appreciation of them all and of their friendly cooperation.

For most of his materials, however, the author is obliged to institutions elsewhere. The liberal use, both in study and in publication, which he has been permitted to make of their resources prompts him to extend his hearty thanks to the American Antiquarian Society, the Massachusetts Historical Society, the Yale University Library, the Library of the Harvard Law School, the New York Public Library, and above all, to the Division of Manuscripts of the Library of Congress where reposes the principal collection of the papers of James Kent. In all these places, the writer has met with an unfailing courtesy which renders the memory of his researches most agreeable.

Furthermore, he wishes to thank Dodd, Mead and Company for permission for the extended quotation from Professor Allan Nevins's edition of the diary of Philip Hone; he thanks the Marshall Jones Company for permission to quote at some length from Professor Roscoe Pound's *The Spirit of the Common Law;* and he acknowledges the courtesy of Dr. Alexander C. Flick, editor of *New York History,* in permitting him to make the freest use of the article, "The Western Eyres of Judge Kent," which appeared in that journal in the issue of April, 1937.

Finally, he cannot close his accounts without expressing his gratitude to the American Historical Association in general, and in particular to Professor John D. Hicks, Chairman of that body's Committee on the Carnegie Revolving Fund for Publications. It is through the largess of that Committee that this study of James Kent now appears in print.

Table of Contents

JAMES KENT

A STUDY IN CONSERVATISM

I

On Mount Parnassus

Haec studia adolescentiam alunt. . .

* * *

IN HIS parish at Portsmouth in New Hampshire, the Reverend Ezra Stiles reflected upon his call to the Presidency of Yale College. He found it hard to make up his mind. The students, thought he, would probably be like "wild fire not easily controlled and governed"; [1] the college itself he knew to be run down. There was no gainsaying that; nor was there much comfort in the reflection that other colleges were no better off. It was a bad time for learning. Stiles said so frankly, and summed it all up in terse Latin—*Toga cedit armis.*[2] It was a bad time for college presidents. Stiles implied that too, if he did not say it; but he hinted that it mattered little, since even good times were bad for them. "At best," he said, "the diadem of a president is a crown of thorns." [3] Nevertheless, he decided to accept the crown and face his martyrdom like a Christian.

The authorities at New Haven applauded his resolution and prepared to install him with pomp. They appointed a July day in 1778 for the ceremonies which, in spite of war, went off to their satisfaction.[4] A procession formed and moved across the Yard, a hundred and sixteen undergraduates leading the way two by two, followed by ten young Bachelors of Arts.

[1] Ezra Stiles, *Literary Diary,* II, 209.
[2] *Ibid.,* II, 213–214, 226.
[3] *Ibid.,* II, 209.
[4] *Ibid.,* II, 282.

Then came the beadle and the butler walking together. A decent space, and the president-elect himself appeared in company with a dignitary of the Council of Connecticut. The corporation, and the two professors and four tutors who composed the faculty, came next, with Masters of Arts and dignified divines closing the procession as the chapel doors swung to.

Within, the proceedings were all that learning and eloquence could make them. Stiles was the orator of the day as the occasion demanded. Speaking in Latin, he told his hearers what he thought they should know if they wished to be considered educated men. They should understand of course how to speak and how to write good English, and to that end he proposed to keep up the practice of public debates and declamations.[5] He wanted the students trained to talk readily of many things, though it was not mere glibness that he was after, for he believed that ease of utterance should spring from a mind well-stocked with ideas.[6]

Whence were these to come? The speaker pointed to humane studies as the proper source, and since such studies had been handed down chiefly in Greek or Latin, he argued the necessity of knowing those tongues.[7] Going further, he held that they ought to be known, even if translators made classical thought accessible in English. The reason for this belief was literary. As Stiles expressed it, there are beauties in the speech of Homer and of Vergil which fade in translation. It is from the well, said he, that we drink the purest water—*purius e fonte bibuntur aquae.*[8] But he did not hold up the ancient authors merely as models of literary form. The matter that they dealt with

[5] Ezra Stiles, *Oratio Inauguralis,* 4. He praises the ability *super quavis re ex tempore liberrimeque dicendi, non de scripto recitato tantum, verum de mente idearum plena.*

[6] *Loc. cit.*

[7] *Ibid.,* 4–5.

[8] *Ibid.,* 6. Graecae utique Latinae amoenitates et idiomatum venustates, in linguis tralatitiis omnino amitterentur. . . . Vergilii . . . Homeri flores latebunt, nisi suis linguis ii legerentur.

was more important than that, however beautiful the form might be. Those authors drew the youthful mind to contemplate heroic things, great deeds and great events, their causes and their meaning; they explained the policies of empires and republics and expounded the principles on which the most splendid states had been fashioned.[9] Thus Stiles seemed to discern values in the classical heritage that answered the needs of his own country and his own time. Inducted into office while war was being waged for independence, he had sworn allegiance not to a king but to a commonwealth. He saw a new nation in the making. He believed that the young men before him, the future leaders of that nation, could learn much from the wisdom of antiquity.

It was not only in the humanities, however, that the new president perceived values. His intellectual interests were varied. He set store by the sciences and urged his hearers to cultivate them.[10] From the sciences he went on to metaphysics and theology whence he proceeded to a discussion of the learned callings. A minister himself, he by no means belittled the attainments requisite for the lawyer or the physician. What he said of legal studies shows well enough how broad were his views concerning professional education in general.

He commended to students of law the study, not of rules and tricks, but of jurisprudence. "Let these youths," he said, "observe how far the English law, whether by custom or by acts of our legislatures, has been embodied in that of America. Students would find it useful also," he continued, "to examine the great principles of the English law, both common and statute, for their own worth; they would find it beneficial to follow the closely reasoned opinions of the English judges by

[9] Ezra Stiles, *Oratio Inauguralis*, 4–5. . . . clarissimarum rerum gestarum rationes, eventuumque causas, rerum publicarum et imperiorum consilia, politiarumque principia splendidissimarum.

[10] *Ibid.*, 10–14.

reading the reports of the cases decided in Westminster Hall."[11] Though no longer a subject of King George, Stiles did not hesitate to express admiration for his judges and his courts. He called the judges worshipful; the cases before them he declared were as honestly tried as they were justly decided. But excellent though the laws of England were, the student should be content neither with study of them alone nor with that of the earlier systems out of which they grew. He should go beyond the feudal customs, beyond the dooms of the Saxon kings, and not rest satisfied until he should have made himself familiar with the Roman jurisprudence itself.[12] From such a course of studies the knowledge of our own legal system ought now to be drawn, said the orator; and he prophesied that if such a course was pursued, a native genius would arise in our midst, an American Bracton, Coke or Selden who would shape and refine American law and expound it in a learned commentary.[13]

Stiles did not know how true a prophecy he spoke; much less that he spoke it in the hearing of the youth by whom it was to be fulfilled. But in his audience that midsummer morning was a lad not yet fifteen whose name, enrolled among those

[11] Ezra Stiles, *Oratio Inauguralis, 25 et seq.* Praeterea animadvertant iuvenes, quatenus leges Anglicanae adoptive inter nos, sive usu diuturno et consuetudine sive senatus nostralium consultis, stabilitate, statuum foederatorum leges iniverunt. Quinetiam iuris Anglicani communis atque statuti grandia nobilissimaque principia, et ratiocinia iudicum reverendorum doctissima perspicere utile foret; narratas item causas sive actiones tum candide litigatas tum iustissime in tribunalibus dijudicatas Westmonasteriensibus. . . .

[12] *Ibid.*, 25–28.

[13] *Loc. cit.* Hac ratione studiorum cognitio legum nostrarum nunc elicienda est; donec postea genius magnus quidam juralis extiterit, quidam sive Bractonus, sive Fleta, Baconus, Cokeus Seldenusve e nobis exoriturus sit, qui mentis Trebonianae acumine doctissimo, acerrimique ingenii vi et cognitionis vastissimae auctoritate, omnia digestis perstrinxerit; extiteruntque ii sive j.' consulti, sive iudices caeterive eruditi iuris atque periti, qui narratas actiones forenses dictaque iudicia, libris commentariisve mandata tradiderint.

of the other freshmen, appeared in Latinized form as *Jacobus* Kent.[14]

* * *

Though born in the province of New York, James Kent had come to Yale with the advantage of belonging to a good Connecticut family already known to the college. His grandfather, Elisha Kent, had been graduated there in 1729, a young man apparently of common birth, as his name had stood next to the lowest on the roll of his class.[15] Yet he must have been a young man of promise, for he married Abigail Moss, daughter of the Reverend Joseph Moss of Derby, a personage of acknowledged position. He was a trustee of the college and was said by Governor Saltonstall to be the fittest man in Connecticut to be head of the colony. A divine who often fell asleep during the psalms, the Reverend Mr. Moss had yet a spark of genius hidden away within his squat and somewhat corpulent body. When he preached it was with the power of Elijah. He was very learned, but not austere. At least he tempered his theology with humor, wooing his third wife from his very pulpit with a persuasive turn of the text: "Then he put out his hand, and took her, and pulled her in unto him into the ark."[16]

If Elisha Kent owed something of his advancement to the family he married into, he had sufficient ability to become a man of mark in his own right. He was ordained a Presbyterian minister, played an active part in the Great Awakening,[17]

[14] Ezra Stiles, *Literary Diary,* II, 286; James Kent *Address Delivered at New Haven before the Phi Beta Kappa Society,* September 13, 1831, 40.

[15] *Catalogue of the Officers and Graduates of Yale University 1701–1898,* 36; *New York Genealogical and Biographical Record,* IV, 83 *et seq.*

[16] *Genesis,* VIII, 9. For the sketch of Moss, Ezra Stiles, *Literary Diary,* II, 502–503.

[17] He was a "New Light." Franklin B. Dexter, *Biographical Sketches of Graduates of Yale College,* I, 384–385.

made a reputation for himself as a preacher, and established such a devoted following that when, after a controversy with the churches of Connecticut, he removed into New York, many of his flock went with him [18] and settled near him in Dutchess County in a parish that was called Kent's parish in his honor.[19] He helped organize the Dutchess Presbytery and remained one of its conspicuous figures throughout the rest of his life.[20] A dominie who was vigilant but genial, Elisha Kent held patriarchal sway over the valley of the upper Croton where he lived to a good age and died jesting. As he lay seemingly unconscious, one of his deacons, a homely man, approached him softly.

"Do you know me?" asked the deacon.

"Ah, yes, deacon," answered the dominie, "anyone who ever saw you, would know you again." [21]

Of the seven children of Elisha Kent and Abigail his wife, the eldest received the name of his maternal grandfather and went in due time to be educated at the college where that grandfather had once been a trustee. Graduated in 1752, with his name near the head of his class, close to the patrician name of Saltonstall,[22] Moss Kent ranked socially at Yale much higher than had his father; but upon leaving, he chose a profession hitherto deemed less distinguished socially than his. He decided to become a lawyer rather than a clergyman.

The choice was a sign of the changes that were occurring in the colonies. People were heeding religion less, their worldly business more. Trade was increasing and was bringing the

[18] E. H. Gillett, *History of the Presbyterian Church in U.S.A.*, I, 148.

[19] "Notes on the Life of James Kent," *Kent Papers*, Vol. XI.

[20] E. H. Gillett, *op. cit.*, I, 146–147; W. M. Engles, *Records of the Presbyterian Church in U.S.A.*, 351.

[21] "Notes on the Life of James Kent," *Kent Papers*, Vol. XI.

[22] *Catalogue of the Officers and Graduates of Yale University 1701–1898*, 41.

colonies in closer touch with one another and with England, where government showed a growing concern with colonial affairs. The King in Council was insisting that colonial laws should be drawn in nicer conformity to the law of England; [23] colonists found their interest stirring a-new in the subject of the rights of Englishmen. Many things conspired to raise the lawyer in esteem; and though old prejudices against him still survived,[24] many were the promising youths who, like Moss Kent, chose that calling in preference to divinity.

If they came from Yale, the chances were that they already knew something of its possibilities. There President Clap had followed the custom of discussing vocational matters from time to time; [25] and when he talked of the law, he should have been especially instructive. He himself had had practical experience of courts; had once argued and won an important case involving rights of the college. Moss Kent must have heard much about the profession from him and it was that perhaps which decided his preference. At any rate, soon after graduation he began to read for the bar. He was fortunate in having a relative to guide him, doubly fortunate that the relative was Lieutenant-Governor Thomas Fitch,[26] who, even at a later time when professional standards had become much higher, was reputed to have been the most learned lawyer who ever lived in the colony of Connecticut.[27] But it was not only in Connecticut and under Fitch that Moss Kent prepared himself for the bar. He returned in time to the province of New

[23] Elmer B. Russell, *Review of American Colonial Legislation by King in Council*, 205. See also Carroll T. Bond, *Proceedings of the Maryland Court of Appeals, 1695–1729*, Foreword and Introduction, xxi–xxix.

[24] Charles Warren, *History of the Harvard Law School*, I, 3, 5–6.

[25] Thomas Clap, *Annals or History of Yale College*, appendix, 80.

[26] Franklin B. Dexter, *Biographical Sketches of the Graduates of Yale College*, II, 288.

[27] *Fitch Papers*, I, 12 (Elisha Kent had married as his second wife Fitch's sister).

York, a place rather more congenial to the tradition of Coke-Littleton,[28] continued his reading for a season at Poughkeepsie where in June, 1755, he was admitted to practice.[29]

A young man of twenty-two, he had every reason to expect a prosperous career. He was well born and well trained and he had influential connections. Moreover, his prospects, good as they were, he presently bettered through a desirable marriage. At Norwalk in Connecticut, where he had studied under Governor Fitch, lived Hannah, daughter of the physician Uriah Rogers, a man of substance; and in the late autumn of 1760, Moss Kent took her to wife.[30] The young pair settled in Kent's parish on the upper Croton in the precinct of Fredericksburgh; and there upon the thirty-first of July, 1763, James Kent, their eldest son was born.[31]

The son of a lawyer, the grandson of a divine and of a physician, the child was the scion of a family in which learning and cultivation had long been prized. It would have been strange if he too had not been destined for a liberal profession; stranger still if he had not been intended to prepare for it through discipline in the liberal arts at Yale.

* * *

Lads who aimed to go thither were expected to know some Latin, less Greek and at least the elements of arithmetic. James Kent, on turning fourteen, was to find himself easily equal to the standard required.[32]

His education began in a humble way at a Dame School

[28] *Documents Relating to the Colonial History of New York,* VIII, 444–445. See also *History of the State of New York* (A. Flick, editor), III, 40.

[29] Franklin B. Dexter, *loc. cit.* "Notes on the Life of James Kent," *Kent Papers,* Vol. XI.

[30] November 27, 1760.

[31] "Notes on Kent's Early Life," *Kent Papers,* Vol. XI. That part of Dutchess County which contained Fredericksburgh was set off as Putman County in 1812.

[32] *Collegii Yalensis Statuta,* Title i, Section 1.

kept by a shoemaker's wife living not far from the house of Dominie Kent.[33] From her the boy learned the alphabet and enough of spelling to piece out for his delighted mother the sentence, "Hold fast in the Lord." [34] At five he went to his maternal grandfather's in Norwalk in order to attend a school there run by two worthy Scots.[35] The old physician, rather more than the schoolmasters themselves, was inclined to be dour. He prided himself upon the religious quiet of his household and he had no mind to see it broken by the antics of a boy. Indeed, he tried to rule his grandson so strictly that holidays came as a welcome respite to them both.[36] The youngster then made off as quickly as he could to his father's farm in Fredericksburgh.[37]

That farm was a pleasant place to spend vacations. A small sister was there,[38] and a small brother [39] with whom it was sport on a rainy day to lie in wait beneath the bed for a certain familiar mouse to come creeping from its hole.[40] Fair weather, and the nearby river invited to keener sport, whether to fish or to swim.[41] Sorrows to be sure visited even that peaceful countryside and sometimes brought vacations unexpectedly. One winter's Sabbath as Uriah Rogers led his grandson to the meeting house, a rider galloped up to say that Hannah Kent lay dying; and her eldest child came home only to see her breathe her last.[42] In spite of the loss, Fredericksburgh continued to

[33] James Kent, "Reminiscences," *Kent Papers,* Vol. XI.

[34] William Kent, *Memoirs and Letters of James Kent,* 7.

[35] Gordon and Galpin by name. See James Kent, "Reminiscences," *loc. cit.*

[36] William Kent, *op. cit.,* 8.

[37] *Loc. cit.*

[38] Hannah Kent, born October 10, 1768.

[39] Moss Kent, Jr., born April 3, 1766. See *New York Genealogical and Biographical Record,* IV, 83 *et seq.*

[40] William S. Pelletreau, "Birth Place of Chancellor Kent," *Magazine of American History,* XVII, 245–246.

[41] James Kent to Daniel Webster, Dec. 21, 1842, *Kent Papers,* Vol. X.

[42] James Kent, "Reminiscences," *Kent Papers,* Vol. XI.

be an alluring place. Besides his brother Moss and his sister, dark-eyed and sprightly Hannah, James Kent had a troop of cousins for companions.[43] Moss Kent the elder was an indulgent father,[44] his household kindly and secure, and in its qualities the whole valley seemed to share, somewhat secluded from the world and inhabited by friendly neighbors many of whom were kin. From the great oaken house where he dwelt, the patriarchal parson, Elisha Kent, presided over this goodly circle and when he rose to preach on Sabbath mornings he could rejoice in a congregation composed in no small part of his children and his children's children. Of them all it was the schoolboy home on holiday who was to bring most honor to the old man's name.

Meanwhile vacations came and went; schooling continued. From the Scottish masters in Norwalk the lad betook himself in the summer of 1772 to a prim little Englishman at Pawling,[45] there to make his bow to Corderius [46] and to prepare for the Reverend Ebenezer Baldwin's more famous Latin school at Danbury.

In placing his son there, Moss Kent showed sound judgement. Ebenezer Baldwin was not only a scholar, a lover of books, owner of a remarkable library; he was young and high spirited; and with interests not limited to books, he cultivated a fine garden and went forth to swing a skilful scythe at the haymaking in his own meadows.[47] He had too a more than passing interest in the Kents; for Moss Kent, marrying a second

[43] *Loc. cit.* Elisha Kent's daughters had married into well-to-do families in the neighborhood, the Cullens, the Kanes, the Morrisons and the Grants.

[44] James Kent, "Memoranda," *Kent Papers*, Vol. X.

[45] James Kent, "Reminiscences," *ibid.*, Vol. XI. At Pawling, Kent lived with his uncle, John Kane, husband of Elisha Kent's daughter, Sybil.

[46] *Corderii Colloquiorum Centuria Selecta*, a set of Latin dialogues for the beginner. The twentieth edition by John Clarke, Boston, 1770.

[47] William B. Sprague, *Annals of the American Pulpit*, I, 637–640; Franklin B. Dexter, *Biographical Sketches of the Graduates of Yale College*, III, 4.

time, became stepfather of a pretty girl named Polly Hazzard with whom the young minister fell in love.[48] Too vital a person to play the pedant, Baldwin was yet an excellent schoolmaster. He took his boys in hand, drilled them in their paradigms and prose, carried them into Eutropius, Justin, Nepos and Vergil, and all this without exciting anything worse in their minds than fondness for himself and respect for the lore which he taught them. As he had been a tutor in Yale, he understood what was expected of entering freshmen; [49] and he seems somehow to have persuaded his pupils that the tongue of Vergil is not dead but deathless.[50]

That discipleship, profitable though it was and pleasant, was to come to an end sooner than either master or pupils had anticipated. Upon the routine of schoolday sports and classical studies, war and the rumors of war broke in:

> At tuba terribilem sonitum procul aere canoro
> increpuit; sequitur clamor caelumque remugit.

And the wars in Latium, and the exploits of Nepos's heroes were read to the realistic accompaniment of a war at home, loud with the fife, tumultuous with the rattle of musketry, and the roll of drums.[51] Tidings of Lexington and Bunker Hill, the news that independence was declared, report and rumor circulated through the countryside. James Kent calling at the house of Mr. Baldwin saw him spread upon the wall a broad sheet printed with bold and eloquent words that spoke of royal tyrannies and of a freedom to be vindicated with lives, fortunes and with sacred honor.[52]

[48] James Kent to William Kent, March 29, 1847, *Kent Papers,* Vol. XI.

[49] *Quilibet studiosus in sermone suo usitato et quotidiano Lingua Latina utatur sub poena idonea ad arbitrium Praesidis et tutorum constituta. Collegii Yalensis Statuta,* Title iii, Section 10.

[50] James Kent, *Phi Beta Kappa Address, supra cit.,* 31.

[51] James M. Bailey, *History of Danbury,* 60. The town became a military depot.

[52] James Kent, "Reminiscences," *Kent Papers,* Vol. XI.

The young minister was deeply moved by the cause. He preached often upon the theme of liberty. He urged men to enlist. He himself donned uniform and marched away as chaplain to a regiment of militia. Kent saw him as he bade farewell to his flock. He heard from him not long afterward when a letter was read in which the chaplain described how in the night amid a thunderstorm the British had landed on Long Island.[53] Baldwin's career, however, was cut short. He fell ill in camp, and in the autumn of '76 returned home to die, "doomed," as Kent said many years later "to fall prematurely in the flower of his age, and while engaged in his country's service." [54]

He left behind him a disciple who like himself followed with interest the careers of armies. In the spring of 1777 Danbury as a military depot attracted the attention of the British. As the militia sallied forth to dispute the enemy's advance, small Jimmy Kent, followed along, too young to fight but none the less keen to see the fighting. As a coign of vantage he chose a gable end behind a broad chimney, clambered up, perched himself on the ridge pole and waited for the action. Across the highway below a barricade of fence rails had been hastily thrown. In discharging a field piece at the obstacle, the British struck the sheltering chimney instead, whereupon the boy, unhurt but scared, got down as nimbly as he could and scampered away.[55] In fact, he left Danbury and sought safety at his father's side.

He had not far to go, for Moss Kent was staying at Phillipi only about eight miles distant, having removed from Fredericksburgh for good.[56] That place had greatly changed. The

[53] James Kent, *Phi Beta Kappa Address*, 32 *et seq.*

[54] *Loc. cit.*

[55] William Kent, *Memoirs and Letters of James Kent*, 4–5.

[56] In 1774 Moss Kent removed to Compo, where he chiefly resided for many years, but in 1776–1777 he was staying at Phillipi for better security from the British. See "Notes on Kent's Early Life," *Kent Papers*, Vol. XI.

venerable Elisha Kent was dead and lay buried hard by the meeting house where he had been wont to preach.[57] Nor had he died too soon. The vale of Croton was no longer secure; his descendants no longer prosperous. Moss Kent had sold his farm for currency of which the dwindling value left him little to show for it.[58] In his new home in Connecticut further losses harassed him. His legal practice ceased and he suffered a good deal from British raids.[59] Meanwhile his kinsfolk in Dutchess were having their own difficulties. Somewhat Tory in their leanings,[60] they were hard pressed in those troublous times. The Revolution ruined and dispersed them all.[61]

These changes affected James Kent but little. His father's farm at Compo in Connecticut had attractions that even Fredericksburgh had lacked; and holidays were as gay as ever. The boy rode horseback, went fishing and swimming in the Sound, and once he sailed to New York City on a sloop.[62] Studies went on apace, and during a long vacation, surveying and navigation were added to the list.[63] Whatever adversities had befallen Moss Kent, he was still resolved upon continuing the education of his son.

The preliminary stage of that process was almost at an end. At Danbury, Stratfield and Newton tutors were found to add the final touches to the preparation which Ebenezer Baldwin had begun.[64] One day in September, 1777, James Kent, a

[57] James Kent, *Journal*, July 29, 1827.

[58] "Memoranda," *Kent Papers*, Vol. III.

[59] *Loc. cit.*

[60] One of Moss Kent's sisters was the wife of Captain Alexander Grant who was killed on the British side at Fort Montgomery. One of his nephews, Charles Kane, went within the British lines.

[61] James Kent to John C. Van Rensselaer, June 1, 1846. *Magazine of American History*, XVII, 247–250.

[62] James Kent, "Reminiscences," *Kent Papers*, Vol. XI; see also reminiscent entries in his journals, 1825 through 1835, *passim*.

[63] James Kent, "Reminiscences," *Kent Papers*, Vol. XI.

[64] *Loc. cit.*

stripling of fourteen, came home from New Haven jubilant.[65] The learned men there had examined him and found him sufficiently well informed to be enrolled among the *recentes.*

* * *

If by some magic a modern boy could be whisked back to the Yale of the eighteenth century, he would no doubt think himself the victim of a cruel trick. When he had bought a copy of the college statutes,[66] he would be first perplexed on finding them in Latin, then plagued on discovering what they meant. They took for granted that the old Adam was strong in college youths and provided many penalties for indulging him. Should a student climb the roof to ring the bell, he lay himself liable to expulsion. If he impersonated a female in a stage play, he would be publicly reprimanded. If he but took part in such a performance, he would be fined; he would be fined for shooting guns or pistols. Heresies would undo him; an oath, uttered in a fit of youthful indignation, would cause him to be bounced for blasphemy. The statutes assumed that he might be tempted to commit both theft and fornication; they suggested the crimes by forbidding them. They showed little confidence in the young gentlemen's native sense of honor.[67]

There were things to be done as well as left undone. The Bible was to be read diligently, private prayers were to be recited and common prayers attended twice a day.[68] Morning and evening the butler rang the bell for chapel while numerous bells between summoned now to meals and now to studies. For half an hour after breakfast, after dinner for an hour and a half and from the close of evening prayer until nine

[65] *Loc. cit.*
[66] *Collegii Yalensis Statuta,* Title i, 3.
[67] *Ibid.,* Title iv, *de moribus conformandis, passim;* also Title vi, 3.
[68] *Collegii Yalensis Statuta,* Title ii, *de vita pia ac religiosa, passim.*

o'clock, the students had comparative liberty to do as they liked;[69] but thrice a day after the allotted intervals the tutors made tours of inspection to see that every boy was in his place. If absent, he was fined. Even when he was permitted to walk abroad, the eye of authority was on him and he was supposed to wear cap and gown that he might the more readily be spotted. Wherever he happened to be, it behooved him to go circumspectly lest beadle and monitors betray him to the faculty and lay him liable to the ever threatening fines, reprimands or expulsions *prout criminis ratio et gradus postulabant.*

However irksome such restraints may seem to a modern generation, they were favorably regarded in the eighteenth century not only by academicians but also by men of the world. "We went to see the College at New Haven," wrote the Marquis de Barbé-Marbois, "its statutes have been drawn up with wisdom and simplicity."[70]

Of this the students were not appreciative. They treated the chief compiler of the code, President Clap, with base ingratitude. They mimicked him as he prayed in chapel; and once, after he had punished an innocent boy for ringing the chapel bell, they worked off their grudge against him by overturning the presidential privy. They sometimes broke into the cellars of Connecticut Hall for wine; for fowl they would occasionally raid a townsman's hen roost.[71] It is not astonishing that Dr. Stiles should have had misgivings about the presidency. In public he propitiated his charges by calling them "dear

[69] *Ibid.*, Titles iii, 1–2, 4; iv, vi, viii, 1–3.

[70] Eugene P. Chase, *Our Revolutionary Forefathers: Letters of François, Marquis de Barbé-Marbois,* 110.

[71] Franklin B. Dexter, *Student Life at Yale in Early Days, passim.*

For the overturning of the President's privy, see William S. Johnson to Samuel Johnson, March 20, 1755, Herbert and Carol Schneider, *Samuel Johnson, His Career and Writings,* I, 214.

Sons of the Muses"; in private they were "a bundle of wild fire." It was true, as he said, that they were not always easy to control.

That young Kent would increase Stiles's anxiety was unlikely; for in spite of a good supply of animal spirits, the lad was not intractable.[72] Moreover in the fall of 1777 when he became a freshman, the authorities could hardly have tried his sufferance very far. The college had been thrown into confusion through the war and had even deserted New Haven temporarily to seek security inland where an effort was being made to maintain it scattered among several towns.[73] Discipline hardly possible in ordinary times was out of the question now. It bothered Kent but little if at all, nor did study trouble him much more. His class in Glastonbury which he had joined only in November [74] did little else than review familiar things. The January vacation came on apace. The pretense of keeping college in any form was given up, and the students were dismissed not to be called together again until the following June with the arrival of the new president.[75] So passed the better part of the freshman year. The experience had been agreeable enough, if not much different from that in Ebenezer Baldwin's school in Danbury. The studies were not difficult; and when they were over, there were friends of the Danbury days, like Simeon Baldwin, to help while away the idle hours.[76] *Recentes* more obstreperous by far than Jimmy Kent might well have looked forward

[72] Simeon Baldwin to William Kent, February 1, 1848, *Kent Papers*, Vol. XI.

[73] Since March, 1777, classes had been kept up at Wethersfield, Farmington and Glastonbury. Ezra Stiles, *Literary Diary*, II, 213.

[74] Kent had gone to New Haven for his examination in September. Between then and November he had been at home.

[75] Simeon Baldwin to William Kent, February 1, 1848, *Kent Papers*, Vol. XI.

[76] *Loc. cit.*

eagerly to what was yet to come. Yale was in fact to captivate the boy and fulfil all his anticipations.[77]

It was a great privilege to be a student there, for of all the colleges in America, Yale, despite her adversities, was the largest and the most fortunate—at least so believed the new president whose carriage came rumbling into New Haven about noon of an auspicious summer day in 1778.[78] The appearance of Dr. Stiles was the signal for the students to return. The Yard began to stir with life as they came trooping in, perhaps six score in all, mostly lads in homespun, but with here and there a beau conspicuous in finer clothes, a ruffled shirt and white silk stockings.[79] The rattle of plate and pewter was heard as the steward set up commons again. Connecticut Hall bustled with renewed activity while from one of its upper windows Kent with his roommate looked down upon the hurrying to and fro and began, as he said, to feel the charm of college life [80] although something like the customary regulations were about to be restored. Classes were assigned to their tutors; the bell summoned to prayers and the president-elect stood forth to be seen by his college congregation. Nor had he as yet remarked any sign of riot or insubordination. Instead, he noted in his diary: "All in town viz. 112 scholars undergraduates were at prayers last night." True, the young gentlemen asked for cannon and illumination in the evening after the inaugural ceremonies but from this they were easily dissuaded, and "all was peace and tranquillity, and evening prayers as usual." [81]

And peace prevailed outside the walls as well as within. For

[77] William Kent to E. C. Herrick, September 12, 1849, *Herrick Papers.*

[78] Ezra Stiles, *Literary Diary,* II, 273.

[79] James Kent, Notes on His Classmates, a detached MS., Sterling Library.

[80] James Kent, "Reminiscences," *Kent Papers,* Vol. XI.

[81] Ezra Stiles, *op. cit.,* II, 282.

the time being the alarms of war were distant and subdued, and the president congratulated the college upon the fact: "*Gratulor vobis, audd. haec otia academica 'nostra; Deus nobis haec otia fecit.' Gratulor vobis restauratas vel in saevissimis hisce belli temporibus renovatasque solemnitates coenobii nostri litterarias.*" The president prayed that war would not again disturb the college: "*Faxit Deus O.M. ut tranquillitate commoremur diurtuna placida simul et jucunda armorum clangoribus periculisque belli ne amplius turbanda.*" [82] To that prayer his hearers no doubt responded with a loud *amen*.

Be that as it may, Providence responded not at all. Even when the drums and musketry sounded from afar, New Haven was unable to resume for long the traditional routine. Economic disturbances continued to vex the college throughout the remaining years that Kent was there. As the currency depreciated the steward found it increasingly difficult to maintain commons; and the students were dismissed again and again.[83] In the intervals when school kept, Kent was present receiving such remittances as his father could afford always accompanied with advice to make the most of his opportunities and above all to "be ever mindful of the one Thing needful." [84]

The fiscal crisis furnished but a small part of the excitement with which New Haven was pervaded. Couriers to and from General Washington went galloping through the town each day; soldiery both American and French marched in and out; distinguished officers, La Fayette and Steuben among them, came and went, and on the Sound vessels and fleets appeared and faded.[85] Early one morning in the summer of '79 James Kent saw some forty sail standing in toward the haven. A little after sunrise and he espied a detachment of British

[82] Ezra Stiles, *Oratio Inauguralis*, 39.
[83] Ezra Stiles, *Literary Diary*, II, *passim*.
[84] Macgrane Coxe, *Yale Law Journal*, XVII, 323; cf. Luke 10:42, 39.
[85] Ezra Stiles, *op. cit.*, II, 287–290, 370–373, 544.

troops coming ashore.[86] Presently he heard firing. As it came nearer he ran to his room, thrust his clothes into a pillowcase, flung them thus across his shoulder and fled.[87] The next evening he slept beneath his father's roof; but even there he found no security. Moss Kent's farm lay defenseless near the shore, an invitation to raiding parties, and on the third night after his son's return, his house was burnt to ashes by the British.[88] That week of July, 1779, was one of perpetual alarms, excursions and cannonading along the ill defended coast of Connecticut. President Stiles summed up the results in indignant language: ". . . in 7 days from Monday morning 5th to Monday 12th or *in one week* [the British] visited three capital towns on Connecticut sea coast, burned three meeting houses and two Episcopal Churches, 80 or 90 dwellings in Fairfield, 130 in Norwalk and plundered and desolated to an amount of damage rendered in to Governor Trumbull of about one hundred thousand pounds sterling. This," he exclaimed, "is a taste of British clemency." [89]

That summer James Kent long remembered, but not for its calamities alone. He had an adventure which determined his career. It was an adventure not with soldiers or in warfare, but with books, with solid volumes written in sober prose upon the solid subject of the laws of England.[90] The author began with a disarmingly simple definition of law and then proceeded to develop and illustrate it in its relation to the jurisprudence of his country. Law, wrote he, is a rule prescribed by sovereign power establishing rights and prohibiting wrongs. The rights of persons as against the state, as toward one another; the rights of property; the courts and remedies to which resort is

[86] James Kent, *Phi Beta Kappa Address,* note p. 40.

[87] James Kent, Notes on His Classmates. He fled in company with another student, Judson Canfield, July 5, 1779.

[88] James Kent, *Phi Beta Kappa Address,* note p. 40.

[89] Ezra Stiles, *Literary Diary,* II, 359.

[90] Sir William Blackstone, *Commentaries on the Laws of England.*

had when wrong is done and those rights violated; the rights of the state against the person and the state's own remedies for wrongs against itself—such was the system which unfolding before the eyes of young James Kent gave meaning and harmony to the miscellaneous array of titles, estates, chattels real and chattels personal, crimes, liberties, forms of action, pleas, rejoinders, sur-rejoinders, and rebuttals, and all the other scraps and lumber of the English law. All was bound together by the ingenious author into an imposing and coherent fabric; and it was all expressed in language lucid, urbane and sometimes eloquent. Through the summer months the boy read on in fascination, and ere New Haven grew composed again and college sessions were resumed, he had chosen his career. He had resolved to become a lawyer.[91] Fortified in that resolution he returned to Yale as soon as possible to finish his classical studies. Such a course the genius of Blackstone may have well approved. As Blackstone himself bore witness, the compatibility of law with letters is complete and striking.

But the *Commentaries,* howsoever suitable for vacation reading, formed no part of the curriculum which the academic authorities intended the boys of Yale to finish for the Bachelor's degree. Of that curriculum the object was not professional skill, but rather a liberal education, a laudable object, though whether attained by following the methods then in use Kent himself in later years had misgivings. It was not that he resented the emphasis placed upon classical studies. Of these he was to remain a staunch defender always.[92] Rather it was that in his mature years he looked back upon the eighteenth century standards of undergraduate scholarship as contemptible, and his own acquisitions of knowledge at the time

[91] James Kent to Thomas Washington, October 6, 1828, *Kent Papers,* Vol. V.

[92] James Kent, *Phi Beta Kappa Address, passim.*

as few and paltry.[93] Nor, except in his extra-curricular encounter with Blackstone, does he appear to have experienced that stimulating sense of intellectual adventure which is said to be the scholar's *summum bonum.* At the same time, it may well be noted that when a boy of sixteen can become excited over a monumental treatise upon law, the fact is by no means a damaging commentary upon the intellectual training that he has received.

That training proceeded almost entirely in the traditional manner. The autumn of 1779 found Kent an upper classman, ready to pass on from geometry and algebra to trigonometry. He had gained some knowledge of geography; understood grammar, was supposed to understand rhetoric and logic, and had cleared the way for the pursuit of philosophy. Latin and Greek he continued without interruption, though the Greek was still only the Greek of the Gospels, and the Latin that of the *de Oratore,* with now and then an ode of Horace. As a junior, Kent remained under the tutelage of a meek little man named Atwater, of whose meekness, however, he seems not to have been disposed to take advantage. He went through the routine without complaining; and as a senior came at last for metaphysics and ethics, for Locke and Montesquieu, to sit at the feet of President Stiles,[94] who as no other teacher, except Ebenezer Baldwin, won the boy's liking and respect.

Thus happily enough, James Kent pressed onward toward his graduation. Slender though his stock of knowledge was to seem when compared to the learning of his riper years, he was yet accounted one of the best scholars in his class. A chapter of the Phi Beta Kappa Society was established at Yale in 1779

[93] James Kent to Thomas Washington, October 6, 1828, *Kent Papers,* Vol. V.

[94] The tutor conducted the students through to their junior year. For the curriculum, Ezra Stiles, *Literary Diary,* II, 387 *et seq.*

and Kent became a member two years later.[95] At the ceremonies attending the midsummer examination of the seniors, it was Kent who delivered, at the president's behest, the Cliosophic Oration; [96] while in the commencement exercises, planned for early September, he was appointed to participate, not only as a candidate for the degree, but as one of the speakers in the disputations.[97] He had evidently overcome by now his former embarrassment at speaking in public. He was ready to step forth upon the stage and try his skill as an orator.

For that accomplishment in self mastery he was indebted in no small part to the goodly fellowship society of Linonia. He had not been long in college, when Jonathan Brace about to be elected chancellor of the fraternity, plucked him by the sleeve and invited him to become a member; [98] and at a meeting held in Brace's room he was formally initiated.[99] The novice was not slow in coming forward. The next meeting took place at Glastonbury, "at the school-house on the green"; [100] and there Kent made his debut, appearing with his friend John Noyes in a dialogue.[101] Three weeks later he delivered a speech,[102] and in January, 1778, just before the long vacation, he appeared again.[103] Important occasions were these for a boy ambitious for a reputation and they were prepared for with great pains, and not without discouragement and tears.[104] It is possible that these early efforts disturbed the gravity of the brethren, for Jimmy Kent was prone to grow excited and to talk too fast, and more than once his audience

[95] *Phi Beta Kappa General Catalogue 1776–1922*, 787.
[96] Ezra Stiles, *op. cit.*, 540.
[97] *Loc. cit.*
[98] James Kent, Notes on His Classmates.
[99] *Records of the Linonia Society*, November 26, 1777.
[100] *Ibid.*, December 3, 1777.
[101] *Ibid.*, December 3, 1777.
[102] *Ibid.*, December 24, 1777.
[103] *Ibid.*, January 7, 1778.
[104] Simeon Baldwin to William Kent, February 1, 1848, *Kent Papers*, Vol. XI.

were at a loss to understand him.[105] As was their wont, they gave him criticism and advice.[106] Kent's friend Baldwin listened to the rehearsal of his speeches; [107] and in time his manner began to improve. The society liked him well; chose him scribe,[108] then chancellor,[109] and at their anniversary celebration in the spring of 1781, assigned him the role of Alonzo in "The agreeable tragedy" of *Ximena* which they enacted in spite of the college statutes, and that with credit and applause.[110]

The good times which the Linonia brotherhood afforded were among the brightest attractions of college life. Two such societies existed in Yale and for several years they had divided the loyalties of almost the whole student body.[111] Literary clubs they were, taking themselves very seriously to be sure, vilifying each other with great animation. Their aims were indistinguishable. Both had acquired libraries. Both, in defiance of the code, indulged in stage plays and both rejoiced in anniversary feasts and celebrations.

The literary pastures in which it was the privilege of a Linonian to browse offered a varied pabulum of the satirical and sentimental, the sacred and profane. There were the *Letters* of Chesterfield and the sermons of divines. There were *Tom Jones* and *Humphrey Clinker* and there was also Edwards on the Will. Shakespeare had not been overlooked, nor Milton; and Hudibras was there to keep the latter company. Had a member's composition been harshly criticized in meeting, he might betake himself to the *Spectator* to see what Addison could do to chasten his style; a style too pedestrian could

105 *Loc. cit.*

106 *Records of the Linonia Society, passim.*

107 Simeon Baldwin to William Kent, *supra cit.*

108 *Records of the Linonia Society:* Several of the entries are in Kent's hand as scribe.

109 *Ibid.*, February 8, 1781.

110 *Ibid.*, March 30, 1781.

111 Ezra Stiles, *Literary Diary*, II, 527.

well be remedied by recourse to *Ossian*. Among biographies, that of Cromwell was conspicuous; and histories had not been neglected. Josephus was there, and Mosheim, Hume and Robertson, and when Gibbon was published, he too was added to the list, as though in the presence of Whitefield to heap ridicule upon an enthusiastic clergy, and in that of Edwards, with sarcastic deference, to disdain to sound the abyss of the mysteries of grace, of free will and predestination. For the boy who was ambitious for the bar, a treatise, *Every Man His Own Lawyer,* had been provided to encourage or dissuade him, as the case might be; and if he chose to probe somewhat into the foundations of legal science, he could look into Locke or Montesquieu as he might desire. Such were a few of the several score of books which Linonia had collected.[112] Whatever the defects of the proffered fare, it had at least a full-bodied flavor of two rich centuries of literary history and it reflected no discredit upon the taste of those who had prepared it; and that at a time too when preoccupation with the vernacular was barely regarded as worthy of credit toward a degree. To busy one's self with Fielding, with Goldsmith or with Pope was still accounted rather a diversion than a discipline. To read Shakespeare and Milton, history or biography or even a treatise upon civil government could be expected of any right-minded boy without imposing upon a registrar the painful duty of chalking up credits to his account in the college archives.[113]

And yet, however excellent the books which they acquired and read, it would not do to conclude that the societies devoted themselves to letters too austerely. They had indeed a serious purpose; and at their ordinary meetings which were of

[112] The list in the *Linonia Records* mentions eighteen titles in divinity, twenty-six in history, seventeen in poetry, seven in law, twelve in novels and romances.

[113] *Belles-lettres* were just beginning to be academically respectable, and Stiles installed Montesquieu in the curriculum.

almost weekly occurrence, they declaimed and debated with a will. Their anniversary celebrations, too, were occasions for prolonged oratory; but these were held abroad in some chamber or tavern in the town [114] and were accompanied with plays and feasting.[115] Ordinarily, however, the society foregathered in the room of one of its members; and though the scribes took care to record that the meeting had dispersed with decorum, they also betrayed that its object had not been exclusively literary when they adopted, as they often did, the style of "the Honorable Fellowship Club" or "the ever respectable Fellowship Society." And one may guess that fellowship it was, quite as much as the love of literature, that drew these lads together in now one and now another of the low beamed rooms of Connecticut Hall, where of some November evening, cold with mist or wind from off the Sound, a new-laid fire would be burning on the hearth, a few well-placed candles glowing softly, and fire-light and candle-light playing together through the shadows upon merry faces, darting fitful gleams through a hovering haze of blue tobacco smoke, touching up with a fresh lustre now and then, as a dip began to gutter or a log to crumble and fall apart, the pewter of a tankard on the table, the blade of a gallant sabre on the wall, the silver buckle of a shoe; while voices now hilarious and now grave would rise and fall to the cheerful crackling of the flames.

Such was the goodly fellowship of Linonia in which James Kent tarried for four pleasant and memorable years; and now as September, 1781, drew nigh, he prepared to take regretful leave. A confident and comely [116] youth of eighteen, he stood waiting for the momentous day, when adorned with the

[114] Ezra Stiles, *Literary Diary,* II, 527.

[115] *Records of the Linonia Society,* 1768–1790, *passim.*

[116] There is a pastel portrait of Kent at about the age of twenty-five, painted by James Sharpless. *Vide, Columbia Alumni News,* XIV, 369; *Yale Law Journal,* XVII, 311.

Bachelor's degree of Yale, he would bid farewell to the abode of the Muses,[117] as he called the college, and descend into the tumults of the world.

By reason of the uncertainties and confusion which had harassed New Haven since the outbreak of the war, there had as yet been no public commencements during the administration of President Stiles.[118] It appeared indeed as though the class of 1781 might be dismissed under no better auspices. On the seventh of the month, the town was terrified with the tidings of Arnold's descent upon New London; [119] and upon the ninth, a fleet having been descried off Killingworth, the alarm was sounded; the militia began to muster, and academic repose was again disturbed with the presence of soldiers.[120] But tidings of a more reassuring kind encouraged the inhabitants. Washington was on his way to Yorktown; [121] and on September eleventh, as the corporation began to assemble, it was learned that the French fleet had arrived in Chesapeake Bay.[122] Though the fear that Arnold would interrupt the solemnities appointed for the following day had hardly been dispelled, nevertheless the college was illuminated in the evening; the chapel was bright with many tapers; [123] and if militia men were in town, so also were the kinsfolk of the "young Sirs" who were to be honored upon the morrow. The Kents were there.[124] Moss Kent the Elder and Moss Kent the Younger together with the sprightly brunettes, his sister Hannah and his stepsister Polly Hazzard,

[117] Kent referred to Yale as, "The delightful abode of the Muses."

[118] Ezra Stiles, *Literary Diary,* II, 554.

[119] Ezra Stiles, *Literary Diary,* II, 553.

[120] *Loc. cit.*

[121] *Loc. cit.*

[122] *Loc. cit.*

[123] *Loc. cit.*

[124] This is probable, since Compo was not far off. Furthermore Moss Kent Sr., had written that the two girls were coming to commencement. Macgrane Coxe, *Yale Law Journal,* XVII, 325.

with James Kent doing the honors and escorting them about. Town and gown, hardly secure behind the muskets of militia men, yet mingled in the streets with sounds of revelry. New Haven hummed with the incompatible activities of war and academic jubilation.

Nor was war to spoil the happy scene. September 12, 1781, witnessed without halt or hindrance the accomplishment of the ceremonies.[125] The brick meeting house filled betimes with spectators. Before the pulpit had been erected a commodious stage, and there upon a raised step in his great chair sat President Stiles in state, listening with benign approval as Sir Kent, in disputation, demonstrated the superiority of classical to modern literature. Kent spoke in English; but the exercises would have been incomplete in English only. The walls of the meeting house resounded with the swelling cadences of Greek and Latin declamation; while to give full measure, and to appall the Yankees and deter the British in a single utterance, the president arising from his throne, launched forth in Hebrew. But eloquence at last could do no more. The time had come to admit the young Sirs to the long coveted privileges of the baccalaureate. Sedately they came up three by three. The president sitting in his chair, with the beadle standing beside him, uttered the magic formula: *Pro auctoritate mihi commissa admitto vos ad primum gradum in artibus*—. As the president spoke, the beadle gave out the diplomas, together with Greek testaments, and the ceremonies came to an end. The day was far spent. No doubt the audience was far spent too.

As for James Kent, leaving Connecticut Hall and the yard and the green and all the other old familiar haunts, he departed for his father's farm at Compo. Before him lay the destiny which President Stiles some years before had prophesied that a fortunate youth of the oncoming generation would

[125] The following description is drawn from Stiles's *Diary*, II, 554 *et seq.*

fulfil: "There shall arise from our midst a great juristic genius, whether a Bracton, a Fleta, whether a Bacon, Coke or Selden. With an acumen worthy of Trebonian, with the strength and keenness of the highest talent, with the authority of a vast erudition he shall give form and system to our laws."

II

A Son of the Muses Descends into the Forum

Cuius vestibulum [*i.e.*, of the study of the law] cum salutassem reperissemque linguam peregrinam, dialectum barbarum, methodum inconcinnam, molem non ingentem solum sed perpetuis humeris sustinendam, excidit mihi (fateor) animus.

—Sir Henry Spelman [1]

Law, I must frankly confess, is a field which is uninteresting and boundless. Notwithstanding, it leads forward to the first stations in the State. . . . The harder the conflict the more glorious the triumph.

—James Kent [2]

* * *

THOUGH Sir William Blackstone, lecturing at Oxford, had taught jurisprudence to speak the language of the gentleman and the scholar, American academicians had been slow to admit that science into the curricula of their colleges. A proposal had indeed been made at Yale, while Kent was there, to establish a professorship of law,[3] but it had not been carried out; and for such knowledge of the subject as they formally received, the students were principally indebted to the president's rather infrequent lectures upon it. Nor was the situation much different elsewhere, except at the College of William and Mary, where in 1779 the first chair of juris-

[1] Quoted by Charles Warren, *History of the Harvard Law School and of Early Legal Conditions in America*, I, 3.

[2] James Kent to Simeon Baldwin, October 10, 1782, quoted by Simeon Baldwin to William Kent, February 1, 1848, *Kent Papers*, Vol. XI.

[3] Ezra Stiles, *Literary Diary*, II, 233.

prudence in America had been actually established.[4] The law, neglected by the colleges, was not as yet taken up by professional schools. When James Kent graduated from Yale no professional law school was to be found in the country. It is true that this want was soon to be supplied. In 1784, such a school, destined to be famous, was started by Judge Tapping Reeve at Litchfield in Connecticut.[5] At the end of the century the colleges themselves began to pay more attention to legal studies; [6] but at the time of Kent's departure from New Haven, all this was still in the future.

A youth, ambitious to enter the profession, had therefore to humble himself to the drudgery of a clerkship, or, if he could afford it, seek out some lawyer of more or less distinction, pay him a fee of perhaps two hundred dollars, and sit patiently at his feet to pick up such scraps of information as the great man in his moments of indulgence might casually let fall.[7] Such a master was not likely to be very helpful; and his resources in books and reports were altogether too likely to be insufficient.[8] Of English reports only about thirty were in familiar use in America, and of American reports none was published or in existence.[9] Blackstone was to be met with frequently, but other textbooks were few, expensive, and, being for the most part mere manuals for sheriffs and peace justices,[10] inadequate. Moreover, even this meager apparatus had been much impaired through the success of the Revo-

[4] Charles Warren, *op. cit.*, I. 1.

[5] Charles Warren, *op. cit.*, I, 180–181.

[6] The College of Philadelphia in 1790; Columbia, in 1794.

[7] Charles Warren, *History of the Harvard Law School and of Early Legal Conditions in America*, I, 134. At a later date, Kent himself illustrates this indifference toward pupils, confessing he was little interested in them.

[8] *Ibid.*, I, 126 *et seq.*

[9] *Ibid.*, I, 119, 126. Cf. "American Reports and Reporters," *American Jurist*, XXII, 108.

[10] Charles Warren, *op. cit.*, I, 126.

lution. Since many of the best informed lawyers had been Tories, they had found it healthful to quit the country, and they had taken their libraries with them; [11] so that it almost seemed as though the venerable common law disdained abiding in a republic and conforming itself to republican conditions. At any rate, few were the Whig lawyers who, upon going to the circuit, could not carry their libraries in their saddle bags. The fact no doubt accelerated their pace as travellers; it hindered their effectiveness as teachers of the law. Nevertheless, to study under their guidance was the preferred method of gaining admission to the bar. But there were others, less expensive if more circuitous. A friend of James Kent, who had finished his studies, settled in Long Island to begin his practice. He was flattered by an invitation from a genial resident to live for a season at his house without expense, a gratifying civility which the young man attributed at first to benevolence. He was soon undeceived; for it transpired that his prospective host was a scheming pettifogger who planned to make use of him to learn some of the rudiments of the profession.[12]

Although the way to the bar was beset with difficulties, many young men were eager to pursue it. To those who had been at Yale with Kent the law appeared by far the most eligible calling [13] and to none more so than to Kent himself, whose happy encounter with Blackstone had decided his career. His father, indulgent as ever, encouraged him in his resolution and in November, 1781, introduced him to the Attorney General of New York, Egbert Benson.[14]

That eminent man dwelt in Poughkeepsie, a town agreeably

[11] *Ibid.*, I, 131.

[12] James Hughes to James Kent, April, 1784. *Kent Papers*, Vol. I.

[13] James Kent, Notes on His Classmates, *Phi Beta Kappa Address*, note p. 46.

[14] James Kent, "Memoranda of My Life," *Kent Papers*, Vol. III.

situated, with perhaps some two score houses clustering below the steeples of its court-house and two churches.[15] It was a prosperous little place, the seat of Dutchess County which boasted almost thirty thousand inhabitants.[16] The Albany Post-Road ran through it and beside it flowed the Hudson, bearing to New York sloops laden at its wharf with the produce of the fertile valley of Wappinger.[17] The town was growing; and new houses were being built [18] but the greatness of Poughkeepsie did not depend upon its size. It boasted great men, Tappens, Duykincks, and Van Kleecks; and the Dutch influence preserved its solid character.

"What, Mr. Benson," Doctor Dwight once asked, "are the peculiar vices of the Dutch?"

"Vices, sir, they have none," was the ready answer.

The Doctor shifted his ground.

"Tell me then their peculiar virtues," he urged.

"They have all the virtues," retorted Benson.[19]

Nor were the virtues of the Dutch the only items in the catalogue of Poughkeepsie's distinctions. The town was not only the county seat of Dutchess; it was for the time being the capital of the infant republic of New York and in its streets famous personages were seen. Governor George Clinton, related by marriage to the Tappens, had his house there. General Washington visited there. Aaron Burr, John Jay, and Alexander Hamilton transacted legal business there,[20] and there lived Egbert Benson, a genial bachelor of thirty-five, the attorney-general, the *amicus curiae* and keeper of the consciences of the Supreme Court.[21] Throughout the recent war

[15] Edmund Platt, *History of Poughkeepsie*, 33.

[16] *Ibid.*, 54. In 1786 the inhabitants numbered 32,636.

[17] *Loc. cit.*

[18] *Loc. cit.*

[19] James Kent, "Memorandum of Egbert Benson," *Kent Papers*, Vol. VII.

[20] James Kent to Thomas Washington, October 6, 1828. *Kent Papers*, Vol. V.

[21] James Kent to William Kent, February 17, 1847, *Kent Papers*, Vol.

his record as a patriot had been distinguished and he continued to live with great reputation, dominating the judicial system of the state [22] and attended by a company of young men frequenting his office as apprentices at law.

A group of gallant blades they were, less fond of law books than of cards and dancing, of wine and pretty girls; [23] and at first they looked upon young Mr. Kent, a true grandson of the old divine of Fredericksburgh, as rather odd.[24] For a while at least he kept aloof from their diversions, and annoyingly enough sat down behind large folios of Grotius and Pufendorf, with quill in hand for the making of copious extracts.[25] Thus, with hardly an interruption, he continued through the winter and into the spring, while the others in all likelihood regarded him with feelings mingled of disgust and wonder. There seemed to be no end to his industry. As the months went by he sought with more than necessary diligence to understand the historical background of the law. Smollett's *History of England* and that of Hume, Rapin in translation on the laws and customs of the Anglo-Saxons, Sir Matthew Hale's *History of the Common Law*, these he added to his list; while parts of Blackstone he read again and again; and his manuscript notes slowly swelled to several volumes.[26] In addition to the study of books, there was attendance on the courts, where, from observing the attorney-general in action, much knowledge of a practical sort was to be gained.[27] It appeared that the boy was ambitious, and so indeed he was, perhaps too ambitious for the good of his health. His friend John

XI. He says Benson was the mainstay of the Court, that he almost dictated everything and was the keeper of the judicial consciences.

[22] *Ibid.*

[23] James Kent to Thomas Washington, October 6, 1828. *Kent Papers*, Vol. V.

[24] *Ibid.*

[25] James Kent, "Memoranda," *Kent Papers*, Vol. III.

[26] *Ibid.*, and letter to Washington, *supra cit.*

[27] James Kent to William Kent, February 17, 1847. *Kent Papers*, Vol. XI.

Cotton Smith warned him: "Let not, my friend, your laudable excess of ambition hurry you too precipitately on—at the expense of your health. Let my advice prevail so far on you as to make a very prudent allotment of your time—lest—the world be deprived of the richest prospects." [28] Whether this advice was much heeded is doubtful. Kent did fall sick,[29] but he returned to his studies, and in one of his letters to his friend Baldwin confided "a determination to put in a claim for some of the honors that imprint immortality on characters. . . ." [30] Such heroic resolution in a youth of twenty, deserved at least a smile of approbation; and the attorney-general, like President Stiles before him, began to take a friendly interest in his disciple.

Even the gay lads about him discovered presently that he was amiable in spite of his diligence, and that in his own way he was capable of liveliness and mirth. His fellows at Yale had long since made this discovery; and from them he received messages of warm, not to say effusive sentiments of friendship. "You deserted the *Alma Mater,*" wrote Smith reproachfully, ". . . left your comrades to deplore your absence, and have never yet alleviated the sorrow by a single visit." [31] And while the Yalensians bore their grief as best they could, the young gentlemen of Poughkeepsie were finding the law apprentice not such an odd character after all. Theodorus Bailey, hardly more than a year after Kent had come to live at his father's house, professed an attachment "bordering on maiden

[28] John Cotton Smith to James Kent, November 4, 1782. *Ibid.*, Vol. I.

[29] Simeon Baldwin to James Kent, January 25, 1783. *Ibid.*, Vol. I.

[30] Simeon Baldwin to William Kent, February 1, 1848, quoting from an early letter of James Kent to himself. *Ibid.*, Vol. XI.

[31] John Cotton Smith to James Kent, August 25, 1783. *Kent Papers*, Vol. I. Though Kent received his M.A. degree in 1783 and was appointed by President Stiles to deliver an oration on law, he did not visit New Haven at the time. Simeon Baldwin to James Kent, May 5, 1784 and September 9, 1784. *Ibid.*, Vol. I.

affection." [32] James Hughes, also a law student and, like Kent, a familiar figure in the Bailey household, upon one occasion took leave of his friend so regretfully as to burst into tears. He kept his countenance until the wood hid him from sight, but then as he confessed, "I blubbered almost to town, like a boy who had lost his top. . . ." [33] It would appear that James Kent in the disagreeable process of acquiring a legal education continued to make friends.

That the study of law was indeed disagreeable Kent discovered to his disappointment, and during the first year at Poughkeepsie the spell which Blackstone had cast over him in the summer of 1779 was almost broken. The fact that he was among strangers whom he had not yet learned to like,[34] accounts in part for his unhappiness; but a more probable cause was the disillusionment from which he suffered. The study was hard and dull, and he detested it.[35] As he bent over the ponderous tomes, memories of the happier days in New Haven all but crowded the black-letter learning from his mind.[36] He was sunk in youthful melancholy, and oppressed with the weight of the task which he had undertaken.[37]

Nor was he much encouraged when his eyes were opened to the actual state of the profession which he hoped to enter. A few consoling facts he might have noticed. Much legal business was being transacted, and the proscription of Tory lawyers enhanced the opportunities of new practitioners.[38] Nevertheless it was inescapable that both law and lawyers were more unpopular than they had been upon the eve of

[32] Theodorus Bailey to James Kent, December 16, 1782. *Ibid.*, Vol. I.

[33] James Hughes to James Kent, February 17, 1783. *Ibid.*

[34] James Kent, "Memoranda," *Kent Papers*, Vol. III.

[35] *Ibid.*, and letter to Simeon Baldwin cited at head of chapter.

[36] *Loc. cit.*

[37] Compare with Joseph Story's early troubles with Coke upon Littleton. Charles Warren, *History of the Harvard Law School*, I, 140.

[38] *Ibid.*, 94.

the Revolution. To James Kent this unpopularity was no matter of mere hearsay and rumor. His friend Hughes, but recently admitted to the bar, wrote from Huntington in Long Island that the profession was disliked there.[39] Simeon Baldwin, now a tutor at Yale and a law student on the side, surveyed in a manner far from reassuring the situation in Connecticut; ". . . the prospects are miserable in this State. We are litigious enough—but they are petty causes, small fees and a multiplicity of needy voracious attorneys to devour them—when this is the case the practice will be viewed with contempt. . . ." [40] To John Cotton Smith it was not only the number of the lawyers but their eminence that seemed a cause for anxiety: "The manner in which the Bar is at present thronged—the number of respectable characters that adorn it—together with the real difficulty there is of shining in the pursuit are considered by many as insuperable objections to engaging in the profession." [41]

Such announcements were not calculated to embolden an apprentice who was now standing upon the threshold of his career. Supported, however, by the prestige of the attorney-general, James Kent in January, 1785, appeared at Albany before Chief Justice Richard Morris and his puisne brethren Yates and Hobart, a bench of unlearned and bibulous judges, who, having a relish at once for pomp and port, were holding ceremonious session in a tavern.[42] Perhaps the aspirant for an attorney's license was informed enough to deserve it. The judges would scarcely have known. Perhaps a hint from Benson predisposed them favorably. At any rate the examination

[39] James Hughes to James Kent, April, 1784. *Kent Papers*, Vol. I.

[40] Simeon Baldwin to James Kent, January 16, 1785. *Ibid.*

[41] John Cotton Smith to James Kent, September 16, 1785. *Kent Papers*, Vol. I. Both Baldwin and Smith, however, became prominent; Baldwin, a judge, Smith, the Governor of Connecticut.

[42] James Kent to William Kent, February 17, 1847. *Ibid.*, Vol. XI. His remarks upon that old court are far from flattering.

resulted fortunately, and Kent received his license to practice as an attorney before their august tribunal.

The occasion was interesting in more ways than one; for an important cause was being argued, involving title to certain lands of Chancellor Livingston, who appeared as his own attorney, with Alexander Hamilton and Egbert Benson arrayed against him.[43] The display of talent was an impressive object lesson in how legal business, when managed by brilliant barristers, could be raised above the level of drudgery. It was an object lesson too in the stiff competition that would have to be met, for Hamilton and Benson were not the only gifted advocates of the New York Bar. John Lawrence, Samuel Jones the Elder, John Cozine, Richard Harison, and Aaron Burr were part of a roster of formidable names [44] which might well make the diffident uneasy. The city of New York alone supported the services of some forty lawyers.[45] Kent's friend Hughes had removed thence for that very reason,[46] and Kent himself was not disposed to try his fortunes in the city. Deluded no doubt by the notion that his family name might prove of some assistance, he returned to the scenes of his early boyhood in the valley of the Croton; and in the late winter of 1785 hung out his shingle at Fredericksburgh. "I think I can at least command business enough to preserve myself in existence with entire independence," [47] he wrote to Theodorus Bailey and settled down to wait for business to come in.

The inhabitants of Fredericksburgh, however, proved indifferent to the hopes of the grandson of Elisha Kent. The small, slight and rather dark young gentleman quite failed to awaken their confidence in his abilities as an attorney. Whether it was that they considered him superfluous, or that

[43] James Kent to Elizabeth Hamilton, December 10, 1832. *Ibid.*, Vol. VI.
[44] James Kent to William Kent, March 7, 1847. *Kent Papers*, Vol. XI.
[45] Charles Warren, *History of the Harvard Law School*, I, 94 *et seq.*
[46] James Hughes to James Kent, April 16, 1784. *Kent Papers*, Vol. I.
[47] James Kent to Theodorus Bailey, March 1, 1785. *Ibid.*

they suspected him because of his calling, or mistrusted him as being somewhat too gently bred remains doubtful. Certainly in his manners he would not have given offense willingly, for he was shy among strangers.[48] Perhaps his very diffidence told against him, for simple folk, as he was later to learn, are prone to esteem a man rather more according to his boldness than his deserts; and if he be a lawyer, to value a ready opinion given in off-hand ignorance as far more trustworthy than one that is halting from a knowledge that authorities disagree.[49] A satirist, writing at the time, drew up a code for the behavior of young advocates, advising them to discard all modesty, and, assuming impudence, thrust themselves forward in the courts, brow-beat witnesses, insult their adversaries at bar, and take a lofty tone to the bench itself. Such conduct, he declared, would win them briefs and reputations.[50] But of such conduct, James Kent was incapable, and if it was necessary to adopt it in order to succeed, he was foredoomed to failure. And the specter of failure was indeed now staring the luckless fellow in the face. He was poor and deep in debt.[51] The folk of Fredericksburgh, callous to his plight, left him alone in solitude and despair.[52]

Besides, he had fallen in love; [53] and the girl of his choice dwelt not in Fredericksburgh, but in Poughkeepsie. Thither after six weeks of gloom and despair, James Kent returned.[54]

* * *

[48] James Hughes to James Kent, March 20, 1784. *Ibid.*

[49] James Kent to Moss Kent, Jr., August 20, 1790. *Ibid.*

[50] *The Boston Gazette and the Country Journal,* June 27, 1791.

[51] James Kent, "Memoranda of My Life," *Kent Papers,* Vol. III.

[52] *Loc. cit.* Lucien B. Proctor in a pamphlet "The Trials and Triumphs of a Young Lawyer," Albany, 1888, says that Kent was waited upon and asked to leave Fredericksburgh. There is no clear confirmation of this in the *Kent Papers.*

[53] James Kent, "Memoranda of My Life," *Kent Papers,* Vol. III.

[54] *Loc. cit.*

Though it was true that Benson's most promising disciple was a serious-minded youth quite indisposed to be daring in his pleasures, yet ordinarily he had a natural gaiety of spirits which his Poughkeepsie friends, like those in New Haven, found attractive. Apparently, too, his gallant companions in the office were not without their influence upon him, for long before he had served out his apprenticeship to the attorney-general he was becoming not only a well-versed student, but also something of a beau. If he was not forgetful of Hale and Blackstone, neither was he forgetful of the ladies. They pleased him; and he strove to be pleasing in return. "I had the happiness a few days since, of seeing Miss Everson of the *City*—who told me she was in company with you at *Pleasant Valley* — She said—so, my friend at college, entirely the scholar and philosopher—now in addition, the courtier—the man of gaiety and fashion. . . ." [55] Thus wrote Hughes; and once when Kent was home at Compo the same friend had assured him: "In truth you have something about you that makes the old women mumble praises in your favor and the young ones chirp them with gladness." [56]

The talk of Kent and his friends was certainly not all of weighty legal matters. They thought much and they wrote much about women and their wiles and charms. Even sage Simeon Baldwin was not above it: "And I will challenge the most experienced philosophers to show me more lively experiments in the science of optics or, with their mirrors and prisms, paint more lively colors than the reflections which beam from [women's] eyes when brightened by virtuous desire." [57] That women lacked the firm and stable character of men was of course assumed. The amiable creatures had their

[55] James Hughes to James Kent, April, 1782. *Kent Papers*, Vol. I.
[56] Same to same, December, 1782. *Ibid.*
[57] Simeon Baldwin to James Kent, January 25, 1783. *Ibid.*

foibles and were excessively vain.[58] Nevertheless they were deserving of serious consideration.

None was more thoroughly convinced of this than James Kent, and at Poughkeepsie he had had opportunity to make useful observations upon the subject. The household of Colonel John Bailey, where he lived, was adorned with the presence of sprightly and good-looking daughters; among them, one in particular was conspicuous with more than ordinary graces. She was very young to be sure, but the law student glancing up from his commentaries and abridgements, could not help remarking how as she grew she became more enchanting. Before he was aware of what had happened, he had fallen violently in love.[59] Elizabeth Bailey did not exactly discourage his attentions. Sometimes she even found occasion to visit Benson's office.[60] In her eyes, young Kent was "a charming little student." [61] Apparently he was something more, for though a year of his apprenticeship remained, they were engaged to be married.[62] Hughes, who had wedded Betsey's sister Polly, congratulated his friend: "You are possessed of one of the best girls in the country—treat her as a rosebud—wear her in your bosom." [63] The advice was superfluous. Had the apprentice been as sure of his prospects as of his passion, he had been supremely happy.

How long the nuptials of James Kent and Elizabeth Bailey might have been postponed is problematical had not Gilbert Livingston, a prominent lawyer in Poughkeepsie, seen fit to take a junior partner. This good fortune, however, at last befell the despairing attorney in Fredericksburgh; and on April

[58] John Cotton Smith to James Kent, September 13, 1784. *Ibid.*

[59] James Kent to Thomas Washington, October 6, 1828. *Kent Papers*, Vol. V.

[60] Elizabeth Kent to James Kent, September 22, 1804. *Ibid.*, Vol. III.

[61] *Loc. cit.*

[62] James Kent, "Memoranda." *Ibid.*, Vol. III.

[63] James Hughes to James Kent, March 20, 1784. *Ibid.*, Vol. I.

3, 1785, a bridegroom of twenty-one, he married his beloved Betsey, a girl of only sixteen.[64] For more than a year after the marriage the pair lived at Colonel Bailey's,[65] while the husband saved money enough to pay his debts and buy a house of his own,[66] a snug little box of a house [67] set in an acre of ground; [68] and there in the autumn of 1786 he brought his bride.[69] Kent, happier than he had been for a long time, read with complacency a merry letter from his friend Baldwin. It was written in legal jargon, saying much about the reciprocal rights and duties of *baron* and *feme*. "Who could have thought," wrote Baldwin, "that the once bashful Jimmy who would have trembled if a female's plumes but shook would have so soon become a conquering soldier in the bold attack —who would have thought that the youngest in our class would have obtained the animating palm before so many of our oldest veterans . . . ?" [70]

Life in Poughkeepsie now became delightful. Law practice, though far from rushing, supported the *baron* and *feme* in perfect comfort. A servant-girl lightened the tasks of Mrs. Kent; and Moss Kent the younger came to keep his brother and sister company and, in a not too absorbing fashion, to read law.[71] There were agreeable neighbors. The house of Theodorus Bailey, brother of Elizabeth and friend of her husband, stood next door [72] and the connection with Mr. Livingston gave access not only to the family of the name,

[64] James Kent to Thomas Washington, October 6, 1828. *Ibid.*, Vol. V.
[65] James Kent, "Memoranda." *Ibid.*, Vol. III.
[66] *Loc. cit.*
[67] Moss Kent, Sr., to James Kent, September 6, 1790. *Ibid.*, Vol. I.
[68] Helen W. Reynolds, "James Kent Sometime of Poughkeepsie." *Year Book, Dutchess County Historical Society*, 1923. Kent's house was not far from the office of his senior partner, Gilbert Livingston.
[69] James Kent, "Memoranda," *Kent Papers*, Vol. III.
[70] Simeon Baldwin to James Kent, September 13, 1785. *Kent Papers*, Vol. I.
[71] James Kent to William Kent, March 7, 1847. *Ibid.*, Vol. XI.
[72] *Loc. cit.*

but through the Tappens and the Crannels to all the other gentle-folk of the shire-town; [73] while Hannah Kent, sister of Moss and James, established another influential connection by marrying into the family of the Platts.[74] There was genial companionship, therefore, and pleasures of a staid and quiet kind. Once a fortnight during winter season dancing assemblies were held and occasionally Mr. and Mrs. Kent attended them and Mr. Kent found the ladies "numerous and brilliant." [75] Jaunts and excursions in the summer and frequent rambles over the surrounding hills gave a little variety to the modest programme of amusements; [76] but it was at home in their cottage and its garden that the Kents took their keenest satisfaction.[77] As evening descended and the candles were lighted, a neighbor would oftentimes drop in to smoke a pipe, drink a glass of wine and talk politics and literature; [78] or if alone with his wife, James Kent would take down a good old English novel from the shelf and read aloud.[79] On Sabbath mornings, obeying the summons of the bell in the steeple of the Dutch Church,[80] the Kents, with their neighbors, would saunter forth through the quiet streets to public worship. They were blessed soon with the birth of a daughter whom they named Elizabeth after her mother. The father observed with pride the perfection of his offspring. "My little child—is full of prattle and activity—," he wrote as she began to

[73] Helen W. Reynolds, "Bartholomew Crannel," *Year Book, Dutchess County Historical Society*, 1922, 48–49.

[74] George L. Platt, *Platt Lineage*, 103.

[75] James Kent to Moss Kent, Jr., December 23, 1791. *Kent Papers*, Vol. I.

[76] James Kent to William Kent, February 21, 1847, March 7, 1847. *Ibid.*, Vol. XI, reminiscent letters.

[77] James Kent to William Kent, February 21, 1847, March 7, 1847. *Kent Papers*, Vol. XI, reminiscent letters.

[78] James Kent to Moss Kent, Jr., February 23, 1799. *Ibid.*, Vol. III.

[79] James Kent, "Memoranda." *Ibid.*

[80] James Kent to Dr. Samuel Miller, September 6, 1847. *Ibid.*, Vol. XI.

grow. "She has a charming skin and a lively eye and in my particular judgement is sweet and beautiful." [81]

The life that he was leading, Kent described as one of classic simplicity.[82] That it was simple there could be no doubt; and if books have any influence upon living, it was classic too. One day Edward Livingston and he fell into conversation upon the ancient authors, and Livingston, drawing out of his pocket a small edition of Horace, commented upon the beauty of the poet's style. Kent feigned agreement. Actually he was embarrassed, for his classical learning had become too rusty for him to appreciate the nicer points of prosody.[83] Ashamed of his ignorance, he presently set about the task of remedying it. His brother Moss was with him at the time, more fresh in his classical studies, and willing in exchange for law to give what he could of literature. The two brothers sat down to study Horace together. There would be no second occasion for chagrin at rustiness in Latin.

Thus to the other amenities of life in the shire-town of Dutchess was added the cultivation of the humanities until the poets and historians of Rome, together with Homer, Hesiod, Demosthenes and Xenophon, all in their own proper tongues, became sources of genuine enjoyment.[84] Though it could not be said that James Kent so far achieved scholarship as to read Thucydides with his feet on the fender, nevertheless his acquisitions were substantial and extensive, and the delight he took in them deep and sincere. When his brother Moss at last departed to seek his fortunes in the wilderness of Canajoharie, a correspondence ensued between them upon the progress they

[81] James Kent to Moss Kent, Jr., December 23, 1791, March 1, 1792. *Ibid.*, Vol. I.

[82] James Kent to Thomas Washington, October 6, 1828. *Ibid.*, Vol. V.

[83] James Kent to William Kent, February 17, 1847. *Ibid.*, Vol. XI; "Memoranda," *ibid.*, Vol. III.

[84] James Kent, "Memoranda." *Kent Papers*, Vol. III.

were making through the ancient authors, whose works they bought when they could, and when unable, borrowed from an indulgent friend like Egbert Benson.[85] For a reason more comprehensible to the eighteenth century than to our own, James Kent set great store by these studies. He considered them bound up with the prosperity of his career; and came to call them "the mine of all [his] happiness and honor." [86] That he should have done so reflects credit not only upon his own, but upon the cultivation of the bar to which he belonged. After all, it had been a member of that bar, a man as young as himself, who had stimulated his lagging interest in classical pursuits; and older lawyers could not but have applauded him in so doing. Humane learning was prized by all the leaders of the profession, and in their arguments whether forensic or political, they lost no opportunity to point an epigram with a deft allusion to the orators and poets. In the bitter controversy of the year 1792 Brockholst Livingston as *Hortensius* and Richard Harison as *Scaevola* debated the issue of the day; and Harison becoming somewhat acrimonious only elicited from his Clintonian adversary the bland rebuke: "It was not thus in the shades of Tusculum that *Scaevola* conversed with *Hortensius*." Harison, however was not to be outdone: "The allusion to the conversations in the shades of Tusculum awakens emotions of mingled pleasure and pain. Those conversations were once delightful, but when *Hortensius* became the advocate of *Verres,* those conversations ceased to be pleasant to *Scaevola*." [87]

Those urbane advocates cordially assented to the observation of Cicero, *haec studia non impediunt foris,* as a generous and pleasing dictum. It was a moot question, however, whether an attorney just admitted could afford to take it too seriously.

[85] James Kent to Moss Kent, Jr., September 15, 1790. *Ibid.*, Vol. I.
[86] James Kent, "Memoranda," *ibid.*, Vol. III.
[87] James Kent to William Kent, April 5, 1847. *Kent Papers*, Vol. XI.

The example of the junior member of Livingston and Kent may be considered as somewhat equivocal evidence in its favor. Indeed he himself appears at times to have had misgivings over his devotion to literature. "I have read fifty lines in the *Iliad* every morning and I want but the labor of tomorrow morning to finish the seventh book," he wrote to Moss, and added immediately by way of warning that his brother should beware of neglecting business for literature. "The requisite share of business," he remarked very justly, "must be acquired as *sine qua non*. . . ." [88] To this end, he resolved to enrich his knowledge of jurisprudence. "I am determined," he said, "law shall receive a daily and competent portion of my time." [89]

Nor was this determination merely verbal. Indeed he had already begun to extend his information in both law and equity, with Sir Edward Coke as his guide for the one, and Peere Williams for the other.[90] Not satisfied with his understanding of the course of earlier legal development he studied the subject afresh in Reeves's history; [91] while for the more recent changes he read the opinions of Lord Mansfield and duly admired the part which that jurist was playing in the adaptation of the law-merchant to the older body of the common law.[92] He read with system as well as with diligence; and mastered the various titles, not only by examining them as they stood in England, but by noting how they had been modified by the Revolutionary legislation of New York. The constitution of that commonwealth declared the English law to

[88] James Kent to Moss Kent, Jr., June 4, 1790. *Ibid.*, Vol. I.

[89] Same to same, August 20, 1790. *Ibid.* He divided his day thus: to 8:30 A. M., Latin; 8:30–10:00, Greek; 10:00–12:00 M., law and business; in the afternoon he studied French and became very proficient in reading it; and in the evening he read English authors with his wife; *Memoranda*, Vol. III.

[90] James Kent to Moss Kent, Jr., February 21, 1790, *Kent Papers*, Vol. I.

[91] Same to same, August 20, 1790. *Ibid.*

[92] *Loc. cit.*

be the basis of its own, though at the same time providing for departure from it in the discretion of the legislature.[93] The modifying process had already set in; and Kent followed it with interest. Describing to his brother the methods of his study he elaborated: "The head for instance of *heirs* had received a full digest. This led me to make remarks on our act regulating descent of lands and on our act regulating descent of chattels of intestates. Both of these are immense deviations from the principles of the common law. . . ." By these changes he observed that primogeniture, the preference of males, the inheriting *per stirpes* and the exclusion of the half-blood were pretty much abolished; and that on these matters, the law of New York was tending to resemble the law of Rome.[94] To that law, then, he found it expedient to pay attention also; and he read the *Institutes* in Latin; and the three chapters of Justinian's hundred and eighteenth novel in Greek. The exercise was not one of pedantry, for from that novel, as he had discovered, the New York statute of distributions had been largely copied.[95]

Such painstaking researches, needless to say, were more than sufficient for the demands of practice in the County Court of Dutchess where Kent most often appeared.[96] Few of the attorneys with whom he contended there, were his equals in information,[97] though some of them were nevertheless strong competitors in action. Among the ornaments of the Dutchess Bar one Silas Marsh was conspicuous, an ignorant lawyer, but resourceful, shrewd, and fearless. The

[93] Constitution of the State of New York (1777), Article XXXV.

[94] James Kent to Moss Kent, Jr., March 5, 1792. *Kent Papers*, Vol. I.

[95] James Kent to Moss Kent, Jr., March 5, 1792. *Kent Papers*, Vol. I. But the English Statute had also borrowed from the Roman law, as Kent at a later time, was to point out in his *Commentaries*.

[96] James Kent to William Kent, March 7, 1847. *Ibid.*, Vol. XI.

[97] Except perhaps Jacob Radcliffe and Edward Livingston.

court one day resolved to punish his impudence, but Marsh invented so many excuses and delays that he had the judges sorely perplexed when Benson, as friend of the court, rose up to extricate them from their difficulties. Marsh, far from being overawed, turned his back upon the bench and said with a bow to Benson, "I beg pardon of your honor—I perceive I have been addressing the wrong tribunal." On another occasion the First Judge of the County, Zephaniah Platt, having administered the oaths to the supervisors, strode into the tavern and with complacency announced, "I have just qualified the whole Board of Supervisors." Marsh, lingering over his liquor, cried out, "Ah, Judge, the whole Board of Supervisors could not qualify you." [98]

This intrepid attorney, showing little reverence for the magistrates, probably showed even less for a young practitioner like Kent; and though the latter in his old age used to refer to him, and to most of the other members of the Dutchess Bar, with something very much like condescension,[99] they were less inept perhaps than he has represented them. That they were not all Harisons by no means made the contests entirely one-sided. Kent sometimes lost, they sometimes won the decisions.[100] Steadily however he advanced in his profession; and he began to develop a spirit of enterprise to supplement his learning. Justice Hobart, holding a term of Circuit Court at Poughkeepsie, waited in vain for certain counselors to come from New York to prosecute a case of trespass in behalf of some plundered Tory traders; and James Kent and Edward Livingston, taking advantage of the non-appearance, petitioned the court to waive its rule that mere attorneys

[98] For both incidents, "Notes on the Life of James Kent," *Kent Papers*, Vol. XI.

[99] James Kent to William Kent, March 7, 1847. *Ibid.*, Vol. XI.

[100] Account Book of Livingston and Kent, *passim*.

should not practice in the circuit term. Hobart granted their petition, and the jury awarded them its decision.[101] It was before the County Court, however, that Kent, as has been said, usually practiced, and the causes which he managed there were fairly simple. It is possible that even without a previous perusal of Justinian he could have handled them as well.

For those causes illustrated some of the most elementary methods by which Anglo-Saxons, living in simple rural communities, have been wont from time immemorial to defend their rights.[102] A bay horse, a grey mare and a colt with a blaze on its forehead broke through the fences of one Van Bunschoten, who catching the beasts as they made damage in his meadow impounded them and refused to surrender them to Anthony their rightful owner. Now Van Bunschoten was a stubborn Dutchman, Anthony a self-assertive Yankee, who, not to be imposed upon, retained Kent and went to law. Van Bunschoten found an advocate in Jacob Radcliffe, like Kent, a former student of Benson, and the two attorneys arrayed against each other in a case of replevin, had a brisk exchange of plea, of replication and rejoinder. When the issue was tried, however, the twelve good men gave in their verdict for Anthony. A yoke of oxen, wandering at large were caught and harnessed by the poor but enterprising Aaron West who set them to ploughing in his own field. Their rightful owners, some of the Livingstons, sought out Kent, who fitting their case into an action of trover, won a verdict for twenty-six pounds. West, however, was fortunate in his poverty, for the sheriff returned *nulla bona*.

But it was not only beasts that wandered when they should have stayed at home. Men, too, were prone to transgress, and

[101] James Kent to William Kent, February 17, 1847. *Kent Papers*, Vol. XI. (Kent was admitted counselor in 1787.)

[102] All these cases are drawn from the Account Book of Livingston and Kent, *passim*.

to diversify business, there were actions of assault and battery, of simple trespass, of trespass *de bonis asportatis,* of trespass *quare clausum fregit;* and for a variety of wrongs, there was the ever present and adaptable action of trespass on the case. Of the kind of legal work which made lawyers unpopular as a class the firm of Livingston and Kent handled their share. They brought actions of ejectment and of debt again and again.[103]

Sometimes they took cases somewhat more unusual. Among the paupers of Fredericksburgh was one Sarah Derbyshire whom the overseers of the poor in that place packed off to Stephen-town in Westchester County. The overseers of Stephen-town, however, were not given to hospitality, and appealing less to charity than justice went to law over the matter. They retained Jacob Radcliffe, while Kent, pleased no doubt to have his professional competence recognized at last, pleaded the cause of his native Fredericksburgh. The day of official sympathy for the underprivileged had not yet arrived; and both Kent and Radcliffe may be supposed to have performed a public service in doing what a lawyer's skill could do to rid each his own respective client of responsibility for the unfortunate Sarah. Paupers were not as yet highly esteemed and infants of dubious paternity were still called by a picturesque, if unpleasant name. A wench gave birth to a child in Clinton-town where the overseers, inferring a father, bestirred themselves with diligence to find him. The embarrassed youth on whom they fastened sought advice from Kent as to what had best be done in this extremity; and while Kent championed the improvident lover, the more callous Radcliffe appeared for the overseers and so far prevailed as to get bond from the defendant's father to indemnify the town for the support of the child.

[103] The majority of cases handled, according to the Account Book, are actions of debt.

Such suits, however, happened seldom. The business of Livingston and Kent consisted chiefly of cases involving debts. Like others, it had its varying fortunes, its good years and lean.[104] It was not, at least to Kent, a fascinating business,[105] but such as it was, it yielded a livelihood, supported a family, made possible the purchase of property,[106] and above all afforded leisure for the cultivation of the classics.

It also made known Kent's name among the Dutchess freeholders and opened the alluring prospect of a political career.

* * *

As might be expected of a young man who had been disciple to Ebenezer Baldwin, Ezra Stiles and Egbert Benson, James Kent was interested in both the theory and practice of politics. The friends with whom he talked and corresponded shared with him their speculations on the subject. They discussed the import to Europe of the American Revolution.[107] They pondered the Declaration of Independence and noticed the inconsistency between the ownership of slaves and the profession of sentiments of equality and freedom.[108] They discussed the Articles of Confederation together with proposals for strengthening them.[109] Not that they all agreed that

[104] James Kent to Moss Kent, Jr., February 21, 1790. *Kent Papers*, Vol. I.

[105] Kent never liked legal practice and said that because of his pride and diffidence, he had "no talents for an attorney." "Memoranda," *ibid.*, Vol. III.

[106] May 1, 1786, Kent and his brother-in-law, Theodorus Bailey, bought a considerable parcel of land in Poughkeepsie. It was Lot No. 6 of the extensive old farm of the Van Kleecks, in an acre of which Kent's cottage with its garden stood. Kent and Bailey borrowed money for the purchase from Anne Maria Jay and gave her a mortgage for one hundred pounds. "James Kent, Sometime of Poughkeepsie," Helen W. Reynolds, *Year Book, Dutchess County Historical Society*, 1923, p. 27.

[107] John Cotton Smith to James Kent, July 22, 1785. *Kent Papers*, Vol. I.

[108] Same to same, May 31, 1785. *Ibid.*

[109] Simeon Baldwin to James Kent, August 1, 1783. *Ibid.*

the Confederation was hopeless—Simeon Baldwin, for example, would have preferred to see it left as it was; for he opined that the Rubicon was already crossed, and that as a matter of principle it is unwise to tamper with constitutions of government.[110]

There were many who agreed with Simeon Baldwin. The senior member of the firm of Livingston and Kent was adverse to meddling with the Articles. Judge Zephaniah Platt was no advocate of innovation.[111] The redoubtable George Clinton, allied by marriage to Kent's neighbors, the Tappens, and himself a householder in Poughkeepsie, was convinced that the republic of New York could prosper handsomely despite the flaws which busy men like Egbert Benson and Alexander Hamilton were bent on discovering in the Confederation; while the yeomen farmers on whose support the power of Clinton rested,[112] held the same opinion. A remote government, operated by the scions of the aristocracy, a government which could itself impose and could itself collect a tax on land, an excise upon liquor, and levy imposts and duties without end, a government designed apparently to put debtors at a disadvantage by forbidding states to issue bills of credit or to impair contractual obligations—such a government was not calculated to appeal to the farmers of New York who for the last twenty years had been growing more conscious of their interests as a class, and hence, more alert to detect conspiracies against them.[113] To the farmers, the handiwork of the Philadelphia Convention was far from acceptable. To their suspicious scrutiny it appeared as little better than a monstrous engine of aristocratic domination.[114]

[110] Same to same, May 10, 1785. *Ibid.*

[111] Both Gilbert Livingston and Zephaniah Platt were Anti-Federalist members of the Poughkeepsie Convention.

[112] E. Wilder Spaulding, *New York in the Critical Period, passim.*

[113] *Ibid.*, 76–77.

[114] It appeared thus to the farmers everywhere. S. B. Harding, *Ratifica-*

The alacrity with which aristocrats arose to defend it gave color to the yeomen's charge and point to their suspicion. Marshalled against them stood the landed gentry and the wealthy merchants, groups drawn together by the ties of kinship into a compact oligarchy.[115] It was of slight moment that Gilbert Livingston disliked the proposed constitution. He, after all, was but a lesser scion of the family whose name he bore. The chancellor approved the instrument. The Lord of the Manor was for it, and Philip Livingston and Henry Livingston followed his example. The Chief Justice, Richard Morris, advocated it; his brother Lewis shared his sentiments, and their talented and aggressive youngest brother, Gouverneur, had helped to draw it up. It won the support of General Philip Schuyler; and Stephen Van Rensselaer cast in its favor the weight and influence of the lordliest of the manorial proprietors.[116] John Jay and Alexander Hamilton, its most brilliant spokesmen, one married to a Livingston, the other to a Schuyler, confirmed their reasoned attachment to the constitution with the strongest ties of kinship and affection. The fact that they were lawyers exerted also its expected influence. The men who most desired the innovation were their clients, the speculators loath to suffer a further depreciation of their securities and lands, the merchants and ship owners impatient at seeing their wharves and vessels longer idle, the squires and manor lords in dread of their restive tenantry.[117] These were the men who had made the constitution; and these were the men whom Jay and Hamilton served professionally. As lawyers it was with their clients' welfare

---

tion of the Constitution in Massachusetts; J. Fiske, *Critical Period;* Charles A. Beard, *Economic Interpretation of the Constitution, passim.*

[115] Dixon R. Fox, *Decline of Aristocracy in the Politics of New York, passim.*

[116] E. Wilder Spaulding, *op. cit.*, 71–72.

[117] Charles A. Beard, *Economic Interpretation of the Constitution of United States, passim.*

that they identified the public interest. As statesmen they identified the public interest with their own. In so doing they precipitated a sharp class conflict out of which they emerged in triumph at Poughkeepsie with the Constitution of the United States as their splendid trophy, cunningly designed at once to promote the glory of the nation and to excite the disgust of George Clinton and the farmers of New York.

The sympathies of James Kent were at once enlisted on the side of aristocracy and the constitution. That perverse or generous ambition which sometimes prompts a well-born man to espouse plebeian causes was entirely alien to his nature. In him no trace or semblance of the Gracchi could be found. He was true to all the traditions—and prejudices—with which he was familiar—to those of his family, of his church, of his college, of his calling and of the complacent class to which by fortune he belonged. He was imbued with a deep sense of the dignity of property, and a new government competent to protect property appealed to him with powerful persuasion.[118]

Nor was his conviction the result of prejudice alone. As one familiar with Locke and Blackstone, the defense of property as a major object of the state seemed to him naturally enough to be justified by both jurisprudence and philosophy. When the *Federalist Papers* began to be put forth, the conviction must have gained in strength; Kent read them eagerly and committed long passages to memory; [119] and the doctrine which they expounded sank into his congenial mind like seed in fertile ground and confirmed his own conclusions with novel, pleasing and ingenious arguments. It came as a corrective to the vulgar sophistries which had been encouraged by the tumults of the Revolution. For some years the rights of

[118] Nathaniel H. Carter, *Reports of the Proceedings and Debates of the Convention of 1821*, 434, where Kent observes the states would have been insufficient by themselves to protect property.

[119] James Kent to Thomas Washington, October 6, 1828. *Kent Papers*, Vol. V.

property had been frequently and successfully assailed.[120] The teachings of the *Federalist* portended a reaction toward more conservative policies; and it may be inferred that James Kent greeted that reaction with a sigh of relief. It is certain that his enthusiasm for the Revolution had been short of extravagant. When the war had receded from New Haven, he had remained in college; when it had approached, he had retreated without delay. However much he may have valued freedom, he had struck no single blow in its behalf, albeit for several years before the war had ended, he had been of age which the laws considered ripe for bearing arms.[121] His loyalty to the cause was doubtless above suspicion; but it may also have been tempered by the knowledge that one kinsman was a royal officer and that another had gone within the British lines. The baiting of Tories, that favorite diversion in the post-revolutionary years, had distressed him greatly, and the appearance of the *Phocion* papers of Hamilton, urging that the time had come to give it up, he had hailed with satisfaction.[122] If a valiant Revolutionary veteran like Hamilton yearned for the oblivion of prejudice and for the reestablishment of orthodox and stable counsels, it can be readily imagined with what enthusiasm such a possibility was viewed by so mild and modest a patriot as James Kent. That young man valued liberty; but like Hamilton, his idol, he valued it most when vigorous government curbed its excesses and made it safe for property.[123]

The influence of that statesman upon Kent was not exerted only through his essays. In October, 1787, an acquaintance,

[120] For example, by the confiscation of the estates of Tories and by the issue of fiat money.

[121] *I.e.*, sixteen years.

[122] James Kent to Elizabeth Hamilton, December 10, 1832. *Kent Papers*, Vol. VI.

[123] James Kent to Elizabeth Hamilton, December 10, 1832. *Kent Papers*, Vol. VI. Mrs. Hamilton had asked Kent for reminiscences about her husband. He responded promptly and in considerable detail.

which was to ripen into friendship, sprang up between them. They met at Albany, whither the rising young lawyer from Poughkeepsie had gone on business before the Supreme Court, and at the hospitable board of General Schuyler they dined together. The talk, to which Kent eagerly listened, was all of the great work which had just been completed at Philadelphia.[124] He was not aware at the time that Hamilton was already planning the *Federalist;* but his happy introduction to the most brilliant of its authors prepared him, as the essays began to appear in print, to welcome them with delight. For the benefit of the citizens of Dutchess he even undertook to abridge and print them in the local newspaper.[125] When sufficient numbers of the original had been published to form a slender volume, Kent and his friend Egbert Benson received a generous supply which they distributed among the freeholders.[126]

Notwithstanding their zeal, the good folk of the shire remained skeptical about the advantages of the proposed constitution; as did indeed the state itself. All the campaigning and arguments of the Federalists barely persuaded the convention, meeting at the court-house in Poughkeepsie,[127] to ratify the instrument. James Kent, putting aside all other business, attended the sessions daily throughout the six weeks of their duration and watched with anxious eyes the vicissitudes of the struggle.[128]

Though a partisan, he admitted that the opposition had

[124] *Loc. cit.*
[125] *Loc. cit.*
[126] *Loc. cit.*
[127] The convention assembled on June 17, 1788, and sat for six weeks. There were sixty-five members of whom nineteen were Federalist and forty-six Clintonians. Gilbert Livingston, Kent's partner, and Zephaniah Platt, his kinsman, were Anti-federalist at first, but later voted for the constitution. James Kent to Elizabeth Hamilton, December 10, 1832. *Kent Papers,* Vol. VI.
[128] *Loc. cit.*

talents as well as numbers. He noted the force of John Lansing's appeal to popular prejudice.[129] He remarked the dignity and good sense with which Governor Clinton presided.[130] He admired the arguments of Melancton Smith, which closely woven, seemed at times to involve the convention in a web of metaphysical subtleties.[131] Such admissions, however, only served to bring out in sharper relief the superior abilities of those who were managing the cause of the constitution; and the peculiar talents of Richard Harison, Chancellor Livingston, John Jay and Alexander Hamilton were listed and appraised by Kent as he looked down intently upon the proceedings.[132] So far as mere logic and persuasion were concerned, the Federalists, as he observed, were more than capable of answering whatever arguments their adversaries might put forth. Nevertheless the struggle was stubborn and protracted. For weeks the delegates, sitting under the presidency of the inflexible Clinton, applauded the eloquence and voted down the proposals of Hamilton and his friends.

The defects of the Articles of Confederation Hamilton exposed in vain.[133] The advantages of a strong government equipped to levy taxes and satisfy its creditors; [134] the perfections of a legislature furnished with a senate to check the follies of the multitude,[135] these and such like themes he developed without avail; and even while his eloquence depicted America as on the very brink of ruin, his appeal to the supernal powers, "O save my country, Heaven," [136] failed somehow to

[129] *Loc. cit.*
[130] *Loc. cit.*
[131] *Loc. cit.*
[132] *Loc. cit.* Kent was not a member of the convention.
[133] James Kent to Elizabeth Hamilton, December 10, 1832. *Kent Papers*, Vol. VI. These were the speeches of Hamilton which his young friend especially admired.
[134] *Loc. cit.*
[135] *Loc. cit.*
[136] *Loc. cit.* Kent thought this appeal sublime and touching!

strike responsive chords in the bosoms of men whose faith was in New York that she could save herself.[137]

That faith, however, was badly shaken when the Convention learned that New Hampshire and Virginia had already ratified, and that, whatever Clintonian New York might choose to do, the constitution was nevertheless in full legal force. Confronted with a *fait accompli,* the state had little willingness to brave the Union. The effect of Virginia's adhesion was especially marked; and thence forward Kent observed a rapid change in the tone and manner of the proceedings.[138] A spirit of accommodation began to prevail; and with the Federalists' concurrence in the proposal to accept the constitution but to get it amended as soon as possible,[139] the convention brought debate to an end. Governor Clinton remained as irreconcilable as ever, but defection had set in among his followers. To the satisfaction of Kent, the Dutchess delegation no longer presented a united front. Melancton Smith, Zephaniah Platt, Gilbert Livingston and John De Witt parting company with their colleagues, voted with the majority for the constitution.[140] The Federalists had won the day.

James Kent though but a spectator was as jubilant over the victory as a seasoned veteran, the first victory at the expense of the Clintonian faction which the New York aristocracy had been able to celebrate since the establishment of their own conservative State Constitution eleven years before. Two bulwarks now rose between them and the restive democracy of little farmers; and with a strengthened sense of security

[137] E. Wilder Spaulding, *New York in the Critical Period,* 218–219.

[138] James Kent to Elizabeth Hamilton, *loc. cit.*

[139] *Loc. cit.*

[140] James Kent to Elizabeth Hamilton, December 10, 1832. *Kent Papers,* Vol. VI. As Kent was only a spectator at the convention, it has been described only as it appeared to him, without investigation of the reports of Childs, which by the way, were drawn up at Kent's house evenings.

gentlemen lifted their glasses and drank a toast to the new regime.[141]

Kent who was with Hamilton in New York when the first Congress assembled, witnessed the inauguration of the new government.[142] What ambitions the historic scene aroused within him it is easy to imagine; though it was to be the irony of his career that despite his friendship for the Federal Union, the offices of that Union were constantly to elude him and to fall not infrequently to the lot of men who had once professed to believe the Federal Constitution an instrument of tyranny.[143] Ironical it was too that while his own party dominated the counsels of the Union, he himself was to enter upon the *cursus honorum* in a state that was dominated by the very party he detested. By 1790 he had become well known to the voters of his county, and though they were predominately Clintonian, they paid him the compliment of choosing him one of their burgesses in the Assembly of New York.

* * *

Of a nature too simple and straightforward to be very proficient in the art of political intrigue,[144] James Kent became notwithstanding a valuable member of the legislature. Howsoever Federalist were his inclinations, he had yet a just sense of the interest and dignity of his state, and when a bill was introduced for incorporating a state bank he was decidedly for it. "It is as requisite to have a state bank to control the influence of a national bank as for a state government to con-

[141] E. Wilder Spaulding, *New York in the Critical Period*, 272–274. The strict limitations on the suffrage franchise; and an elaborate system of checks and balances made the State Constitution less flexible to the demands of the Clintonians than it would otherwise have been.

[142] James Kent to Elizabeth Hamilton, *loc. cit.*

[143] *E.g.*, Theodorus Bailey and Smith Thompson who were Anti-federalist.

[144] He had read the *Prince* and confessed to his brother, "I don't know what to make of (it)." James Kent to Moss Kent, Jr., August 20, 1790. *Kent Papers*, Vol. I.

trol the influence of a general government," was the opinion he expressed to Theodorus Bailey, and he descended to particulars in observing that money would be carried to Philadelphia unless there were a bank to receive it in New York.[145] Nor was a bank the only major object of state policy in which Kent was interested. The federal census had just been taken and in the light of the information thus furnished the legislature set about the task of readjusting the State's representative system. Of the joint committee to whom this labor was entrusted, Kent was a member.[146] Between the Hudson valley and the settlements westward toward Canandaigua and the Genesee communication was difficult and precarious. A committee was appointed to examine methods for improving it, and Kent was a member of this committee too.[147] The claims of the creditors of the state, as those claims were affected by federal assumption of state debts, became the study of yet another committee to which he also belonged.[148] These were more than routine tasks; but the energetic member from Dutchess had his share of those as well. He handled petitions and reported out private bills; and, what was probably more to his liking, introduced a bill of his own to permit executors to sell the lands of deceased debtors for the satisfaction of claims against their estates. For the Committee of Ways and Means he recommended the rejection of a revenue bill sent down by the Senate as an infringement upon the privilege of the lower house.[149]

[145] James Kent to Theodorus Bailey, February 27, 1791. *Ibid.* The bank was incorporated with a capital not to exceed $1,000,000. The President was Isaac Roosevelt, and Nicholas Low and Gulian Verplanck were among the directors—*New York Daily Advertiser,* March 26, 1791.

[146] *Assembly Journal,* 1791, p. 13. James Kent to Theodorus Bailey, January 16, 1791. *Kent Papers,* Vol. I.

[147] *Assembly Journal,* 1791, p. 17. Internal improvement of the State was a favorite object of Federalists.

[148] *Assembly Journal,* February 15, 1791. *New York Daily Advertiser,* March 10, 1791.

[149] *Assembly Journal,* 1791, pp. 17, 32, 36, 47, 52, 56, *et passim.*

The office which he held was one of the least important in the gift of party. Nevertheless in the city of New York which had possessed, until very recently, the distinction of being the capital of both the state and nation, and in politics in which state and national issues were confused and blended, even an assemblyman enjoyed an influence which the most eminent politicians could not ignore. Mr. Kent became a guest at the tables of Governor Clinton,[150] Chancellor Livingston,[151] and Chief Justice Jay.[152] He was flattered with the civilities and exposed to the fascinations of Attorney-General Aaron Burr with whom he dined and breakfasted.[153] Dinners, as he wrote home to Dutchess, multiplied upon him like the hydra-head.[154] New York abounded with politeness and hospitality; and none was more polite, none was more hospitable than the Attorney-General whose refined taste, subtle mind and graceful, insinuating manners reminded the young assemblyman of Lord Chesterfield.[155]

With his breeding and cultivation James Kent was apt to grace the tables of the great. However, he was not deluded with the notion that Burr's hospitality was prompted by mere social motives.[156] The term of General Schuyler as a Federal Senator was about to expire; [157] and Aaron Burr, supported by the Clintonians, was ambitious to succeed him. As the fate of his candidacy rested with the New York Legislature, it was politic to be as agreeable as possible to all the members. Burr, however, in practicing his arts upon James Kent was courting

[150] James Kent to Theodorus Bailey, January 27, 1791. *Kent Papers,* Vol. I.

[151] *Loc. cit.*

[152] James Kent to William Kent, February 21, 1847. *Ibid.,* Vol. XI.

[153] James Kent to Theodorus Bailey, January 12, 1791. *Ibid.,* Vol. I.

[154] *Loc. cit.*

[155] James Kent to Theodorus Bailey, January 16, 1791. *Ibid.*

[156] James Kent to William Kent, February 21, 1847. *Kent Papers,* Vol. XI.

[157] DeAlva S. Alexander, *A Political History of New York,* I, 49.

disappointment. The mind of the assemblyman from Duchess was already made up.

A man who had favored the adoption of the new federal system would have stultified himself had he preferred to see it operated by others than its tried friends. Kent was nothing if not consistent; and the secure establishment of the Hamiltonian system, he, like other Federalists, regarded as the sequel of the constitution.[158] So far as banks were concerned, his reading of Adam Smith had convinced him of their usefulness, and Hamilton's views upon the subject confirmed his own.[159] Nor were the other items in the secretary's programme less desirable. Both the funding and the assumption measures he deemed equally wise. Their bearing upon the fortunes of both his country and his family he had already discussed with his brother Moss. Their father, he suggested, should subscribe to the new federal loan to the amount of his certificates; [160] and he added that the second session of Congress, having fairly well complied with the secretary's recommendations, had concluded auspiciously for the credit of government and the accomplishment of the great objects of national concern.[161] Such a convinced partisan was not likely to be much influenced by the cajoleries of Aaron Burr; and even as he ate his bread and drank his wine, Kent hoped for his defeat.

To avow his stand openly required honesty and courage. Dutchess County was still suspicious of Hamilton and all his works and the Dutchess assemblymen generally reflected the local prejudice.[162] But Kent, whatever his faults, never

[158] Charles A. Beard, *The Economic Origins of the Jeffersonian Democracy, passim.*

[159] James Kent to Theodorus Bailey, February 20, 1791. *Kent Papers,* Vol. I.

[160] James Kent to Moss Kent, Jr., August 20, 1790. *Ibid.*

[161] *Loc. cit.*

[162] James Kent to Theodorus Bailey, January 16, 1791. *Kent Papers,* Vol. I.

deserted his convictions. With the minority of the legislature he cast his unavailing vote for General Schuyler [163] and informed his Clintonian friend, Theodorus Bailey, of his action: "I saw the administration of Hamilton which I conceive essential to the prosperity of the nation violently opposed—to send a character there who has always been regarded as unfriendly to the government and its administration and who was brought forward by persons always hostile to it and who himself possessed talents that might be exerted in a powerful degree, was with me to contradict the most obvious dictates of good policy and of faithful attachment to the success of the constitution. I therefore voted from the conviction of my judgement." [164] This frank declaration to a political opponent revealed a strong simplicity of character on which the wiles of Aaron Burr could only have been wasted.[165] Kent had no more of Machiavelli in his nature than of the Gracchi.

Perhaps it was this very forthrightness that appealed to the free-holders who had his political fortunes in their keeping. It is obvious that they liked him in spite of his Federalist bias for they invited him in 1791 again to represent them.[166] Not until the following year, however, when "the whole phalanx of the Federalist party took the field with some gallantry," [167] did he accede to their wishes.

The state campaign of 1792 was hard fought. Since the post of governor, together with seats in the legislature, was the prize, the struggle provoked an intensity of competition in which men forgot all scruples. It was a campaign poisoned with the prejudices of caste.[168] Arrayed behind Governor Clin-

[163] *Assembly Journal*, 1791, p. 23.

[164] James Kent to Theodorus Bailey, January 27, 1791. *Kent Papers*, Vol. I.

[165] Kent says that after the vote Burr's attentions ceased.

[166] James Kent to William Kent, February 21, 1847. *Kent Papers*, Vol. XI.

[167] *Loc. cit.*

[168] DeAlva S. Alexander, *A Political History of New York*, I, 53.

ton stood the rough democracy of small farmers. Persons of quality and wealth supported Jay.[169] Between the candidates were drawn sharp contrasts which confirmed the prejudices and intensified the convictions upon either side. If Jay was a stately patrician, Clinton was a sturdy tribune of the people. If Jay well understood how to conduct government with ceremonious dignity, Clinton knew better how to manage it with the simplicity becoming a republic. If Jay's prudence was the more reliable assurance of continued constitutional protection from the assaults of the rabble, plain citizens could count more certainly upon the inventiveness of Clinton to extend their privileges and redress in their favor the balance against contumelious aristocrats. Such were the representations [170] which excited to life the most dangerous animosities and made the campaign of 1792 long memorable in the annals of New York.

Of themselves they would have sufficed to make it bitter. The injection of federal issues rendered the controversy still more acute. The measures of Hamilton for assuming and funding of the debts [171] had resulted through stimulated speculation in widening the breach between rich and poor. From the transactions of the treasury, the yeoman, the veteran of the recent war and the common folk in general had profited but little. The fortunes of the wealthy had been greatly amplified.[172] With a deep sense of grievance, therefore, the cohorts of the tribune Clinton flung themselves into the tumults of the

[169] That was the general rule. The Livingstons, however, were from personal reasons exceptions to it. As Henry Adams has shown the New York democracy relied upon persons of quality for leadership.

[170] DeAlva S. Alexander, *op. cit.*, I, 53–54. Scandals in the land-office aggravated the already ugly situation.

[171] DeAlva S. Alexander says the assumption of state debts and the ensuing speculation were the chief issues. *Loc. cit.*

[172] Charles A. Beard, *The Economic Origins of the Jeffersonian Democracy, passim.*

campaign. The Federalist phalanx took the field with equal ardor.

Fresh from his perusal of Livy and from his contemplation of the classic antagonisms between plebeian and patrician, James Kent stepped into the fray upon the side of privilege.[173] The challenge of the contest summoned forth other young ambitious champions [174] not all of whom were wise or virtuous enough to espouse the proper cause. But upon whichever side they stood they fought with animation for their principles, and some of them like Smith Thompson, De Witt Clinton and Ambrose Spencer were destined to go far upon the road to fame. To Kent it must have been most vexing that Thompson in particular, who had been studying law under his very guidance, was so perverse as to be Clintonian. More annoying still no doubt was the fact that Gilbert Livingston professed the same adherence. It was hardly conducive to harmony in the firm of Livingston and Kent that the partners should be competing as they were for the suffrages of the Dutchess freeholders.

Such however was the situation. At a meeting called in Poughkeepsie by Judge Platt for the express purpose of renominating Kent assemblyman, a faction headed by Judge Tappen tried in vain to put Livingston in nomination also.[175] The support thus given to his rival Kent attributed to family connections; [176] and indeed the intermarriages of Livingstons, Clintons and Tappens ought ordinarily to have secured sufficient influence to insure their candidate's success. But it was the influence of Platt that predominated in the meeting he had

[173] James Kent to Moss Kent, Jr., March 1, 1792. *Kent Papers*, Vol. I.

[174] De Witt Clinton, Ambrose Spencer, Smith Thompson, Joseph Yates, Samuel Mitchill, Cadwalader Colden *inter alios*, DeAlva S. Alexander, *A Political History of New York*, I, 56.

[175] James Kent to Moss Kent, Jr., March 1, 1792. *Kent Papers*, Vol. I.

[176] *Loc. cit.*

called and Kent alone was nominated there.[177] Equally flattering to him were the results of the election; for though Dutchess out of six assemblymen returned four Clinton partisans, yet Kent himself, staunch though he was for Jay, received the highest vote of all. His partner put forward as his particular opponent [178] was badly beaten.[179]

Sure of his own election Kent awaited anxiously the returns from Jay's campaign for the governorship. His hopes were high that with the Chief Justice seated in the governor's chair halcyon days, as he put it, would ensue.[180] And as he was persuaded of Jay's integrity, so he was convinced, possibly through the land-office scandals, that Clinton was dishonest. "If Providence should but grant us success," wrote he, "we may rationally expect a sudden death to the little intrigues of favorites and party . . . I shall feel signally devout to Providence for his goodness if he has but permitted us this time to remove so corrupt a man as Clinton from the administration of the government." [181] Thus Kent waited in growing impatience to learn the outcome of the campaign. He kept minute account of the returns as they came in. From his friend Colonel Troup in New York he learned that the city by a small majority was for Jay; [182] and it appeared too that Ulster and Westchester were to be of the same persuasion.[183]

[177] James Kent to Moss Kent, Jr., March 1, 1792. *Kent Papers*, Vol. I.
[178] James Kent to Moss Kent, Jr., May 2, 1792. *Ibid.*, Vol. I.
[179] James Kent to Moss Kent, Jr., June 6, 1792. *Ibid.*, Vol. I.
He lists the votes there as follows: James Kent—1257, Barnabas Payne—1034, William Radcliffe—966, Jonathan Akin—960, Josiah Holley—955, Ebenezer Mott—933, Matthew Patterson—917, S. A. Barker—812, Martin Wilkie—799, I. Oakley—752, Gilbert Livingston—735, William Wheeler—600, Morgan Lewis—502. Of the six elected only Kent and Payne were Jay men.
[180] James Kent to Moss Kent, Jr., March 1, 1792. *Ibid.*, Vol. I.
[181] James Kent to Moss Kent, Jr., March 1, 1792 and May 2, 1792. *Ibid.*
[182] James Kent to Moss Kent, Jr., May 2, 1792. *Ibid.*
[183] *Loc. cit.*

Though Dutchess had elected four Clintonian assemblymen, Jay seemed there fairly secure with a majority of two hundred votes; [184] and that though the tenant farmers on the lands of the Livingstons had voted solidly for his opponent, a fact probably explicable from other reasons than the one assigned by Kent, that they had been driven to it "like sheep to the slaughter." [185] Tenant farmers hardly required pressure from their landlords to vote for George Clinton. For years it had been from them that he had derived his most numerous support.[186] The apostasy of the Livingstons from Federalism furnished their tenants but a superfluous inducement to remain democrats; and it is not impossible that if any compulsion was resorted to, it was Federalist landlords who may have been guilty of the practice. Be that as it may, it presently transpired that if mere ballots meant anything, the tribune Clinton was defeated, and the Chief Justice by a slim majority [187] elected the Governor of the State. Ballots, however, the Clintonians refuse to take seriously; and in June, James Kent was writing indignantly to his brother upon the subject of the reelection of Clinton: "This event," said he, "though it would have been melancholy if it had been the voice of the people, yet it is rendered doubly afflicting from the consideration that it takes place in violation of the law and of justice." [188]

The defeat of Jay resulted from the Board of Canvassers' decision to ignore the votes which had been cast by the electors in Otsego [189] where lived Moss Kent and where the Federalist

[184] *Loc. cit.*

[185] James Kent to Moss Kent, Jr., May 2, 1792. *Kent Papers*, Vol. I.

[186] E. Wilder Spaulding, *New York in the Critical Period* shows clearly that even when the Livingstons in 1787 had been strong for the Constitution, their tenants had been against it.

[187] Kent reckoned it at near 500 votes; *vide* James Kent to William Kent, February 21, 1847. *Kent Papers*, Vol. XI.

[188] James Kent to Moss Kent, Jr., June 15, 1792. *Ibid.*, Vol. I.

[189] The validity of the returns from Tioga and Clinton counties was also drawn in question; but it was principally upon the rejection of the Otsego

influence owed much to the exertions of his patron, Judge William Cooper, the wealthiest if not the only squire in the new county. But the electioneering efforts of the judge and his young friend were thwarted through a technicality. According to the requirement of law, the sheriff was entrusted with the formal duty of delivering the ballot-box to the Secretary of State; and this duty, as was thought, had been properly performed. The canvassers, however, had not been reckoned with; and as good Clintonians they feigned to believe that Otsego had no sheriff at all who was legally competent to deliver in the vote. The situation was anomalous. Sheriff Smith, if Sheriff he was, had overrun his commission. Sheriff Gilbert, if Sheriff he was to be, had not yet received his or been sworn in.[190] Hence arose the legal question whether an act is valid and official when performed by a sheriff whose commission has expired but whose successor has not yet qualified. Such an act the canvassers declared illegal; and upon this pretext, threw out the Otsego votes and saved the day for their chieftain, Governor Clinton.

Their imprudent zeal kindled a conflagration [191] and gave the angry Federalists an opportunity to pose in a new light as the champions of the people's freedom. They published pamphlets; they held meetings; they passed resolutions; they collected opinions from leading lawyers within the state and without. Rufus King, Richard Harison and Robert Troup upheld the validity of the Otsego returns while Richard Stockton in New Jersey and Tapping Reeve from his law school in Litchfield added the weight of their testimony to that of the

---

ballots that the controversy hinged. DeAlva S. Alexander, *History of Political Parties in the State of New York,* I, 56–62.

[190] James Kent to Moss Kent, Jr., June 15, 1792. *Kent Papers,* Vol. I. James Kent to William Kent, February 21, 1847, *ibid.* Vol. XI; *vide* DeAlva S. Alexander, *History of Political Parties in the State of New York,* I, 56–62.

[191] James Kent to William Kent, February 21, 1847. *Ibid.,* Vol. XI.

Bar of New York [192] where only Aaron Burr presumed to sustain the much belabored canvassers. "The latter has *shamefully* prostituted his talents to serve a desperate and abandoned party," [193] declared Kent, as he himself ransacked the precedents, harangued the populace, moved resolves against the administration, and advocated a convention to condemn the canvassers and order the whole electoral process to be repeated.[194]

With such energy did he bestir himself that the Clintonians, sitting hardly secure in the seats of authority, branded him as the ringleader of sedition in Dutchess.[195] The novel appellation, rather awkwardly worn by one whose well-shaped nostrils were wont to twitch at the very mention of demagoguery, Kent strove with all his powers to deserve. Polished gentleman though he was, he called hard names. Governor Clinton was an odious tyrant. The urbane Brockholst Livingston, who, apostatizing from orthodoxy, supported the tyrant's claims, was an abandoned character.[196] On the other hand, the people usually contemptible, by an amusing vicissitude of fortune, became now the virtuous citizens righteously resentful at the tyrannies their rulers had practiced upon them. Ordinarily the sight of liberty poles filled Kent with disgust. But the pole set up in Cooperstown before the court-house was an exception. In the autumn of 1792, as he visited the outraged shire of Otsego, he viewed it with approval. It was an emblem of the just indignation of the people at the recent attack upon their liberties.[197]

[192] *Loc. cit.*, and James Kent to Moss Kent, Jr., June 15, 1792. *Ibid.*, Vol. I.

[193] James Kent to Moss Kent, Jr., June 15, 1792. *Ibid.*

[194] For these activities *vide* James Kent to Moss Kent, Jr., June 6, 1792, June 15, 1792, July 4, 1792, July 11, 1792, *Kent Papers*, Vol. I, and James Kent to William Kent, February 21, 1847. *Ibid.*, Vol. XI.

[195] *Loc. cit.*

[196] James Kent to Moss Kent, Jr., June 15, 1792. *Ibid.*, Vol. I.

[197] "Memorandum of a Journey to Lake Otsego 5–19th September, 1792,"

But all the furor of the Federalists came to naught. Judge Cooper might have furnished whole forests of liberty-poles and the people generally throughout the state would have yet willingly acquiesced in the authority of Governor Clinton. Their representatives in the legislature had no thought of seriously questioning his title. With tolerance but without anxiety the assembly permitted an investigation and attended James Kent and his Federalist colleagues as they conducted a long and expensive examination of many witnesses.[198] The findings, though not creditable to Clintonian methods, were barren of any results except the strengthening by legal evidence of what the Federalist minority had all along suspected.

Kent, despite his indignation, bore himself with restraint throughout the proceedings. He had checked his original impulse to seek redress by means of a convention; [199] and as he examined the witnesses from Otsego and the other injured counties, he strove with lawyer-like skill to establish evidence that would warrant impeachment of the canvassers. The evidence might be, indeed it was, as damaging as he could desire. The assembly had nevertheless not the remotest thought of impeachment. James Kent, Josiah Ogden Hoffmann and their coadjutors were leading a forlorn hope.

As their revelations grew more embarrassing, once again their opponents resorted to a quibble to extricate themselves from danger. A resolution was adopted that since canvassers had not been chosen by the Council of Appointment, they were not officers within the meaning of the Constitution and that hence the assembly's impeaching power was inadequate

---

Kent Papers, Vol. I—Kent was accompanied thither by his father, Moss Kent, Sr., and by his wife.

[198] *New York Daily Advertiser,* January 3, 1793, *et seq.*

[199] James Kent to Moss Kent, Sr., December 23, 1792. *Kent Papers,* Vol. I.

to reach them.[200] In vain did Kent retort [201] that if the canvassers were unimpeachable, so too were the many other important functionaries who owed their places elsewhere than to the Council of Appointment, and who by reason of their power were capable of inflicting great damage upon the state. More bold than diplomatic in his argument, he pointed out that the resolution would exempt the commissioners of the land-office, and he sought to know how else and where else redress could be obtained than by impeachment in the assembly in the event such bodies were guilty of mal-conduct. Should the governor through the attorney-general set in motion the machinery of the law against them? But suppose the governor himself were an accomplice in the mischief? What then? Was redress against a powerful officer to be sought by the ordinary citizen in the ordinary courts of justice? Was that the only means of remedy? If so, remedy was impossible. Furthermore, if the individual citizen could seek redress, though fruitlessly, how much greater was the assembly's right to seek it by impeachment, being deputies as they were of all the citizens together. Was there an apprehension that guiltless officers might be victimized? Or, granted for the sake of argument that a given functionary like a commissioner of the land-office or a canvasser—granted that he was exempt, yet even then would an impeachment be a very gross mistake? If the law does indeed exempt him, let him plead that exemption before the senate in abatement. If the assembly should exceed its power, still no irremediable injury would ensue, because in the senate there exists another tribunal to examine and correct their mistakes before final judgement can be pronounced. On the contrary, if the assembly voluntarily curtail an authority with which the Constitution clothes them, both their own

[200] James Kent to Moss Kent, Jr., January 27, 1793. *Ibid.*

[201] The following summary is derived from the report of Kent's speech in *The New York Daily Advertiser*, January 8, 1793.

reputation and the welfare of their constituents will permanently suffer. For that mistake no correction is forthcoming.

For full power of impeachment then, of all officers, regardless of the mode of their appointment, argued Assemblyman Kent. His address was temperate, well-reasoned, and impressive, if not eloquent: "The power of impeaching," he said, "is granted to us in the emphatic language of the Constitution as the *representatives of the People.* We sit here as their trustees and we ought to have the eyes of eagles to watch over the trust and prevent its diminution." [202]

The assembly, however, were not persuaded. Kent expended his words and energy in vain. Some debate was had but the net result was nil. George Clinton remained the Governor and the Board of Canvassers escaped without rebuke.[203]

The affair was not without its influence upon Kent's fortunes. It had served to bring him conspicuously to the notice of prominent Federalists and the party determined to reward him. The national House of Representatives offered a suitable theatre for the ambition of a well-informed lawyer and an enterprising partisan who would be able as well as willing to cooperate effectively with Secretary Hamilton. To the House of Representatives, therefore, it was proposed Kent should go.[204]

It would have been a grateful change for him to enact a role upon the federal scene, for state politics dominated by Clinton had become thoroughly distasteful. "I have finally arrived," he confided to Moss Kent, "to a most zealous and fearful detestation of the present administration in this State." [205] But the change was not to be. Federalist politicians might propose his candidacy and put him, as they did, in nomination. It was

[202] *The New York Daily Advertiser,* January 8, 1793.
[203] James Kent to Moss Kent, Jr., January 27, 1793. *Kent Papers,* Vol. I.
[204] *Loc. cit.*
[205] James Kent to Moss Kent, Jr., March 22, 1793. *Ibid.*

the voters of Dutchess who disposed; and with the fickleness that well-born men were wont to consider characteristic of the multitude, they disposed of Kent without ceremony. Though he had pretended to hope little from his candidacy,[206] the young man was nevertheless chagrined. It had not assuaged the soreness of his discomfiture that old friends had turned against him.[207] Judge Platt had worked for his opponent. Gilbert Livingston had done likewise, perhaps impelled to do so by the rankling smart of the defeat which a year before he had suffered at the hands of his more than equal partner. The sharpest hurt of all was that inflicted by his sometime friend, the brother of his wife, Theodorus Bailey who, nominated by the Clintonians as his competitor for the congressional honor, had carried off the prize. To the hypocrisy of these, his neighbors, and to the calumnies which he fancied that they had circulated against him, Kent attributed his defeat.[208] Perhaps it was rather the expensiveness of the assembly's inquest upon the canvassers that was in fact the fundamental cause. Citizens sometimes find dishonesty in government more tolerable than the cost of eradicating it, and to say that Kent was the author of the expense of the assembly's investigation was but legitimate tactics, an argument *ad hominem* that was telling and by no means untrue.[209]

Whatever the cause of his being defeated, Kent found his present situation disagreeable. From a long and wearisome session of the assembly, he returned to Poughkeepsie. The town had lost its former charms. For some time he had been toying with the possibility of removal to New York. The city had proved hospitable and attractive. Among its foremost lawyers

[206] James Kent to Moss Kent, Jr., January 27, 1793. *Ibid.*

[207] James Kent to Moss Kent, Jr., March 22, 1793. *Ibid.*

[208] James Kent to Moss Kent, Jr., March 4, 1793; March 22, 1793. *Kent Papers*, Vol. I.

[209] That the argument was actually used, *vide* James Kent to William Kent, February 21, 1847. *Ibid.*, Vol. XI.

he had made good friends. It offered prizes and held out professional inducements, which Poughkeepsie, now sinking into the obscurity of a mere county town, could never hope to equal. Besides, the thought of practice there in the firm of Livingston and Kent, was now, after all that had happened, hardly to be supported.[210] The time had come to make a change and to launch forth upon a more adventurous ocean.

One day therefore, in the spring of 1793, James Kent with his little family and his few belongings boarded a sloop and was borne down the river toward the beckoning metropolis.

[210] Kent seems never to have liked his law-partner. In his "Memoranda," *Kent Papers*, Vol. III and in his letter to Thomas Washington of Tennessee, frequently cited, he speaks of him as "dull" and of the partnership "unequal."

III

A Sojourn in the City

Sunt lacrimae rerum et mentem mortalia tangunt.

Aeneid I, 462

Haec studia secundas res ornant, adversis perfugium ac solacium praebent; . . . Ego vero fateor me his studiis esse deditum. Ceteros pudeat, si qui ita se litteris adbiderunt ut nihil possint ex iis neque ad communem adferre fructum neque in aspectum lucemque proferre; . . .

Pro Archia Poeta Oratio

* * *

AMONG the treasures which James Kent brought with him to the city were his books. He brought besides a hundred pounds in cash and more than a third of the sum he laid out in the purchase of more books.[1] His wife, who had a strain of thrifty Dutch in her blood,[2] may well have been alarmed at his extravagance. One day when a wheel-barrow was trundled up to their door bearing the wisdom of Thuanus in several volumes, Mrs. Kent turned in dismay to ask her husband how the costly acquisitions were to be paid for. Rushing into the street to see if something could be done to extricate himself from his embarrassment, he came upon Edward Livingston who was interested in the building up of a new library for the young metropolis.

"Are you aware," inquired Kent with eager concern for

[1] James Kent to Moss Kent, Jr., July 10, 1793. *Kent Papers,* Vol. I.

[2] Elizabeth Bailey's mother was Altie Van Wyck, daughter of Theodorus Van Wyck, *Collections of New York Historical Society Abstracts of Wills, 1777–1783*, IX, 280–281.

public education, "that your library wants the works of the great Thuanus?"

Livingston, though the future codifier, seems to have been as innocent of Thuanus as Kent upon a former day had been of Horace. He nevertheless agreed that the lack was lamentable and expressed satisfaction that his friend knew how it might conveniently be supplied. Kent, losing no time, hastened home, and to his relief saw the wheel-barrow trundled off bearing the volumes to fill the gap upon the public shelves.[3]

Livingston had unwittingly rendered a service to his friend that was probably more substantial than that which at the same time he had rendered to the city. The Kents were upon the verge of poverty. The practice of the firm in Poughkeepsie had always been more leisurely than lucrative. About five hundred dollars a year had been the average income which it had yielded to the junior partner,[4] who by dint of an economy possible where the bookstalls were infrequent had contrived to support his family in comfort. But the eve of his departure to New York had found him with only books, some scanty furniture and the hundred pounds in cash wherewith to tempt his fortunes in the city.[5] Upon these slim resources to live with anything resembling the easy style to which the county town had accustomed him, he naturally considered as beyond his scope, at least until an established practice should offer some assurance of security. This, however, was a consummation less easily achieved than desired; and in spite of his acquaintance with influential persons, a succession of briefless months repeated the unhappy experiences at Fredericksburgh and threatened to repeat the Fredericksburgh failure upon a bigger and a more disastrous scale. The slender sum he had fetched with him down the river dwindled at an alarming rate, and had

[3] "Notes on the Life of Kent," *Kent Papers*, Vol. XI.
[4] James Kent to William Kent, March 7, 1847. *Kent Papers*, Vol. XI.
[5] "Memoranda," *ibid.*, Vol. III.

it not been for the timely largesses of brother Moss in Otsego he would have been presently sunk again in debt.[6] With the cost of living high,[7] and a family on his hands, it was not strange that the young paterfamilias should have wondered how much longer he could endure the city. "I will try a year or two yet," he informed his brother, "and if it will not do here, I must go to the woods somewhere as you have done." [8]

A cabin in the woods could hardly have been a less attractive dwelling place than that which New York offered to the impecunious. Not yet extended beyond the tapering end of Manhattan, the city crowded within that narrow compass a swelling population of more than thirty thousand.[9] It was a dirty and unwholesome seaport town with crooked, ill-paved and dimly lighted streets through which pestilence came stalking without pity. The Kents, unable to afford anything better, lived in an uninviting corner near the tip of the island without other advantage than nearness to the Battery and the Bowling Green. But the Battery as an abode of fashion could only have sharpened their discontent with the squalor of their own dingy little street; [10] where they strove in vain to make the best of their situation, anxious for the health of their child, and yearning for the snug cottage and its wide and fragrant garden in Poughkeepsie.[11]

Poverty was not the only misfortune which beset the struggling lawyer and his wife. They had not been long settled in New York when Moss Kent the Elder, feeble with sickness

[6] James Kent to Moss Kent, Jr., July 10, 1793. *Ibid.*, Vol. I.

[7] James Kent to Moss Kent, Jr., October 2, 1793. *Ibid.*

[8] *Loc. cit.*

[9] *The First Census of the United States*—New York, 1790, 8–9. The city had an exact population in 1790 of 33,131, the state 340,120.

[10] James Kent to Moss Kent, Jr., May 29, 1793. *Kent Papers*, Vol. I; James Kent to William Kent, March 29, 1847. *Ibid.*, Vol. XI. He doesn't name the street, but says it was between Broad and Broadway near Marketfield.

[11] James Kent to William Kent, February 21, 1847. *Ibid.*, Vol. XI.

and with years,[12] came down from his new home in Lansingburgh to pay them what was to be his final visit. He was suffering with the ravages of a stroke from which he never recovered and in February, 1794, he ended his days and was buried by his eldest son who was too poor, however, to afford the customary scarves for the funeral.[13] The death of Moss Kent Senior was the more lamentable as it occurred just as he stood again upon the threshold of prosperity. His career had not been wholly fortunate—the loss of property and the encumbrance of a wife becoming more ill-tempered [14] had sorely vexed his latter years, until leaving Connecticut behind and separating from his uncongenial spouse,[15] he had sought serenity in the solitudes of northern New York. There, waited upon by Jack, his faithful negro, and tilling his new farm and discharging the duties of peace-justice and surrogate,[16] he had been looking forward to a comfortable old age solaced by the kindness of his children. His daughter Hannah, wife of William Pitt Platt of Plattsburg was living not far away in easy circumstances, a daughter whose house furnished the old man a hospitable retreat whenever he chose to go there.[17] One son was prospering as a merchant-lawyer in Otsego,[18] and the other, more remote to the southward, was a man of parts sure to prosper eventually. The brothers had been one in their determination to look after their aging parent with solicitude; and with their minds ever intent upon classic lore, had taken pride in their filial devotion and referred to themselves the epithet which Vergil had meant for Aeneas, *insignes piet-*

[12] Moss Kent, Sr., *natus* January 14, 1733. O.S. *New York Genealogical and Biographical Record*, IV, 84.

[13] James Kent to William Kent, March 29, 1847. *Kent Papers*, Vol. I.

[14] James and Moss Kent, Jr., called their step-mother "the old woman."

[15] Moss Kent, Sr., to James Kent, February 20, 1791. *Kent Papers*, Vol. I.

[16] James Kent to Moss Kent, Jr., April 6, 1793. *Ibid.*

[17] Moss Kent, Sr., to James Kent, July 9, 1792. *Ibid.*

[18] Moss Kent, Jr., to James Kent, February 7, 1792. *Ibid.*—Later he failed, but regained prosperity. *Vide infra.*

ate.[19] The old man's death had left them in unfeigned sorrow.

With the elder brother that death aggravated a still more bitter loss. He had no more than set foot in the metropolis when its fevers laid hold upon his infant daughter. She was a promising young lass whose charms the doting father had been wont to describe in letters to his brother. "Our little child is growing finely," he had written, "[She] is now nine months old [and] can almost stand alone by a chair and is full of bloom and beauty." [20] She had lived but a little more than two years when the pestilential atmosphere of the city put an end to her brief days. Kent whom much desired but untimely business had taken up to Albany returned home only to mingle his tears with his wife's in mourning their dead child.[21] The humble house in the dingy little street was more forlorn than ever. Amid increasing discouragements James Kent sought to forget his sorrows in his books; but despite the winged words of Tully the effort was unavailing.[22] The image of his little child rose up before him and blurred the poet's verses and the pages of the reports.[23]

* * *

The church steeples which pricked their way upward among gables, roofs and chimneys to dominate the sky-line of New York, bore witness that the city sometimes worshipped a more

[19] Moss Kent, Jr. to James Kent, March 9, 1793; James Kent to Moss Kent, Jr., March 22, 1793. James Kent visited his father in Lansingburgh and had him draw up his will in March, 1793. The old man had a modest estate of about £600. He still had his farm at Compo from which he received rent. He willed the bulk of his estate to his younger son. *vide, New York Genealogical and Biographical Record,* IV, 85.

[20] James Kent to Moss Kent, Jr., July 8, 1791; December 23, 1791. *Kent Papers,* Vol. I.

[21] James Kent to Moss Kent, Jr., May 29, 1793. *Kent Papers,* Vol. I. The child died of the fever, after an inoculation against the smallpox; and was buried within an hour after Kent's return.

[22] James Kent to Moss Kent, Jr., October 2, 1793. *Ibid.*

[23] James Kent to Moss Kent, Jr., July 25, 1793. *Ibid.*

gracious Deity than Mammon. Its life was lived by no means wholly at the Tontine or in the counting-house. Bills of lading and of exchange, invoices, charterparties and disputes and litigation over marine insurance did not exhaust the topics of its conversation. Though not yet the abode of a Cardinal nor the dwelling-place of a thousand Levites, the metropolis even in its wayward youth was not an irreligious town. Over the place the genius of Protestantism still presided, conducive alike to the fostering of pure manners and the accumulation of profits. From the first derived the desire, from the second proceeded the means of sustenance for the growth of learning; and General Sir Guy Carleton had hardly embarked his regiments when liberal minded citizens began to bethink themselves of the grateful task of restoring under republican auspices that royal foundation with which King George the Second had once been pleased to adorn his city of New York.

Facing southward toward the spire of Trinity Church, King's College arose within the ample boundaries of its Green, a commodious, three-storied building of severe and solid Georgian elegance.[24] Except for the royal crown that once had glittered on the weather-vane of its neat belfry, its outward aspect was but little changed since the days before the Revolution. From the calamities of that war the institution itself had suffered great damage, illustrating even more aptly than Yale the force of Doctor Stiles's observation: *Toga cedit armis.* King's College, converted by turns into a barracks and hospital and situated, moreover, in a town the last to be relinquished by the enemy, had all but expired under the strain of its vicissitudes.

It was fortunate, however, in its alumni whose influence and

[24] Thomas A. Janvier, *In Old New York,* map 54–55. The Green sloped from Church Street toward the Hudson and was bounded on the north by Murray, on the south by Barclay Streets. There is a plate representing the college as it was in 1790 at page 14, in *Columbia University: Dedication of the New Site, May 2, 1896.*

respectability made it possible for their loyalty to manifest itself in the most constructive benefactions. Many of them having played honorable parts in the recent war, were still present in the city where they could be counted upon to lend aid in the resuscitation of their *Alma Mater*. Among them were Richard Harison, Egbert Benson, Robert R. Livingston and John Jay by whose hands, in the days when they were undergraduates together, had been planted the sycamores which were now waving their wide shadows across the College-Green.[25] A few years later Gouverneur Morris stepped boldly forth from the same portals to be followed in turn by Robert Troup and Alexander Hamilton.[26] If any college could be confident of patronage and favors, that college was King's whose alumni made the bead-roll of the city's distinction.

Nor was it to be disappointed of its hopes. Its old privileges were confirmed with new charters, which proceeding from the legislature of a republic changed the now meaningless name of King's to the more appropriate appellation of Columbia.[27] From the same bountiful republican source grants of money followed the bestowal of charters [28] until the college began so to flourish once again that the regents presently reported that it was about to be raised "to a pitch of exalted prosperity." [29]

In the varied intellectual fare which she set before her

[25] John B. Pine, "Kings College: Now Columbia University" in *Historic New York*, 337–338.

[26] *Catalogue of the Governors, Trustees, etc., of Columbia University*, Harison and Jay, 1764; Benson and Livingston, 1765; Morris, 1768; Troup and Hamilton, 1774; 49–52.

[27] The Charters of 1784 and 1787. The first placed the College under the regents of the University of the State of New York directly. The second committed its management to an autonomous corporation of trustees. *A History of Columbia University, 1754–1904*, 59, 68.

[28] *Ibid.*, 63 *et seq.*

[29] *Regents Report to the Legislature: Assembly Journal, November*, 1796, 146.

students,[30] Columbia was more generous than either Yale or Harvard. Her destinies were for the time being committed to such far-sighted trustees as Samuel Provoost, John and Brockholst Livingston, James Duane, Richard Varick, John Jay and Alexander Hamilton, who like their contemporaries, still believed that the classical languages and mathematics composed the core of a liberal education. They would have been at a loss to comprehend the teaching of salesmanship and folk-dancing as an academic function, and so too would the President, Doctor William Samuel Johnson, statesman and philosopher, the friend of Lord Mansfield and the English Johnson. Yet both President and Trustees discharged their duties according to their lights, which sufficed to reveal the value of other tongues than Greek and Latin and of other sciences than mathematics as cultural disciplines. The traditional studies continued to be approved [31] while the invention of novel courses augured well for the catholicity of the future curriculum.

Interesting and talented men in the faculty of the college symbolized the widened scope of its studies. Vilette de Marcellin taught French; [32] and for a brief period Doctor John Daniel Gros added instruction in German to his graver duties as Professor of Moral Philosophy, Geography and History. Doctor Gros, an eminent Lutheran divine, educated at Marburg and Heidelberg,[33] had a fellow-countryman as his colleague, John Christopher Kunze, sometime student at Leipzig, and like Gros a learned Lutheran. Arabic and Hebrew rolled from his tongue with fluency, and he graced the chair of oriental languages without, however, attracting many disciples to sit at his feet.[34] More successful in his professorial

[30] *Loc. cit.* The exact number was 124.

[31] *A History of Columbia University, 1754–1904*, Appendix B, 450–451.

[32] *Catalogue of the Governors, Trustees, etc., of Columbia University*, 23.

[33] *Dictionary of American Biography*, VIII, 15–16.

[34] *Ibid.*, X, 512.

career was John Kemp, an acute Scotch mathematician whose students deserved such acclaim in their first public exhibitions that the trustees who had hired the master for but a single year, thought better of it, extended his appointment indefinitely and ended by making him a Doctor of Laws, an honor which he also received from his native Aberdeen.[35] But Kemp, like Doctor Rattoone, the Professor of Greek and Latin, fitted into the traditional pattern of academic pursuits. Of their colleague, Samuel Latham Mitchill, native of Long Island but graduate of Edinburgh, the same could not be said, for that accomplished *savant* personified the spirit of innovation wherewith Columbia was being leavened.[36] A pretense at least was made of teaching economics,[37] a task allotted to Doctor Mitchill, whose competence, at least in his own conceit, for he was a vain man,[38] was not lessened by the fact that his favorite *fach* was chemistry. He apparently taught that science with some appreciation of the developments brought about by Lavoisier and Priestley, with the latter of whom he managed to cultivate a friendship. Furthermore he was an expert in theoretical agriculture, and by offering instruction in this subject, he perhaps added to the number of the liberal arts and certainly diversified his usefulness to the expanding college.

Indeed, strictly speaking, Columbia could have been called a college no longer. She was beginning to assume the character of a university. Of the hundred and twenty-four students who dwelt within her gates the majority continued to pursue the liberal arts,[39] but a school of medicine had been already established and Doctor Samuel Bard, himself an alumnus of

[35] *Ibid.*, X, 319–320.

[36] Courtney R. Hall, "Samuel Latham Mitchill, A Queen's County Polymath," *New York History*, XIV, 113–124.

[37] *History of Columbia University*, 80.

[38] So Kent described him when they were members of assembly in 1792.

[39] *Regents Report to the Legislature: Assembly Journal, November, 1796*, 146.

Kings, presided over a medical faculty of six professors who taught obstetrics, surgery, anatomy, botany, the theory of physic and the *materia medica* to a group of thirty students.[40] Of the competence of Doctor Bard there could be no doubt. Like Gros, Kunze and Mitchill he had studied abroad and he brought back to his *Alma Mater* the best scientific knowledge that London and Edinburgh could give.[41]

The ambition of the trustees of Columbia for the development of a university was not satisfied merely with a medical school or with an enriched curriculum of liberal arts. As might have been anticipated in a community where increasing population and commerce made the relations among men more intricate than hitherto, a desire had been stimulated in the citizens to investigate more curiously than had been the custom the rules and principles wherewith those relations were wont to be regulated in long established societies. The study of law began therefore to assume new importance and to receive fresh encouragement. Indeed reasons of the most practical kind rendered it indispensable. Lawyers whose clients had ships afloat upon the seven seas were finding an ignorance of the lengthening list of decisions in commercial and admiralty cases to be an expensive luxury; and they were applying themselves to their books with an assiduity at which an earlier generation would have been amazed.[42] They were, as a rule, impelled to their researches through no disinterested love of jurisprudence. Their motives were less lofty, their rewards less intangible than those which prompt the pursuit of learning as an end in itself. Nevertheless among their number a few practitioners were genuinely interested in the broader implications of the law as an intellectual discipline concerning itself with

[40] *Loc. cit.*

[41] Edinburgh M.D., 1785. *Dictionary of American Biography*, I, 598–599.

[42] This will be further developed below.

the great objects of society. Of these John Jay and Alexander Hamilton were the most eminent; and as members of the corporation they were in a strategic position to make their wishes count. That body, influenced it seems by them,[43] resolved to establish a course of legal studies in the university. The plan, it is true, had been considered before. On the eve of the Revolution, Governor William Tryon had proposed to become a patron of legal education and a Tryonian Professorship of the Laws of England had been intended as a monument to his vanity and good will.[44] The project, however, had not matured, though the idea that law should somehow be represented in the curriculum still survived and for the three years immediately preceding independence, a Professorship of Natural Law had had at least a nominal existence.[45] That subject the trustees in 1784 voted to revive, but the law of nations as well as that of nature was to be included in the scope of instruction; while at the same time, two additional chairs, one of the municipal law, the other of the *Jus Civile* were also to be established. But the proposal was too ambitious at the time, and for want of money to support it came to naught.[46] Nine years later the bounty of the legislature partially supplied the lack, and made possible, if not a separate law school, at least a professorship within the college itself. The trustees, looking about for an incumbent, were guided in their choice by the recommendations of Judge John Sloss Hobart and of the Chief Justice of the United States, John Jay.[47] On December 24, 1793, they assembled in the hospitable house of Simmons the Innkeeper, and there upon Doctor Bard's nomina-

[43] *A History of Columbia University, 1754–1904*, 336.

[44] *Ibid.*, 36.

[45] The incumbent was the Rev. Mr. Vardill, a class-mate of Benson and Chancellor Livingston. He turned out badly, for, like President Cooper, he was tainted with Toryism.

[46] *A History of Columbia University, 1754–1904*, 336–347.

[47] James Kent to William Kent, February 21, 1847. *Kent Papers*, Vol. XI.

tion, they elected James Kent to occupy the newly established chair at a stipend of £200 a year.[48]

The eagerness with which the appointment was accepted can be readily guessed. It was not only that it gave relief from penury. The occupation promised to be agreeable, while the title in itself could be regarded as a recognition of arduous researches from which, at last, something could be brought forth into the public light for the pleasure and advantage of the community. Through the summer of 1794 the professor devoted himself with renewed diligence to his studies,[49] examining his authorities and composing his lectures with scrupulous care. When in the following November his course began, he had fortified his knowledge with a reading of Bynkershoek, with a more extended study of the English Reports down to Burrows, and for the sake of form and elegance, with a perusal of Cicero and Quintilian.[50] It was, therefore, a well-grounded scholar whose introductory lecture an audience, assembling at noon [51] of a November day in the college hall, awaited with some interest, perhaps more curiosity, to hear. A little man in a black silk gown [52] appeared presently upon the platform and began to read from his manuscript.

"This is the first instance," said he, "in the annals of this seat of learning, that the science of our municipal laws has thus been admitted into friendship with her sister arts, and been invited to lend her aid to complete a course of public instruction." [53] The speaker was much concerned to defend the propriety of this innovation and he undertook to demon-

[48] The official notice is in the *Kent Papers* near the end of Vol. I.

[49] James Kent to Moss Kent, Jr., January 7, 1794. *Ibid.*, Vol. II and *ibid.* James Kent to Moss Kent, Jr., October 9, 1794.

[50] *A History of Columbia University, 1754–1904,* 336.

[51] James Kent to William Kent, April 5, 1847. *Kent Papers,* Vol. XI.

[52] *Loc. cit.*

[53] James Kent. *An Introductory Lecture to a Course of Law Lectures Delivered November 17, 1794.* This has been reprinted in *Columbia Law Review,* III, 330–343, and future citations will be to that reprint.

strate the compatibility between the liberal arts and law. Since the legal mind should be precise and orderly, it is expedient that it should be disciplined by logic and mathematics.[54] Since it must attend to numerous questions involving rights and duties, it should be informed with the precepts of moral philosophy.[55] All the arts indeed are necessary to furnish forth the complete lawyer who, the lecturer declared, "should resemble Tully whose fruitful mind as [Quintilian] observes was not bounded by the walls of the forum but by those of nature." [56] To the storing of such an intellect no contributions are more apt than those which the Greek and Roman authors alone can give, for they impart good taste, information and moral wisdom all at once; [57] while even from the narrower view-point of professional advancement, they may be regarded as useful, since they necessitate an acquaintance with the language of the civil law, the tongue of Ulpian and of Papinian.[58]

Moreover, if a knowledge of the liberal arts is beneficial to the lawyer, to the layman equally beneficial is a knowledge of the law. Since the science deals with the subject of government and public policy, it enables him better to understand his times, for those times are preoccupied with nothing more absorbing than thought and speculation upon that very subject.[59] The study therefore is not without its philosophical value. It has its practical advantage also, even for him whose calling is elsewhere than to the bar. In a commonwealth such as ours, to the layman as well as to the lawyer, public office is accessible.[60] The consequence of that fact is clear. The lay-

[54] *Columbia Law Review*, III, 339.
[55] *Loc. cit.*
[56] *Ibid.*, 338.
[57] *Ibid.*, 339.
[58] *Loc. cit.*
[59] *Ibid.*, 330.
[60] *Ibid.*, 331.

man himself should be familiar with the laws over against the day when he may be called upon to assume public responsibility. Although this should not happen, he will yet discover that legal knowledge can be useful to the private citizen. As it did among his ancestors, it will promote in him the desire to watch with a jealous eye the conduct of the magistrates, arouse him to be ever on his guard against the usurpations of tyranny.[61] Nor less in his private than in his public relations will that knowledge prove its desirability, for "The science of law has expressly for its object the advancement of social happiness and security. It reaches to every tie which is endearing to the affections and has a concern on every action which takes place in the extensive circles of public and private life. According to the lively expression of Lord Bacon it may justly be said to *come home to every man's business and bosom.*" [62]

Having established the propriety of jurisprudence as an academic pursuit, the speaker addressed himself more directly to the public and political aspects of the study. It was, he declared, especially appropriate for young men of talent, as it opened the way to the highest honors of the commonwealth.[63]

That these youths might be grounded in correct doctrine, the lecturer spent some time in discussing the sources from which they should obtain their knowledge. He stated emphatically that the common law of England was indispensable; [64] but at the same time he warned his hearers against the unequal and oppressive maxims which, as he believed, still remained a blemish upon it.[65] That law confirmed and accentuated what Kent called "the adventitious advantages of

[61] *Ibid.*, 332–333.
[62] *Ibid.*, 342.
[63] *Ibid.*, 331–332.
[64] *Ibid.*, 334.
[65] *Ibid.*, 333.

birth or fortune," [66] for which he professed no liking; though his acceptance of property and of the rights of inheritance as defined in American law, may have laid him open to a charge of inconsistency. As John Adams, in criticizing his lecture, pointed out, the inheritance of any property is an adventitious advantage whether it be the title to an earldom or a farm.[67] Just though the observation was, Kent nevertheless was right in believing that the English laws in the process of adaptation to American circumstances had been shorn of their greatest inequalities; and the system which had resulted from that process he indicated as the proper source of doctrine for American students. The position was sensible enough, for after all, it was the American commonwealth to whose honors young lawyers were to aspire. As for Kent himself, like his contemporaries of the New York Bar, he had sought and would continue to seek his own knowledge of jurisprudence chiefly in the English sources; and many of the doctrines that he found there he was often to praise and apply in his subsequent career. The concern of the common law for liberty was a feature of the system which compelled his admiration again and again. Nevertheless, as a lecturer he chose to emphasize the monarchical and reactionary traits of English jurisprudence; nor did he hesitate to express his partiality for American laws which he said were the best "take them for all in all, of any people that ever united in the bonds of civil society." [68]

So thoroughly persuaded was he of their excellence that he seemed to think that there was little chance of improving upon them. At any rate, he cautioned his audience against novelty,[69] and bade them beware of further change as if

[66] *Columbia Law Review,* III, 331.

[67] John Adams to Charles Adams, February 14 and 15, 1795. *Kent Papers,* Vol. II.

[68] *Columbia Law Review,* III, 343.

[69] *Loc. cit.*

American experiments with republican principles had produced all that was necessary to political progress. If he appeared to dislike certain of the more aristocratic features of the English law, he was by no means ready to go along with the French in urging extreme democratic doctrines; and he expressed the belief that as society here had escaped the burdensome establishments which oppress, so it should avoid the wild innovations which disturb the transatlantic world.[70] Extreme measures might be necessary to Europe where the tyranny of pope and feudal lord had first to be overthrown before the fabric of true freedom could be raised.[71] Fortunately they were not needed in America; and learning imbued with the Jacobinical ideas of the French would be even more dangerous to American freedom than it would if colored by the aristocratic prejudices of the English.[72] Let students of law shun both English reaction and Gallic revolution, let them seek their inspiration in America and "imbibe the principles of republican government from pure fountains."[73] Such was the injunction which the professor laid upon his pupils.

The study of American jurisprudence was to be regarded, then, as the most conducive to the just esteem of liberty. Indeed according to Kent liberty depended for its continuance upon the maintaining of that jurisprudence in its pristine vigor. How that might be done was another consideration which rendered it imperative for American lawyers to be conversant with American principles. Of these none was more characteristic than the power of our courts to bring the validity of a statute to the test of the constitution.[74] The expediency of the principle had already been demonstrated, as Kent believed, in the case of *Trevett* v. *Weeden* where the

[70] *Ibid.*, 333.
[71] *Ibid.*, 343.
[72] *Loc. cit.*
[73] *Ibid.*, 333.
[74] *Ibid.*, 334.

Rhode Island judiciary had nullified the scheme of the legislature to wipe out debts with an issue of fiat money.[75] Lest the privilege of the courts to intervene in similar cases in the future should be doubted, he proceeded to expound and defend the doctrine of judicial review.[76]

Dangers to liberty arise not only from the caprice of monarchs. They proceed as well from the passions of majorities; and it is from that source that in America they are to be feared. A principal object of our constitutions is to guard against them by establishing "certain rights to be deemed paramount to the power of the ordinary Legislature" where the passions of the majority are reflected. The legislature therefore cannot properly be itself the judge of the extent of its own authority, for being such, it would be able to explain away those very limitations with which the instrument, in the interest of the minor faction, has sought to restrain it. This contradiction, were it possible, could lead to only one conclusion, the overturn of private rights and the sacrifice of the minority to the vindictiveness of the multitude.[77] Against this danger the power of a firm and impartial tribunal, lifted above the rage and malice of party,[78] is the surest and the most logical safeguard, keeping the legislature within the charter of its authority by testing the dubious statute according to the standard of the fundamental law.

Armed with their weapon of review, the courts do more than assuage the force of the collisions between the few and the many. They do more than protect the rights of the minority against popular assault. By holding even the balance of authority among the great departments, they maintain that

[75] *Loc. cit.*, and note at bottom of page, *Columbia Law Review*, III, 334.

[76] The discussion occurs, *ibid.*, 334–337.

[77] *Columbia Law Review*, III, 335.

[78] Of course, a Federalist judge, by his very nature, would be above partisan malice—*e.g.* Mr. Justice Chase or for that matter a little later, Judge Kent himself.

equilibrium of government itself without which, as Montesquieu had shown, liberty is impossible. Of these departments the judiciary is the least, the legislature the most, likely to commit encroachments upon the others,[79] a process which when consummated, produces tyranny; for then all power is vested in a single body and can be exercised without any external check or hindrance. This the constitution has tried to prevent by a nice delimitation of the respective spheres of governmental authority. If these can be at will transcended by the legislature, the very constitution itself becomes a nullity; and indeed it deserves to become so, unless it has somewhere provided a check to prevent the transgression. That check is furnished by the courts, and "to contend that the courts must adhere implicitly to the acts of the legislature without regarding the Constitution, and even when these acts are in opposition to it, is to contend that the power of the agent is greater than that of his principal and that the will of only one concurrent and coordinate department of the subordinate authority, ought to control the fundamental laws of the people." [80]

Such was the unique role which Kent, nine years before *Marbury* v. *Madison,* assigned to the courts of justice. He regarded it as the essential means of preserving the fabric of American government in its original perfection. To preserve it, he declared, is a trust, and it is a trust which by its very nature can be the most safely committed to the men of law, not only to those who are already distinguished in the profession, but also to such of the youth "as are animated with the generous passion of becoming hereafter distinguished as lawyers, magistrates and statesmen. . . ." [81] And he concluded his discourse by defining the purpose by which his

[79] *Columbia Law Review,* III, 337.
[80] *Columbia Law Review,* III, 336–337. Cf. *The Federalist,* No. 78.
[81] *Ibid.,* 343.

instruction would be guided: "If he to whom is entrusted in this seat of learning the cultivation of our laws, can have any effect in elevating the attention of some of our youth from the narrow and selfish objects of the profession to the nobler study of the general principles of our government and the policy of our laws—if he can in any degree illustrate their reason, their wisdom and their propitious influence on the freedom, order and happiness of society and thereby produce a more general interest in their support, he will deem it a happy consolation for his labors." [82]

Those labors lasted for a period of some four years during which Kent succeeded in surveying with a fair degree of comprehensiveness the whole field of American government and law.[83] He examined the nature and duties of government in general, and he reviewed the several forms of polity which have appeared in the world from time to time. He traced the political history of the United States to the making of the Constitution. From that point, he proceeded to a discussion of the consequences of America's independence upon her relations with the foreign world and the numerous incidents of war, peace and of neutrality to which those relations were subject. From the law of nations, he returned to dwell at length upon the domestic constitutions; and the federal government and the governments of the states, especially of New York, received their just share of attention. From public law he descended to the humbler but more difficult theme of private law to deal with the rights of property both real and personal, with the methods by which they are acquired and transferred, with contracts, with the forms of action and with crimes and punishments,[84] all these as they were at the

[82] *Loc. cit.*

[83] A synopsis of the future course occurs in the preliminary discourse, *Columbia Law Review,* III, 341, from which the above synopsis is taken.

[84] He was uncertain that his course would extend to the subjects of actions, crimes and punishments, however. *Loc. cit.*

time embodied in the jurisprudence of New York State.

The course was more comprehensive than successful. Whether its content was too professional for the student of the arts, or too academic for the apprentices-at-law, is doubtful. At any rate, the hopes of the professor were disappointed. In December, 1794, he had written to his brother that the lectures were well attended and that he believed the fees would reach £200; [85] but in the following year, the account was less gratifying. The lectures by that time were indifferently received, only two students had appeared for the term, and them the professor instructed in his office without much concern for their advancement.[86] The fate of the course, however, seems not to have been exceptional. With all their learning and experience, Judge Parker at Harvard and Judge Wilson at the College of Philadelphia met with no better success.[87] That fact, had he known it, might have afforded consolation of a kind to Professor Kent. Be that as it may, he was too much dissatisfied with his results to accept his stipend any longer, and in the spring of 1797 he sent in his resignation.[88] The trustees, however, were unwilling to accept it, until the bestowal upon him of an honor more distinguished than that of a chair in Columbia, induced them at last to let him go.[89]

But they did not bid him farewell without paying tribute to his learning. At ceremonies in May, 1797, when honorary degrees were being conferred, up rose Brockholst Livingston with the pertinent query: "Why do we pass by our learned law professor who does the college so much honor?" [90] His colleagues of the corporation seem to have countered with a

[85] James Kent to Moss Kent, Jr., December 11, 1794. *Kent Papers,* Vol. II.

[86] James Kent to Moss Kent, Jr., January 4, 1796. *Kent Papers,* Vol. II.

[87] *A History of Columbia University 1754–1904,* 340.

[88] James Kent to Moss Kent, Jr., May 18, 1797. *Kent Papers,* Vol. II.

[89] They accepted the resignation a year later when Kent was appointed Justice of the Supreme Court of New York.

[90] James Kent to William Kent, April 5, 1847. *Kent Papers,* Vol. XI.

"Why indeed?" And so, for the first time in his life, though not for the last, James Kent was adorned with a Doctorate of Laws.[91]

* * *

Kent had accepted the professorship of law in the hope that it might be a source of edification to the community and of benefit to himself. From the authority which he believed it would lend his name he had expected an enlarged and more lucrative practice to result.[92] The fact was that his business had begun to mend even before his appointment.

The sudden improvement in his fortunes he owed to the merchant, James Greenleaf, who with his partner James Watson, and with Robert Morris and John Nicholson of Philadelphia, had speculated on a grand scale in real estate in the future city of Washington.[93] Many years later, writing in a reminiscent vein to his son, Kent invoked the aid of Vergil to describe the changes which the appearance of the Capital had undergone in half a century:

> ac rara domorum
> tecta vident, quae nunc Romana potentia caelo
> aequavit, tum res inopes Evandrus habebat:
> —Capitolia—
> aurea nunc, olim silvestribus horrida dumis
> —passimque armenta videbant
> Romanoque Foro et lautis mugire Carinae.[94]

The verses were a summary, more or less apt, of the developments which Greenleaf and his associates had foreseen, no doubt, in 1793; and they had laid out a considerable fortune

[91] *Catalogue of the Governors, Trustees, etc., of Columbia College,* 212—James Kent LL.D., 1797.

[92] James Kent to Moss Kent, Jr., January 7, 1794. *Kent Papers,* Vol. II.

[93] James Kent to William Kent, March 29, 1847. *Kent Papers,* Vol. XI.

[94] Quoted in the above letter; Aeneid viii, 98–100, 347–348, 360–361.

in what to the unseeing eye appeared very much like thicket, swamp and sand-hill. The purchase of six thousand lots at £25 and £35 each[95] was certainly no niggard investment in the future of the Federal City. In December, 1793, Greenleaf proposed a journey to inspect his properties, and considering it wise to have counsel at his elbow, he lent James Kent a coat[96] and paid him a liberal retainer to accompany him.[97] It was the first remunerative employment which the impecunious attorney had had since his arrival in New York.

From the trip he returned with money in his purse and with his spirits and his prospects much improved. It was not long before he himself, following the example of the whole coterie of Federalist lawyers and politicians,[98] began to tempt the favors of fortune by those speculations in real estate for which the virgin wilderness of northern and of western New York opened up a boundless opportunity. In the spring of 1794 he sold his house and lot in Poughkeepsie for £400, paid the balance of what he still owed upon the property, and let out the remaining £200 at interest.[99] Presently he was invited by his friends, Robert Troup and Samuel Boyd, to join with them in a purchase on credit of 69,000 acres at four shillings an acre within the boundaries of the future county of Steuben. He considered the proposal, assented to it; but before the papers had passed, prudently sold his interest in the scheme

[95] *Loc. cit.*

[96] *Loc. cit.* Kent's own coat was too thin for a winter-journey, he says, and this gives a fair idea of how low his fortunes had fallen.

[97] *Loc. cit.* This letter, and the "Memoranda of Tour to Washington, December 5, 1793–January 3, 1794," at the end of the first volume of the papers describe the incidents of the trip. Rufus King rode in the stage with them to Philadelphia, and introduced Kent to President Washington. Kent met also James Madison, and saw John Adams "talking all around with more self-importance than Washington himself." At Georgetown he dined with General "Harry" Lee.

[98] Dixon R. Fox, *Decline of Aristocracy in the Politics of New York*, 120, *et seq.*

[99] James Kent to Moss Kent, Jr., June 2, 1794. *Kent Papers*, Vol. II.

for a neat profit of $2500.[100] Nor was that the only lucrative transaction in which he participated. He bought an interest in a township in the county of Ontario, and sold it at a gain of £1000.[101] With the Baileys and the Platts, from whom his estrangement had proved but temporary, he joined in another and a more extensive speculation; this time in the northern part of the state near Plattsburgh where his sister Hannah and her husband, William Pitt Platt, were settled. At twenty shillings an acre, the associates bought a tract of 4300 acres which Kent found to be a good investment also.[102] A saw-mill and a grist-mill were built upon the property, settlers were coming in; and in a short time the price of the land was rising toward thirty shillings an acre; [103] while Kent never forgetful of his brother's kindness, invited him to come in upon the speculation.[104] Such operations were no doubt somewhat dangerous, and they proved the ruin of more substantial men than Kent whose prudence, however, was sufficient to save him from catastrophe. "Everything," as he wrote to Theodorus Bailey, "has been reared up and supported by the Dedalian wings of paper credit and has approached too near the sun." [105] The resulting crash he anticipated with uneasiness; but he escaped unhurt and considerably enriched, one of those temperate speculators, as he had said complacently enough, who had provided the means when they created the debt.[106]

[100] James Kent to William Kent, April 5, 1847. *Ibid.*, Vol. XI.

[101] James Kent to Moss Kent, Jr., February 4, 1795. *Ibid.*, Vol. II.

[102] James Kent to Moss Kent, Jr., March 12, 1796. *Ibid.*

[103] James Kent to Moss Kent, Jr., October 13, 1796. *Ibid.* Kent appears to reckon his profits now in dollars and cents and again in pence, shillings and pounds.

[104] Moss Kent, Jr., to James Kent, October 23, 1796. *Kent Papers*, Vol. II, Moss accepted the offer.

[105] James Kent to Theodorus Bailey, December 31, 1796. *Ibid.*

[106] *Loc. cit.* He sold out to William and J. Bailey a good part of his northern holdings, some of which he kept, and visited in the course of one of his northern eyres. James Kent to Moss Kent, Jr., June 13, 1797. *Ibid.*, Vol. II.

Enticed no further into such transactions than he thought it safe to go, Kent devoted his best energies to the law; and the place which he won for himself among the lawyers of New York, soon demonstrated the wisdom of his removal to the city. Though the first few months of his sojourn there might well have led to a contrary conclusion, his reputation as a gifted advocate had preceded him nevertheless, and as his appointment at Columbia had proved, he was known and respected by both the bench and bar. "Is not Mr. Kent admitted into this court?" asked Chancellor Livingston with some surprise one March day in 1794 when Kent applied for his license as a chancery solicitor. "He ought to have been long ago," declared Livingston and added, "I want no examination. Let his license as solicitor and counsel be made out and he may be sworn in to both degrees at once." [107] It was no sooner said than done, and thus Kent made his first contact with the Court of Equity which was to become in time so much his own handiwork. From the chancellor's house he walked up Broadway to encounter in the person of John Glover his first business in chancery. Glover who had been stopped in the building of a new house by an injunction obtained on the ground that it blocked his neighbor's alley, applied to Kent for aid. Straightway the case was accepted; the answer drawn, and the notice served on Robert Troup, the opposing counsel, of a motion before the chancellor at Clermont to dissolve the injunction. To the astonishment of Troup, the chancellor granted his opponent's prayer. The injunction was dissolved. Glover proceeded with his building while Kent, fifty dollars richer for his pains, felt as he long afterward confessed "the triumph of a Caesar." [108]

Despite this auspicious beginning, it was not in equity, however, that he found his most frequent employment. That field

[107] James Kent to William Kent, April 5, 1847. *Ibid.*, Vol. XI.
[108] James Kent to William Kent, April 5, 1847. *Ibid.*, Vol. XI.

of jurisprudence had not yet been seriously cultivated in America,[109] and its doctrines would not be well understood until Kent himself should become chancellor. Meanwhile the law proper was being investigated with such unprecedented thoroughness as to astound the judges themselves. The Supreme Court of the now independent State of New York was not especially impressive as a judicial body. Their sessions were not punctually held; [110] and if Kent is to be believed, the Chief Justice, Richard Morris and his successor Robert Yates, were both of them too ignorant and too bibulous to be truly ornamental to the bench.[111] Their colleague, John Sloss Hobart, was more austere in his deportment, but he knew less law even than they; [112] and he owed his ermine to political services in the Revolution. In the early 1790's the number of the judges was increased to five as Yates and Hobart welcomed to their company John Lansing, Morgan Lewis and Egbert Benson.[113] Of these the first was supposed to be, the third undoubtedly was a great improvement; for Benson, as Attorney-General, had more than once supplied the deficiencies of the court of

[109] James Kent to William Kent, February 17, 1847. *Ibid.* Kent there says the chancellor was then *pro forma* as there was almost no chancery business. However, he himself, as a Master in chancery, had plenty of business.

[110] *Loc. cit.*

[111] *Loc. cit.* and James Kent to William Kent, March 7, 1847. *Ibid.*

[112] *Loc. cit.* Cf. the opinion of Judge Hobart expressed in the Albany *Register*, September 28, 1801:—"This gentleman may be a good farmer, but God Almighty never intended him for a judge."

[113] Richard Morris, Chief Justice, retired in 1790 and Robert Yates succeeded him. That left John Sloss Hobart as the sole puisne-judge until the almost immediate appointment of John Lansing. Morgan Lewis was added in 1792 and Egbert Benson in 1794. *Vide* beginning of the first volume of *Johnson's Cases.* According to some contemporary opinion Benson was not brilliant as a jurist:—"His Honor has always claimed the prerogative of expressing himself in dark and unintelligible terms. The rules of the Supreme Court, which are of his inditing, will long remain a monument of the confusion of his ideas." Albany *Register*, September 28, 1801.

which [114] he now became a member. But even then, much was still wanting to make the tribunal influential in the development of law.[115] Nevertheless the law, like a crab, began to progress by going backward, by returning to ancient principles. The source of this impulse was the New York Bar, whose members, well-informed though they may have been, had never until now been either so curious about their science or so well-supplied with materials for satisfying that curiosity. Law books were scarce even yet; but the means of information, woefully meager in the days when Kent was studying under Benson, were slowly but steadily enlarged in the closing decade of the century.[116] The older learning of the common law represented by the names of Coke and Littleton was being more accurately explored than ever before.[117] It was no academic exercise. As has been shown concerning Kent himself, the lawyers of New York were much preoccupied with the business of becoming landowners. For many centuries, the ownership of land had been the foundation of aristocracy; [118] and the Federalists, to whose company most self-respecting lawyers belonged, were well aware of the fact and, in spite of correct republican principles, strove to affect the manners and the habits of a landed gentry.[119]

[114] James Kent to William Kent, February 17, 1847. *Kent Papers,* Vol. XI.

[115] James Kent to William Kent, March 7, 1847. *Ibid.*

[116] See the Appendix to the end of this chapter, pp. 120–122.

[117] James Kent to William Kent, March 7, 1847. *Ibid.*, Vol. XI. I have followed Kent in stressing the revived interest taken in the law at this time. But it seems that the New York Bar had always throughout colonial times sustained a high reputation. *Vide* Julius Goebel, "The Courts and the Law in Colonial New York" in Alexander C. Flick's *History of the State of New York,* III, 3–42.

[118] Esmein, *Cours élémentaire d'Histoire du Droit Français,* "La Condition des Terres et l'état des Personnes," 187 *et seq.* How much of Pollock and Maitland's *History of English Law* is concerned with land-tenures needs hardly be called to mind.

[119] Dixon R. Fox, *Decline of Aristocracy,* Chap. vi *passim.*

To this end, they bought the virgin acres of New York in parcels of fantastic extent; [120] and though they sold at speculative prices, they were not speculators merely. They built fine houses in the country and to their estates they gave the names of their families.[121] Here they dwelt in very decent style indeed, drinking their Madeira, reading their Latin histories,[122] riding about on their spirited horses, entertaining their friends with open house, and condescending to the pioneers who, busy with their axes in the woods, had better things to do than gape in wonder at such outlandish affectations. Perhaps the woodland-farmer paid a gruff respect to all this alien quality, for the gentlemen were by no means mere dandified ornaments. They were oftentimes, like Squire William Cooper, hard-headed, somewhat choleric landlords, and they discharged with zeal and pleasure the duties of local magistrates; were sheriffs, justices-of-the-peace and surrogates; and like the gentlemen of England, they attended the judges at assize.

Into the pattern of such activities the traditions of Coke-Littleton fitted nicely, and that ancient jurisprudence which had been land-law ere it became the law of the land [123] was not alien, despite the obsolescence of feudal tenures, to the broad acres of New York where titles were often confused and dubious, and where most civil cases, tried before the justices-in-eyre, were concerned with ejectments and the acrimonious disputes between tenant and landlord.[124] It was therefore by no means accidental that as the eighteenth century drew toward its close, Robert Troup, Egbert Benson, Richard

[120] *Loc. cit.*

[121] *Loc. cit.*

[122] Moss Kent at Cooperstown writes to his brother about being found by Hamilton reading Tacitus in the Squire's library. James Kent on his eyres saw evidences of classical scholarship in *Bath* and *Canandaigua.*

[123] The phrase is Professor Plucknett's.

[124] James Kent to William Kent, March 7, 1847. *Kent Papers,* Vol. XI.

Harison, Samuel Jones the Elder, James Kent and Alexander Hamilton should have sought familiarity with the lore of *Coke-Littleton.*[125] They were land speculators, land owners and the attorneys to landed gentlemen. It was their business to be conversant with the doctrines and traditions of the land law.

That, however, was not their sole, or even their most serious concern; nor did it prevent them from assuming an amphibious character to deal with the new questions of maritime law which the rising commerce of the city, the renewed strife between France and England and the neutral position of America combined to bring conspicuously forward. Though cases involving the older principles might predominate on the dockets of the courts in the hinterland, litigation in the metropolis arose more frequently upon questions to which those principles afforded little guidance.[126] The causes there smacked of the atmosphere of wharves and of the salty tang of the seas whence ships came sailing in laden with fortunes for the enterprising merchant. Him the common law, like the gentlemen whose interest it had long subserved, had until recently been inclined to hold unworthy of high regard. As long as wealth had consisted almost entirely in the possession of land, the attitude was intelligible, and rationally enough it was with land that the common law had been preoccupied. "I am sure," says Mr. Justice Park, "I rather go beyond the bounds if I assert that in all our reports from the reign of Queen Elizabeth to the year 1756 . . . there were sixty cases

[125] James Kent to William Kent, March 7, 1847. *Ibid.*, and James Kent to William Kent, February 17, 1847. *Ibid.* Troup, Benson, and Jones, Sr., "the oracle of the law" seem to have been more proficient in the older learning than in the new. Harison and Hamilton excelled in both. *Vide et* James Kent to Elizabeth Hamilton, December 10, 1832. *Ibid.*, Vol. VI.

[126] James Kent to Elizabeth Hamilton, December 10, 1832. *Ibid.* He says commercial causes and especially those relating to marine insurance contributed the bulk of litigation.

upon matters of insurance." [127] Few and unimportant also were the cases which had to do with charter-parties and with bills of lading and exchange.[128] This disregard of merchants and of mercantile transactions was becoming by the mid-eighteenth century a thing of the past. It was then that the process of assimilating commercial custom to the common-law, a process tentatively begun by Coke,[129] somewhat haltingly carried on by Holt,[130] was boldly consummated by the brilliant Scot who in 1756 donned the robes of Lord Chief Justice and proceeded to win lasting renown as the Earl of Mansfield. In the reports of his decisions,[131] the Federalist lawyers of New York found and appropriated new resources to aid them in their litigation. The discovery was a boon to themselves, and to their clients, the merchants; and in the skilful hands of Harison, Kent and Hamilton it became an added stimulus to the growth and development of cis-atlantic law.[132] It was through them especially, and in New York naturally enough because of its rapidly expanding trade, that the learning of Mansfield and the doctrines of the law-merchant were introduced into America as though to demonstrate the adaptability of the common law to American needs and to compensate for the obsolescence of its feudal titles. But Sir Edward Coke was not forgotten; and thus, supported by him upon the one side, and by Mansfield upon the other, the law-

[127] Quoted by Thomas E. Scrutton, *Select Essays in Anglo-American Legal History*, III, 7.

[128] *Loc. cit.*

[129] Theodore F. T. Plucknett, *A Concise History of the Common Law*, 227–228.

[130] *Loc. cit.*

[131] Sir James Burrow, 1701–1782: *Reports of the Cases Argued and Determined in the Court of the King's Bench during the time of Lord Mansfield's Presiding*, 4th edition, 5 vols., 1790. *Dictionary of National Biography*, VII, 448. Mansfield, *Obiit*, 1793.

[132] James Kent to William Kent, February 17, 1847. March 7, 1847. *Kent Papers*, Vol. XI; James Kent to Elizabeth Hamilton, December 10, 1832. *Ibid.*, Vol. VI.

yers of New York pursued their career like agile performers in the circus who, standing erect with their nimble feet planted well apart, ride two horses at a time. By both the landed gentry and the merchants [133] they were loudly applauded and upon both they levied with impartial hand for fame and fortune.

Proud as they were of American law, they did not pretend to find it sufficient for their needs. Nor were they content to confine their investigations to English sources. Following the example of Hamilton, who seems to have got the lion's share of commercial causes,[134] the New York lawyers began to extend their studies to the continental codes, and to take Emerigon and Valin within the range of their observation.[135]

But commercial law in many of its aspects is related to maritime law which in turn affects not only the rights of individuals but also those of neutral and belligerent countries; and thus from their study of marine insurance, to choose but a single instance, Hamilton and his fellow attorneys were led by natural steps to a study of the law of nations.

To this they were induced by political as well as professional expediency. The Federalists had succeeded in 1795 in electing John Jay the Governor of the State; and with characteristic fervor they congratulated themselves upon the event. "I believe now I may say *redeunt Saturnia regna,*" [136] wrote Kent to his brother; but less than a month later, the advent of the golden age was jeopardized by the disclosure of the treaty which Jay had brought with him back from England. The unpopularity of the instrument threatened to rob the Federalists of the sweetness of their victory, and upon the very day

[133] As has been remarked above, the interests of these two groups pretty well coincided in New York. See Spaulding, *supra cit.*

[134] James Kent to Elizabeth Hamilton, December 10, 1832. *Kent Papers,* Vol. VI.

[135] *Loc. cit.*

[136] James Kent to Moss Kent, Jr., June 17, 1795. *Ibid.,* Vol. II.

when its terms became known, Kent informed his brother that the whole town was in a ferment.[137] "When the treaty comes to be correctly seen," he said with naïve faith in the efficacy of legal arguments to assuage popular indignation, "When it comes to be correctly seen and maturely considered, compared with other treaties and the impartial law of nations, it will be found to be right and that we have cancelled no more than what justice and true policy required and have obtained what we might reasonably have expected." Kent's view was that of the Federalists in general, but their opponents were not easily convinced. The governor was burnt in effigy; [138] and the polite Federalists must have been not a little disturbed when they read the placard posted up conspicuously in a New York street: "Damn John Jay! Damn everyone that won't damn John Jay!! Damn everyone that won't put lights in his windows and sit up all night damning John Jay!!!" [139] The words had an ugly sound; and in a day when the bare mention of *Jacobin* made gentlemen nervous, they may well have suggested the howling of Parisian mobs for the heads of aristocrats. At any rate the populace of New York was unmannerly, if not exactly lusting after blood; and they impelled Kent, with other prominent attorneys, to write to the newspapers in an attempt to show, beside other things, that Grotius, Vattel and Pufendorf, had they been alive, would have approved the treaty.[140]

Of that instrument one of the objectionable articles was the tenth which provided that "Neither the debts due from individuals of the one nation to individuals of the other, nor

[137] James Kent to Moss Kent, Jr., July 2, 1795. *Kent Papers*, Vol. II.

[138] DeAlva S. Alexander, *Political History of New York*, I, 65.

[139] *Loc. cit.*

[140] James Kent to Theodorus Bailey, August 7, 1795. *Kent Papers*, Vol. II. He says there that the excitement about the treaty had prompted him to a renewed study of international law. James Kent to Moss Kent, Jr., July 27, 1795: Numbers 6 and 7 in the *Minerva* he says are by him.

shares nor monies which they may have in public funds, or in the public banks, shall ever in any event of war or national differences be sequestered or confiscated." [141] The subject was one of utmost delicacy, for Americans were extremely sensitive about the debts which they owed to the subjects of their former King; though from another point of view, it might more fittingly be said that they were callous rather than sensitive, since they had never discovered any impulsiveness to pay. Moreover, while the debts which they owed to Englishmen were numerous, the debts owed by Englishmen to them were few; and while Englishmen had money in the public banks and in the public funds of the United States, Americans had few if any similar investments in Great Britain. Hence the article was an easy mark for democratic politicians who aimed to show that Jay had brought home an unequal treaty which sold out and betrayed the interests of America.

Kent, writing under the pseudonym of *Decius*, assured his fellow-citizens that the provision was supported by the authority of Vattel,[142] and by that of the judges of England in 1753 when they had answered a Prussian memorial on a kindred subject. To cite Vattel was perhaps a little pedantic. To cite the judges of England was inept, for the democrats were as little enamored of English precedent as Kent himself in his inaugural lecture at Columbia had pretended to be. The writer was not, however, entirely without shrewdness; and playing upon his opponents' notorious sympathy for France, he reminded them that the convention had already renounced the practice of sequestering the property of the subjects of those powers with which the Republic might happen at a

[141] Quoted by Kent, number 6 of the papers written by him and Noah Webster and published in the *Minerva* during the controversy and later published under the title *Vindication of the Treaty of Amity, Commerce and Navigation with Great Britain*. The book is in the New York Public Library. References are to it as *Vindication*.

[142] *Ibid.*, 227.

given time to be at war.[143] He noted too that the same enlightened policy had prevailed with the government of the United States when, despite the bitterness of the Revolutionary conflict, it had not attempted to annul the debts which were owed at the time to the British; [144] and he added: "I think it will be evident from the authorities which I have adduced, that the sequestration and confiscation of debts and public stock, are not *now* the customary admissible weapons of war." [145]

Having marshalled his authorities, he proceeded to demonstrate how expedient it would be to abide by their doctrines. The popular argument that the article was unequal, since almost all the debts in question were owing from Americans to the British, he disposed of in characteristic Federalist fashion. "We have," said he, "immense territories of waste land to clear and settle; an abundance of raw materials for nourishing the manufacturing and mechanic arts: but to answer these ends, requires an unceasing supply of capital, or credit, which in most cases is its eligible substitute. In short there are no people upon earth who have so many inducements as the United States to declare unequivocally to the world, that the claims of their creditors shall always be deemed sacred in peace and in war." [146] Expedience, therefore, as well as reason, dictated the acceptance of the article as wise and just.

So far as the provisions which had to do with commerce were concerned, Kent admitted that they were less liberal than might have been desired.[147] At the same time, when he had a view to the rigorous mercantilistic practices which had long prevailed among the maritime powers, he could not but

[143] *Vindication*, 228.

[144] *Ibid.*, 229. What legal right the Continental Congress would have had to do so, he does not explain.

[145] *Loc. cit.*

[146] *Ibid.*, 230.

[147] *Ibid.*, 233.

conclude that the concessions which Jay had won were evidence of great ability as a negotiator.[148] As an admirer of Adam Smith, Kent disclaimed the intention of vindicating the justness of mercantilism. "The only question is," he declared, "whether there was any reasonable prospect at present of our obtaining better terms; and if not, whether it was not upon the whole for our interest to accept the trade upon *these* terms?" [149] He believed that it was; for American trade would thereby be put upon a footing of legal right.[150] Like an astute attorney who steals his adversary's thunder by invoking as his own the authority on whom that adversary most relies, Kent quoted Thomas Jefferson to the effect that commercial intercourse with a foreign country at the pleasure of that country's government, must always labor under the disadvantage of uncertainty.[151] But when it is based upon treaty-rights, that uncertainty is dispelled. Hence, however much restricted the rights might be which the treaty had established, to accept the instrument was still to the best interest of America for without it "our trade to every British port can be interdicted by a nod of the British executive." [152] Nor ought the narrowness of the concessions to be dwelt upon exclusively. Narrow they were no doubt, but they were, nevertheless, argued Kent, more generous than any other to be met with in commercial treaties between Great Britain and the European powers for more than a century past.[153]

Whether his reasoning had any effect or not upon the fate of Jay's treaty, Kent watched the progress of the instrument through the Senate with grave concern; and at the attempt

[148] *Vindication*, 239.
[149] *Ibid.*, 235.
[150] *Ibid.*, 236.
[151] *Ibid.*, 237.
[152] *Loc. cit.*
[153] *Ibid.*, 238. He cites the treaties between Great Britain and Spain in 1667 and Great Britain and Russia in 1766.

of the House to prevent ratification by asserting its rights to withhold the laws which would be needed to carry the treaty into effect,[154] he waxed vitriolic from impatience. In concerting the obstructionist measures to which the House resorted, his friend, Edward Livingston, that lover of Horace and that apostate from the Federalist proprieties, played an important part; while Kent looked on with disgust and expressed his rancor by calling him an "unprincipled and malicious incendiary," and by labelling the notion that the House could refuse to carry out the treaty as a "cursed doctrine." [155] To his relief, however, and to the relief of all the merchants and of all the lawyers whose hopes for continued income depended much upon keeping the peace with England, the treaty was ratified at last; and Kent wrote with satisfaction to his brother Moss, "the faith of the nation is preserved, the law obeyed and our peace and prosperity confirmed." [156]

For a second time now, Kent had shown enterprise and courage in defending the merits and policies of Jay. Election to the assembly in 1796 gave him an opportunity of taking an official part upon the legislative side in Jay's administration as governor.[157] The relations between them were cordial; but it was sound ability and faithful party service that deserved the appointments with which the governor now began to reward his friend. Early in 1796 he made him a Master in Chancery,[158] and though chancery business was not extensive, the position was profitable, since besides Kent there was but one other Master in the city. The office kept its new incumbent well occupied and its perquisites would alone have been almost

[154] Allen Johnson, *Readings in American Constitutional History,* Chap. xxii *passim.*

[155] James Kent to Moss Kent, Jr., March 12, 1796. *Kent Papers,* Vol. II.

[156] James Kent to Moss Kent, Jr., May 8, 1796. *Ibid.*

[157] Return of the Canvassers for New York City, June 3, 1796. *Ibid. Assembly Journal,* 1796, *passim.*

[158] James Kent to Moss Kent, Jr., March 12, 1796. *Kent Papers,* Vol. II.

sufficient for his support.[159] But there were even better things in store for him. In the next year, he was appointed Recorder of the City of New York.[160]

The position was the most honorable in the judicial system of the state below a judgeship in the Supreme Court. The tribunal over which the Recorder with the Mayor of New York presided was in fact the Court of Common Pleas for the City and County; and it had been given a solid reputation by James Duane, the first Mayor after the departure of the British troops.[161] It was a court before which the best lawyers of the city were not ashamed to appear; and Josiah Ogden Hoffman, Edward and Brockholst Livingston, Egbert Benson, Robert Troup and Aaron Burr had argued before it,[162] while Hamilton had made law there in the celebrated case of *Rutgers* v. *Waddington*. The appointment of Kent did not dim its lustre; for he had emerged from the crowd of competing advocates, as one of the most learned and successful in the profession, and he had received his place by the unanimous voice of the Council of Appointment.[163] At the same time, to the great annoyance of Senator Ambrose Spencer who wanted the inferior post for a friend of his own, the governor signified his wish that Kent should continue as Master in Chancery.[164]

Thus in the enjoyment of two offices at once, the one dignified, the other lucrative,[165] James Kent was exempted from

[159] James Kent to Moss Kent, Jr., May 8, 1796. *Kent Papers*, Vol. II.

[160] James Kent to Moss Kent, Jr., May 18, 1797. *Ibid.*

[161] James W. Brooks, *History of the Court of Common Pleas of the City and County of New York*, 22; *vide et* Richard B. Morris, *Select Cases of the Mayor's Court of New York City, 1674–1784*, esp. 302 *et seq.* for Rutgers v. Waddington.

[162] James W. Brooks, *op. cit.*, 22.

[163] Robert Morris to Judge William Kent (undated). *Kent Papers*, Vol. XI.

[164] *Loc. cit.*

[165] But for Jay's intimation that he should keep both, Kent would have resigned the Chancery appointment which though more profitable, was the

the necessity of contending any longer at the bar. The fact caused him no regret; for though he had been on friendliest terms with the first lawyers of the city [166] and from professional encounters with them [167] had wrested his honors, nevertheless, forensic collisions were not to his taste; [168] and he welcomed an appointment to the bench as a deliverance.

But he was soon to ascend to higher honor and responsibilities. Changes were happening in the Supreme Court. The retirement of Chief Justice Yates and of Puisne Judge John Sloss Hobart gave Governor Jay an opportunity to improve the bench by nominating James Kent and Jacob Radcliffe to fill the vacancies.[169] And so, happily enough, the ways of these two old friends once more converged. The occasion must have been agreeable indeed, and was no doubt enlivened with many reminiscences of the old days in Poughkeepsie, when as young lawyers starting out together they had argued causes for the overseers of the poor about the disposal of paupers and of children born out of wedlock; and had clashed in a case of replevin concerning a horse, a mare and a colt which had broken through the fences to make damage in the field of the Dutchman, Van Bunschoten. It must have enhanced their satisfaction that they put on their judicial robes together to sit down beside Egbert Benson and expound the laws with him who years before had been their own preceptor of the laws.

* * *

---

less honorable of the two. *Vide* James Kent to Moss Kent, Jr., May 18, 1797. *Kent Papers,* Vol. II.

[166] James Kent to William Kent, February 21, 1847. *Ibid.,* Vol. XI.

[167] *Loc. cit.* He mentions having argued causes particularly with Samuel Boyd, Robert Troup and Richard Harison.

[168] James Kent to Moss Kent, Jr., May 18, 1797. *Ibid.,* Vol. II.

[169] Kent in February, Radcliffe in December, 1798.

For some years past, the bench had been the object of Kent's ambition [170] and he received the profferred dignity in full knowledge that it meant pecuniary sacrifice.[171] It meant other things as well, a withdrawal from distasteful practice at the bar,[172] a post of honor of which the tenure was secure and long, a retreat in the countryside where he could expect again the leisure to make a garden and to cultivate the classics more intensively. Such was the life which seemed to him more rational than one devoted merely to money making; [173] though he was too prudent to forget that pecuniary independence is the foundation-stone of well-ordered and successful living.[174]

Such independence he had won for himself in ample measure during his five years' sojourn in New York. The eve of his departure thence found him in as eligible circumstances as most men could have desired. He lived no longer in the dingy little street where his infant daughter had died. Since that event he had twice moved, the second time into Pine Strcet, into a neat, white house of his own,[175] where the welcome cry of a child was heard once again within the walls.

This infant was a daughter also, and the name Elizabeth was likewise given to her; and as the little girl, who was now dead, once had done, so this child delighted her parents, "prodigiously handsome," as she was, "in her eyes and skin." [176] As

[170] "Memoranda," *Kent Papers,* Vol. III; James Kent to Theodorus Bailey, January 29, 1798. *Ibid.*, Vol. II.

[171] James Kent to Theodorus Bailey, January 29, 1798. *Kent Papers,* Vol. II, and "Memoranda," Vol. III.

[172] *Loc. cit.* and "Memoranda," Vol. III.

[173] James Kent to Moss Kent, Jr., January 4, 1796; June 22, 1796; September 22, 1796. *Ibid.*, Vol. II; also May 18, 1797.

[174] James Kent to Moss Kent, Jr., May 18, 1796. *Ibid.*, Vol. II.

[175] In the spring of 1795, James Kent to Moss Kent, Jr., May 11, 1795. *Ibid.*, Vol. II; James Kent to William Kent, February 21, 1847. *Ibid.*, Vol. XI. He had lived at 69 Liberty Street prior to his removal into Pine.

[176] James Kent to Moss Kent, Jr., May 18, 1796. *Ibid.*, Vol. II.

before, Kent furnished his brother with timely bulletins on her development. "She now lays [*sic*] asleep," he wrote, "in her mother's arms close at my elbow and beside the evening fire. Her sweetness and bloom are to me very interesting." [177] Anxious the parents were for the health of their babe; for as Kent once remarked, New York is the "grave-yard of children"; and pestilence continued to walk its streets. But the little Elizabeth survived; and in time was to become a lady of fashion in a New York much richer, much more populous, perhaps a little more healthful than the city into which she was thus happily born.

Serenity pervaded the household of the Kents where from time to time the quiet routine was agreeably varied with visits paid by persons of quality. That great lady, Mrs. Jay, came to drink tea with Mrs. Kent; [178] and Mr. Justice Hobart dropped in of an evening to talk politics and to pull contentedly at the long pipe which his obliging host had sent out to have fetched for his enjoyment.[179] President Dwight, descending from the abode of the Muses at New Haven, called to inquire how Kent was faring, and remained to discuss in appreciative company the merits of Pope and Addison.[180]

Literary interests, then, were not forgotten in the midst of prosperity. On the contrary they became more keen than ever. The library which had begun to be accumulated in Poughkeepsie, now increased very rapidly,[181] as to the law books and the classics were added modern authors, both French and English. In the English novelists especially did Kent delight; and Defoe, Smollett, Richardson and Fielding found their appointed places on the well-stocked shelves.[182] Of these

[177] James Kent to Moss Kent, Jr., November 27, 1796. *Ibid.*
[178] James Kent to William Kent, February 21, 1847. *Kent Papers,* Vol. XI.
[179] James Kent to William Kent, April 5, 1847. *Ibid.*
[180] *Loc. cit.*
[181] James Kent to Moss Kent, Jr., May 18, 1796. *Ibid.,* Vol. II.
[182] James Kent to Moss Kent, Jr., September 22, 1796. *Ibid.*

the last was held in first esteem. "No writer that ever lived was superior to Fielding," opined Kent,[183] in a justifiable exaggeration which at a later day Thackeray himself would have been willing to applaud. Nor did a reading of the English writers preclude an increasing familiarity with the French among whom Voltaire, in particular, made a strong appeal.[184]

This interest in Voltaire might seem surprising; for that Kent had not entirely cast aside his ancestral religion the pew which he rented in the Wall Street Presbyterian Church was evidence.[185] It is certain, however, that he entertained the fashionable doubts concerning orthodox religion; and in the literary club to which he belonged, he aired them. The playwright and painter, William Dunlap, recorded in his diary: "Kent remarked that men of information were now nearly as free from vulgar superstition or the Christian religion as they were in ye [*sic*] time of Cicero from pagan superstition —all, says he, except the literary men among the clergy." [186] From this skepticism it may be inferred that Voltaire's ideas as well as his wit and grace had exercised their fascination upon the mind of the grandson of Elisha Kent, the Dominie, and the son whom Moss Kent the Elder had used to admonish always to remember the one Thing needful. But it was a skepticism, perhaps more affected than genuine; and it restrained itself within the limits of good taste. As his conduct upon the bench was presently to prove, James Kent could not tolerate the vulgar flaunting of infidelity in public and rose chivalrously on occasion to defend the dignity of the Virgin Mary.[187]

[183] *Loc. cit.*

[184] Kent owned Voltaire's works in 92 volumes. James Kent to Moss Kent, Jr., July 17, 1796. *Ibid.*, Vol. II.

[185] James Kent to William Kent, February 21, 1847. *Kent Papers*, Vol. XI.

[186] William Dunlap, *Diary,* I, 151, entry for September 30, 1797.

[187] *The People* v. *Ruggles,* 8 *Johns. Rep.* 290.

Like other members of the club,[188] he allowed himself considerable latitude for theological speculation; notwithstanding that there were divines as well as free-thinkers in the little circle.[189] But other subjects than religion were discussed, for though there were neither Burkes nor Gibbons there, Garricks, Boswells, Johnsons or Goldsmiths, nevertheless the group was representative of all the major interests of the city. There was no Thrale, the Brewer, to be sure, but there was the rich merchant, William Woolsey; no Garrick certainly, but William Dunlap, actor, playwright, stage manager and painter, represented both letters and the theatre. Charles Brockden Brown, less versatile, stood only for literature, while Samuel Latham Mitchill spoke for science, and Kent himself for law and government; and each freely vented his opinions upon whatever matter it was that suggested itself for controversy and discussion. Like the fellowship society of Linonia, it was a friendly, congenial gathering; and since several of its members were Yale alumni, conversation may well have struck at times a reminiscent vein. However that may be, the club offered agreeable companionship and added to the amenities of living in the metropolis.

Even so, Kent, unreconciled to the town, yearned for the day to come, when he could establish himself again in the country. The noise and squalor of the city annoyed him,[190] and when he could, he fled them. Both he and Mrs. Kent were fond of travel; and both were quickly susceptible to the

[188] *E.g.*, Dr. Elihu Hubbard Smith, the physician, whom in his old age he called "a terrible free thinker," James Kent to William Kent, April 5, 1847. *Kent Papers,* Vol. XI.

[189] The membership is partially listed by Kent in the letter to his son of April 5, 1847. *Ibid.*, Vol. XI; more completely in the preface to Dunlap's *Diary*, I, xviii: William Woolsey, G. M. Woolsey, Charles Brockden Brown, E. H. Smith, S. L. Mitchill, Edward Miller, Rev. Dr. Samuel Miller, Anthony Bleecker, James Kent, William Johnson. *Ibid.*, September 23, 1797, I, 149; January 13, 1798, I, 206; August 6, 1798, I, 323.

[190] He calls the city "hot, noisy, hateful." James Kent to Moss Kent, Jr., June 22, 1796. *Kent Papers,* Vol. II.

beauties of mountain, lake and shore. Even before Cooper made it famous, they had admired the Glimmerglass in Otsego County nor did they need the help of Irving to discover the enchantment of the vale of Hudson. In 1795, in company with Colonel Bailey, they journeyed by stage and by boat to Cumberland Head on Lake Champlain, upon whose waters Kent trolled for salmon; but more than in the fishing, he delighted in the varied scenery, and with notes and sketches, he attempted to catch something of the charm of what he saw.[191] From Cumberland Head he pushed on with Colonel Bailey to Montreal to observe the manners of a foreign country and to return with a renewed appreciation of his own; [192] but after the majesty of mountains and the loveliness of lakes, the city must have seemed more cramped and uninviting than ever. Moreover its ignorant neglect of sanitation was giving rise again to plagues; and in the early autumn of the same year, he fled up the river with his wife and child to take refuge in Poughkeepsie.[193] His alarm was well-grounded. During his absence, more than five hundred persons were carried off, though he consoled himself with the fact that those who died were mostly Irish immigrants.[194]

Even after this purgation, the city was a crowded place, and the following summer found it as noisy, hot and hateful as before. "I hope to quit New York at some not distant day," was the repeated burden of Kent's letters to his brother in cool, sequestered Otsego. To quit the metropolis and to live in the country "surrounded by quiet, books, fields, gardens and my lovely wife and daughter," [195] became a desire more

[191] "Memorandum of a Journey to Montreal 17 May–22 June 1795." *Kent Papers,* Vol. II.

[192] *Ibid.* His remarks on the Canadians are far from flattering.

[193] "Memorandum of Tour to Poughkeepsie September 17–October 31, 1795." *Ibid.,* Vol. II.

[194] *Loc. cit.*

[195] James Kent to Moss Kent, Jr., June 22, 1796. *Ibid.,* Vol. II.

and more urgent. The appointment to the bench made possible the gratification of that desire; and losing but little time, Kent sold his house in Pine Street, and ascended the river to dwell once again in the shire-town of Dutchess where the old animosities that had prompted his removal thence, were long since buried and forgotten.

But though Poughkeepsie proved as attractive as had been anticipated, the Kents did not remain there long. For the sake of the judge's convenience, they removed presently to Albany, the new capital of the state, where they made their home throughout the rest of his official career. Their house became a center of social life,[196] and there was no member of the family but fitted into the patterns of the old-fashioned, somewhat ceremonious style characteristic of the city's quality. The dowager, Mrs. Seton, leaving the house after a formal call, curtsied to her host repeatedly, and to each curtsey he returned a deep bow, until they both, exchanging bow and curtsey, found themselves outside upon the steps.[197] Mrs. Kent, though an active woman, who sometimes rode the easier circuits with her husband,[198] and in his absence, with her own hands prepared the garden to bloom at his return,[199] found leisure to cultivate a less ostentatious but a no less pleasing grace. Her conversation was sprightly, she had graciousness and charm,[200] and her drawing-room attracted distinguished men, governors, judges and members of the bar.[201]

After the removal to Albany the family was increased by two more children; a lusty boy was born in 1802, and chris-

[196] There is mention of this in William Kent's *Memoirs and Letters of James Kent,* 119–120.

[197] James Kent to Elizabeth Kent, August 25, 1807. *Kent Papers,* Vol. III.

[198] *Kent Journals,* 1798–1799 (No. 2), July 2, 1799. 1802–1811 (No. 5), 1810, *et passim.*

[199] Elizabeth Kent to James Kent, April 25, 1804. *Kent Papers,* Vol. III.

[200] This may be inferred from her sprightly and good-humored letters.

[201] *Vide* William Kent *op. cit.*

tened William;[202] and some five years later there was another daughter named Mary.[203] Meanwhile Bess, the eldest, went to dancing school, then finishing school, and in a few short years, was attending the governor's ball in a low-necked gown that put her father into a good-natured fret.[204] His pride, however, was unbounded, and in it shared his brother Moss, a bachelor still, who was now a man of consequence in the western counties, a Senator at Albany, and, as of old, a lover of classical lore in which with satisfaction he saw his young nephew properly initiated.[205]

The Kents continued their genteel connections in New York. Whether there or in Albany, the doors of the elect swung open at their touch; and when he held the assizes in the City, the judge was bidden to dinners almost every evening.[206] Especially memorable were those of Mrs. Rufus King where the best Federalist, and hence the best, society of the metropolis foregathered. Yet that lady's entertainments were without ostentation, were marked above everything else by what Kent called "simple elegance,"[207] and he apparently admired them more than all the others, though he was no stranger even at the house of Hamilton. On an afternoon in April, 1804, he might have been seen riding in the General's carriage toward the Grange where a supper was waiting to which Gouverneur Morris had also been invited. But the affair turned out contrary to expectations. While the Judge and General waited for the other guest, a storm arose; the house rocked in the tempest, and as windows rattled and candles flared, Morris sent word that the "Jacobinical winds" would

[202] James Kent to Moss Kent, Jr., December 8, 1802. *Ibid.*, Vol. III.
[203] James Kent to Elizabeth Kent, May 24, 1807. *Ibid.*
[204] James Kent to Theodorus Bailey, April 16, 1814. *Ibid.*
[205] A strong friendship developed between uncle and nephew.
[206] James Kent to Elizabeth Kent, May 13, 1804. *Kent Papers*, Vol. III.
[207] James Kent to Elizabeth Kent, April 20, 1804. *Ibid.*

prevent his coming, whereupon Kent and Hamilton sat down to sup alone.[208]

Appendix to Chapter III—Section 3: That the materials from which a knowledge of the law could be derived were increasing in extent and variety is shown by booksellers' notices published in the newspapers. The following notices are taken from newspapers in the Ebling Collection in the Widener Library:

New York Gazette and General Advertiser, April 5, 1797—
Thomas Roberts, Law books
Dunlap's American Daily Advertiser, New York, October 12, November 17, 1791
Lists of law books advertised for sale by John Sparhawk, William Prichard and by Rice and Company
The Diary or Loudon's Register, New York, April 2, 1792
A long list advertised by Hugh Gaine
The Albany Register, Albany, April 29, 1796, June 20, 1796
Long lists by Spencer and Webb—*Ibid.,* September 30, 1800—List by Gaine and Ten Eyck
The Albany Gazette, October 28, 1796, June 19, 1800
List by Thomas, Andrews and Penniman and by Gaine and Ten Eyck

Some of these lists are inconveniently long. Among other items they contain:

Bacon's Abridgement, Blackstone's Commentaries, Blackstone's Reports, Beccaria's Crimes and Punishments, Burlemaqui, Burrows' Reports, Campbell's Reports, Coke on Littleton, Comyn's Reports, Douglas' Reports, de Lolme, Dyer's Reports, Espinasse's Reports, Fitzherbert's *Natura Brevium,* Hale's Pleas of the Crown, Harison's Chancery, Impey's Practice, Kyd on Bills of Exchange and Promissory Notes, Modern Reports, Montesquieu, Newman's Complete Conveyancer, *Nisi Prius* Causes, Peere Williams, Raymond's Reports, Saunders Uses and Trusts, Strayer's Reports, Vernon's Reports, Vattel's Law of Nations, Wood's Conveyancing.

[208] James Kent to Elizabeth Kent, April 26, 1804. *Ibid.,* and *Kent Journal* 1833 (No. 11), a reminiscent entry, September 11, 1833, when Kent visited the Grange to see Mrs. Hamilton.

The longest list is furnished by Thomas, Andrews and Penniman, *Albany Centinel*, August 14, 1801, and is given *in extenso:*

Ambler's Reports
Andrew's Reports
Attorney's *Vade Mecum*
Attorney's Pocket Book
Blackstone's Commentaries
Bacon's Abridgement
Bunbury's Reports
Barton's Equity
Blackstone's (H) Reports
Burrows' Reports
Boscawen on Conviction
Crokes Reports
Comyn's Digest
Comyn's Reports
Coke's Reports
Cowper's Reports
Crompton's Practice
Christian's Notes on Blackstone's Commentaries
Cases in Equity
Costs in Chancery
Cook's Bankrupt Law
Clerk's Magazine
Collection of Interrogatories
Clarke's Penal Statutes
Davie's Reports
Doctor and Student
Dyer's Reports
Dogherty's Crown Circuit
Dogherty's Crown Circuit Assistant
Douglas' Reports
Durnford's and East's Reports
Equity Pleaders Assistant
Ever's System of Pleading
Eunomus or Dialogue of the Laws of England
Every Man His Own Lawyer
Espinasse's Reports
Foster's Crown Law
Fearn on Remainders
Finche's Chancery
Fitzherbert's *Natura Brevium*
Gilbert on Replevin
Gilbert on Executions
Gilbert on Equity
Gilbert on Rents
Gilbert on Law of Evidence
Harison's Chancery
Hardres Reports
Hurd's Practice
Heywood's Digest
Hale's Common Law
Hargreave's Law Tracts
Hawkins' Pleas of the Crown
Impey's Modern Pleader
Justice's Assistant
Jones's Law of Bailments
Kyd on Bills of Exchange and Promissory Notes
Kyd on Awards
Landlord and Tenant
Laws of New York
Laws of United States
Law of Simony
Law of Attorneys
Lily's Entries
Morgan's Essays
Mallory's Entries
Moseley's Reports

Martin's Law of Nature
Newman's Conveyancer
Plowden's Reports
Pleader's Assistant
Pigott on Recovery
Powell on Contracts
Powell on Powers
Parke on Insurance
Peake's *Nisi Prius*
Raymond's Reports
Reeve's Law of Shipping
Reeve's English Law
Richardson's Practice
Runnington on Ejectments
Ridgeway's Reports
Sherridan's Practice
Saunders on Uses and Trusts
Swift's System of the Law of Connecticut
Sullivan's Lectures
Strange's Reports
Sellon's Practice
Town Officers
Tidd's Practice
Tomlin's Digested Index
Trials per Pais
Vesey's Reports
Vesey Junior
Vattel's Law of Nature
Vernon's Reports
Viner's Abridgement
Wentworth's System of Pleading
Woddeson's Lectures
Williams's Conveyancing
Williams's Justice
Yelverton's Reports

It is interesting to compare these lists with those of the colonial book seller, William Bradford of Philadelphia, which between 1760–1770 were supposed to be very long and to offer evidence that even then the law in America was becoming a stable and known system, and ceasing to be *arbitrium boni viri* only. *Vide* John W. Wallace *An Old Philadelphian, Colonel William Bradford, the Patriot Printer* pp. 16–88, especially p. 92. The list there is good evidence that the eve of the Revolution found a knowledge of law in increasing demand; but it was still elementary as compared with that which was developed in the closing decade of the eighteenth century.

IV

Giving Laws to the Land of Leatherstocking

And Samuel judged Israel all the days of his life, and he went from year to year in circuit, to Bethel and Gilgal and Mispeh, and judged Israel in all those places.

1 Samuel vii; 15, 16

And this Convention doth further, in the name, and by the authority of the good people of this State, ordain, determine and declare that such parts of the Common Law of England and of the Statute Law of England and Great Britain, and of the Acts of the Legislature of the colony of New York, as together did form the law of the said colony on the nineteenth day of April in the Year of Our Lord one thousand seven hundred and seventy-five, shall be and continue the law of this State.

The Constitution of New York, 1777, Art. XXXV

. . . be an enlightened and intrepid guardian of true old English and of common law liberty and constitutional security.

James Kent to Moss Kent, Jr., May 21, 1799

* * *

JAMES KENT'S manner of living was genteel. It was also strenuous. His duties as a judge of the Supreme Court required him not only to sit with his brethren meting out justice in the central curia, but to attend the governor and chancellor in the Council of Revision to pass upon bills sent up from the legislature. The hardest task of all, however, was riding the circuits. On these occasions Kent traversed a country which, except for the valley of the Hudson, appeared almost too primitive to receive that mature jurisprudence which the constitution declared to be New York's basic law.

This thought the judge may well have pondered as he departed for the western shires.[1] The beauty of the landscape excited his admiration and the farther west he travelled, the more his wonder grew until gazing spellbound at Niagara he came near treading on a rattle-snake.[2] But the beauty that he beheld, whether of Niagara, the Genesee or of the Lakes of the Five Nations, was the wild romantic beauty of a wilderness which the pioneer's axe was only beginning to subdue. For many lonesome hours the learned justice, carrying his commissions toward the assizes in the county towns, picked his way on horseback along dim forest trails where brooded an ancient solemn stillness that rebuked the noisy doings of men and made the formalities of courts seem vain and trivial. Though normally of a cheerful disposition, Kent admitted that the primeval solitudes depressed him. "I saw not a soul," he wrote of one stage of his first circuit journey. "The sky was intercepted by the lofty boughs—the eye in vain attempted to penetrate far on either side. The mind was drove into itself for reflections, and became sedate and grave." [3] For such a wilderness a painted Indian armed with bow and tomahawk seemed better fitted than a justice-in-eyre furnished with commissions of gaol-delivery and *nisi-prius.*

And indeed, though the war-whoop no longer echoed among the hills and though the bosoms of Seneca and Cayuga were no longer cloven by the war canoes of befeathered braves, the Indians still tarried in their ancestral haunts. As he penetrated deeper into the western country, Kent saw them frequently, and admired the dignified melancholy of their squaws and the lithe grace of their straight and comely children.[4] But he

[1] *Kent Journal,* 1798 (No. 2). The text from I Samuel which appears at the head of the chapter, was cited by Kent and applied to his own circuit-riding. William Kent, *Memoirs and Letters of James Kent,* 123.

[2] *Kent Journal,* 1802–1811 (No. 5), June 9, 1802.

[3] *Ibid.,* 1798 (No. 2), Memoirs of Journey from Manlius to Camillus.

[4] *Ibid.* Entry dates are not always given.

observed that the Nations were declining, that their blood was being diluted with an alien strain, that their "ancient dominion" was constantly narrowing. "The axe," said he, "is heard all around them, and like the Rhine," he added with a sense of pathos, "they will dwindle in the sands before they are lost in the ocean." [5]

That ominous ringing of the axe sounded an alarm at which the unhappy braves were no longer capable of rising; portended a disseisin without hope of remedy. Deeper with every succeeding year their domains were being penetrated by the relentless Saxon invaders, whose population was yet sparse, to be sure; and as Kent was informed by the sheriff of Steuben, hardly adequate in that county to the needs of juries.[6] That this deficiency would be soon supplied, the judge, however, had no doubt, for he was much impressed at the speed with which the number of settlers was increasing. "They come," he said, "in a continual stream," and he noted the places of their origin, Virginia, Maryland and Pennsylvania [7] to whose sons the Susquehanna and its tributaries gave easy access northward, while the Mohawk, opening its hospitable valley to the east, received the swelling volume of New Englanders, who passing through it hurriedly, spread out among the western shires to mingle with the southerners and Pennsylvanians and with them to make common cause against the wilderness. If the pioneers left much to be desired in cultivation and politeness, they had at least increasing strength of numbers for the task they had undertaken. "This country populates with great rapidity," [8] Kent observed again at the close of a training day at Geneva where he had seen the reassuring sight of five hundred militia-men assembled under arms. The observation was just. The pioneers, like the sons of Noah on the

[5] *Kent Journal,* June 5, 1798.

[6] *Ibid.,* 1798–1799 (No. 3), June 26, 1798.

[7] *Ibid.*

[8] *Ibid.,* 1798 (No. 2).

morrow of the flood, were multiplying and replenishing the earth.

What was the character of this people that was so rapidly supplanting the lordly Iroquois? Upon this question Kent ruminated long and seriously; nor was he wholly pleased with the conclusions at which he arrived. The frontiersmen presented a sharp contrast to the elegance of life and manners to which he had been accustomed since his birth, and Kent, who like some other philosophers discerned or fancied that he discerned a close relation between dress and conduct, drew from the slovenly garb of the frontiersmen certain inferences that were damaging to their reputation. If they looked rude, he was certain that they were; and in several of the counties, he resigned himself to expect the behavior as well as the appearance of the *sans-culottes*. His expectation was often fulfilled. At Willsborough [9] by Lake Champlain on the northern circuit, at Aurora [10] by Lake Cayuga on the western, the people who came jostling into his court were uniformly unprepossessing; and their attire was the outward and visible sign, as he believed, of an inner rudeness. At any rate, he pronounced whole communities immoral, though it was for the counties of Delaware and Tioga that he reserved his severest censures. Those counties in his opinion were more than rude, worse than immoral. They were fierce; they were licentious; they were profligate—and most damning sin of all, they were Democratic.

Any offense but that the judge might have been willing to condone; but Democracy was unpardonable, not only because it was evil in itself, but because it was the root of all other evils. It summed them all up and it explained them all; and as Kent attached bad manners to rude dress, and low

[9] *Kent Journal*, 1800–1811 (No. 4), June 20, 1800. "Jurors and people looked rude in their manners and dress and gave me an unfavorable opinion of the morals of the country."

[10] *Ibid.*, 1798 (No. 2).

morals to bad manners, so he traced low morals to Democracy and he used the two expressions as practically synonymous. The inhabitants of Delaware and Tioga furnished capital illustrations of his thesis. "They are a rude, fierce people," he exclaimed of the settlers in the latter county, "very democratic and licentious, and there is little government among them." [11] In Kent's estimation they proved the truth of the prophecies of degradation with which the Federalist seers had execrated the advent of Thomas Jefferson to power. That calamity had been the more deplorable inasmuch as it had been followed presently with a kindred misfortune in the state, when George Clinton, coming out of retirement, had been elected to succeed John Jay as governor. These events, while they made the backwoodsmen of Tioga jump for joy, afflicted Kent with the most painful apprehensions for their future. He saw their county as a veritable cave of Jacobinical winds where little that was honest, just and seemly could be preserved. "The pernicious effects of the violent Jacobin administration in this and the United States begins to be sensibly and strongly felt," said he, and he added with misgiving, "The best men are no longer in office and government becomes degraded and feeble and threatens to pervert the administration of justice and introduce violence and oppression." [12] Such was the state of affairs in the county of Tioga which was now successfully competing for the bad preeminence which the judge had formerly assigned to Delaware. That shire he had not hesitated to describe as morally deformed; and from its inhabitants, consisting, as he disdainfully said, "of raftsmen, squatters, insolvent emigrants and demagogues" [13] he had expected little but tumults and seditions. Tioga, however, promised nothing better. "This

[11] *Kent Journal,* 1802–1811 (No. 5), May 26, 1802.

[12] *Ibid.,* 1802–1811 (No. 5), 1802.

[13] *Ibid.,* 1800–1801 (No. 4), Circuits in Ulster, Orange and Delaware, August, 1801.

county," cried Kent with great travail of spirit, "now rivals Delaware county in Democracy and profligacy." [14]

It appeared that the two shires were bent upon making a rake's progress together toward perdition. Either seemed equally well personified in the young lawyer who attended the assizes in Aurora. He was amiable in early life, declared the judge, but "subsequently he degenerated into a Democrat and became a drunkard and licentious. . . ." [15]

These cantankerous judgements seem to have been provoked by something more than mere contempt. If Kent had genuinely despised the backwoodsmen, he should have expressed his feeling in mockery, not in humorless diatribe. He should have regarded the part which they aspired to play in public affairs as farcical, not tragic. Moved to laughter rather than to lamentation, he might thus have displayed true patrician scorn. Of this, however, in the circumstances the little judge was incapable. He was too sincerely apprehensive to remain unruffled and complacent; and his fears arose as well from personal as from partisan considerations. The frontiersmen even in the presence of the court were sometimes prone to be

[14] *Ibid.*, 1802–1811 (No. 5), May 26, 1802. Over against Kent's attitude as a Federalist may be set that of the frontiersman as expressed by a writer in the Albany *Register,* April 14, 1801, urging voters to elect Clinton:—"Our *seaport nobility* still cherish the hope that they shall yet be seated on the backs of their fellow-citizens of the country—and that the free happy proprietor will become the degraded, wretched *peasant.*"

Cf. also the letter of *Ploughboy, ibid.*, April 4, 1801:

"I doubt not but what there are men in this state, that are now swinging the axe to raise necessary food for their families that are better for governor than he is [*i.e.*, Van Rensselaer, Clinton's Federalist opponent]. What a thought must this give one that is used to breathe free republican air, on the spacious plains of Columbia, that men of birth must be more honored than men of worth.

"Fellow citizens, beware of the whited sepulchre, for I can assure you it is sometimes full of all manner of rottenness and dead men's bones that may hereafter rise to our sorrow, if we put too much confidence in our *Modern Moguls.*"

[15] *Kent Journal,* 1798 (No. 2).

disorderly.[16] That courts were seldom popular among them, the justice knew full well,[17] and he knew also that the frontier and its inhabitants were no respecters of persons. This fact was demonstrated at Newtown (afterwards Elmira) in Tioga, where a certain gentleman of Kent's acquaintance was so ill-advised as to exclaim in indignation at the liberty pole which he saw erected in the place. Backwoodsmen roistering before the tavern, heard his remark, closed in upon him with clenched fists and proceeded to punish him with a sound beating.[18] Kent was furious at the outrage,[19] but it was an impotent fury, and it expressed itself with such nervousness and choler, that one may infer that he was himself affrighted.

Fortunately for him, not all the inhabitants of the western country proved to be so obstreperous as the men of Delaware and Tioga. If those counties made him despair, others gave him reason to hope; and more than once agreeably surprised him at the firmness with which they upheld law, decency and order. If the aspect of their society was not uniformly pleasing, yet it presented sufficient quality to permit even a critic to take heart. In Oneida, as in Tioga, objectionable liberty poles, raised in protest against federal taxation, provoked Kent to impatience and disgust,[20] but the shire presently redeemed itself in his eyes by the unexceptionable behavior of the inhabitants at court. "The jurors, and constables," he noted with satisfaction, "as well as the judges and justices were very punctual in attendance and great order was observed." [21] Oneida, however, lay only upon the threshold of the west, and consequently more might be expected of the settlers there than of those in counties farther inland. Yet quite contrary

[16] *Ibid.*, 1798 (No. 2); 1800–1811 (No. 4) June 20, 1800.
[17] William W. Van Ness to James Kent, July 16, 1806.
[18] *Kent Journal,* 1802–1811 (No. 5), May 26, 1802.
[19] *Loc. cit.*
[20] *Kent Journal,* 1798 (No. 2).
[21] *Ibid.*, June 5, 1798.

to his anticipations, Kent discovered that propriety was not wholly wanting even in remote Steuben. "The court [in that shire] was held at Bath," said he, "and though the county is composed of a great mixture of foreigners and Americans, I found unexpectedly the people at court very punctual and orderly." [22] Still more gratifying was the reception of the judge at Canandaigua, a town that he praised unstintedly. The court which he held there was a model of decorum. "I never saw," he said, "more decent and respectable manners in a court of justice." [23]

There were other reasons for the praise of Canandaigua than the fact that the people behaved themselves at the assizes. In the first place, they came principally from Massachusetts and Connecticut; [24] and that alone would have been sufficient to endear them to James Kent, who being himself of Yankee stock, was much inclined, like other Yankees, to glorify the breed and take its superiority for granted. "The Yankees are a glorious people," [25] was his considered opinion, and he never tired of contrasting them with the "dull Germans" [26] and the "churlish, ignorant and unenterprising Dutch" [27] whom he had encountered especially in Oneida, where otherwise he had found much to commend.[28] In Canandaigua fortunately, at least so far as his own views were concerned, these alien and somewhat sluggish strains were to be met with rarely. The population was almost purely Yankee, and to that, as a prime cause, Kent attributed the wholesome conditions of the place. "This orderly, moral people," he wrote in his journal, "though without a clergyman, still preserve the steady and excellent

[22] *Ibid.*, 1798–1799 (No. 3), June 26, 1798.
[23] *Ibid.*, 1798 (No. 2), June 19, 1798.
[24] *Kent Journal*, 1798 (No. 2), June 19, 1798.
[25] *Ibid.*, 1803–1813 (No. 6).
[26] *Ibid.*, 1798 (No. 2).
[27] *Ibid.*, 1803–1816 (No. 6).
[28] *Ibid.*, 1798 (No. 2), comments on Rome and Utica.

moral institutions of New England of which public worship and the sobriety of the Sabbath constitute a distinguished part." [29]

But the Canandaiguans had more than orderly and sober conduct to recommend them to the esteem of the justice-in-eyre; and they had translated from the Connecticut to the Genesee other things besides the New England conscience. They had carried with them the New England land system; and their new county of Ontario was becoming, as a result, the abode of a sturdy and upstanding race of yeomen farmers resembling those of the Connecticut communities among which Kent had passed the years of his early youth. It was natural then that he should have regarded them with special favor; and should have paused to compare them, to their own advantage, with settlers in shires less fortunate. Indeed it was not always possible to make a comparison. Between the Ontario farmers, each with what Kent was pleased to call "a fine, independent little estate," [30] and the raftsmen, squatters and insolvent emigrants in Delaware and Tioga there was little in common. The situation of the inhabitants of the Mohawk valley was fairly fortunate; but even among them, great landlords, like the Bleeckers at Fort Schuyler, continued to retain title to such broad acres that leaseholders were more frequent [31] than owners in fee simple. The county of Steuben was likewise dominated by a landlord, Sir William Pulteney, the absentee, whose agent, Captain Charles Williamson, exercised over the tenants an influence which Kent likened to that "of lord of a clan." [32] From such a domination he believed the inhabitants of Ontario county happily free; and in their freedom he rejoiced with them. Here there was little danger that liberty would degenerate into license, for it was a

[29] *Ibid.* (No. 2), June 18, 1798.
[30] *Kent Journal*, 1798–1799 (No. 3), July 2, 1798.
[31] *Ibid.*, 1798 (No. 2), note on Fort Schuyler (Utica).
[32] *Ibid.*, 1798 (No. 3), July 2, 1798.

liberty that was based upon an attachment to the rights of property and restrained by the traditions of New England piety and common sense.

This favored place enjoyed still other advantages. The year before he had ascended the bench, Kent and his wife had made a tour of Connecticut,[33] where they had admired "the salubrious and beautiful characteristics" [34] of the towns. Those characteristics were being reproduced in Canandaigua against a background of natural beauty that, hardly to be rivalled even in New England, served to set off with more than ordinary charm the academy, the besteepled court-house and the neat frame dwellings, almost two score in number, with which the young village was already furnished.[35] Several of those dwellings, among which that of Oliver Phelps was conspicuous, had the size and elegance of mansions,[36] and as Kent discovered, they housed the most polite and hospitable gentry that he had encountered this side the Mohawk valley.

It was his good fortune to tarry among them over the Sabbath,[37] when he attended meeting, heard music that he pronounced admirable, and listened to Mr. Burt, a common pleas attorney, read a sermon of Dr. Stowe. When meeting was over, the judge was entertained at dinner by another lawyer, Mr. Saltonstall, whose "genteel table" was graced by the presence of his three sisters, of Major Hoops, "a gentleman of the old school," and by the whole Canandaigua Bar, which included three other members, besides the host himself. Here was a thoroughly congenial company, hardly inferior to what was to be found to the eastward; and though it boasted no demigod, like Alexander Hamilton, it displayed an exemplary appreciation of the merits of a demigod, and, to

[33] *Ibid.*, 1797, 1817–1819 (No. 1), Connecticut tour, 1797.
[34] *Loc. cit.*
[35] *Kent Journal,* 1798 (No. 2), June 16, 1798.
[36] *Loc. cit.*
[37] *Ibid.*, June 17, 1798.

Kent's delight, made Hamilton the principal topic of conversation.[38]

An obvious conclusion, therefore, to be drawn from the judge's experience at Canandaigua was that the western country possessed a saving remnant of staid and substantial citizens in whose influence faith could be reposed to counteract Jacobinical poisons. Nor did it seem to be beyond the bounds of possibility that that influence would increase in strength. Such a view may have been too sanguine, and yet there were several reasons to warrant holding it. As Kent himself bore witness, the settlers were coming in a continual stream; and he bore witness also that they came for the serious purpose of reducing the wilderness to cultivation. "The *Western Country* is wonderfully advanced in improvements," he observed during his circuit of 1810,[39] and with interest he continued to watch the progress of improvement through the succeeding years,

[38] *Loc. cit.* The Canandaigua bar consisted at the time of Kent's visit of two counsellors of the Supreme Court, Howell and Porter, and of two common pleas attorneys, Burt and Saltonstall. Kent gives only their surnames. They can be identified as follows:

Peter B. Porter, born in Salisbury, Connecticut, had become a resident of Canandaigua in 1795. He was credited with having engaged in the first jury trial conducted in the courts of Ontario county. George S. Conover, *History of Ontario County*, 165.

Nathaniel W. Howell came to Canandaigua in 1796 from Tioga county. He had been legal adviser to Captain Williamson, and in the same capacity was connected with the Holland Land Company. At the time of Kent's visit in 1798, he was assistant attorney-general for the five western New York counties. In the thirteenth congress he succeeded Porter, and was in turn succeeded by him. He was long a common pleas judge of Ontario county. *Ibid.*, 164–165.

Timothy Burt, of whom little is known. He was town clerk of Canandaigua in 1799, and supervisor in 1806 and 1807. *Ibid.*, 168.

Dudley Saltonstall, a scion of the old Connecticut family, Yale, 1791, a law student of the famous Judge Reeve of Litchfield. Surrogate of Ontario county, 1798–1809. Franklin B. Dexter, *Yale Biographies and Annals* (Fourth Series), 730.

Mr. Hoops, "a gentleman of the old school," was Major Adam Hoops, the surveyor.

[39] *Kent Journal*, 1802–1811 (No. 5), May 28–July 13, 1810.

as canals and turnpikes increased the facilities of communication and made possible the rise of commerce.[40] The effect of these rapid developments was not solely the accumulation of wealth. It was social and political as well as economic. As the virgin lands of a recent wilderness were brought under tilth, those who had once been needy pioneers often became well-to-do, if not opulent farmers, and their novel situation tended to steady them in their habits and attach them more firmly to the rights of property. Expanding commerce necessitated the growth of the mercantile and professional classes, the weight of whose influence was thrown oftenest into the scales to redress the balance in favor of conservative counsels in law, in morals and in politics. Furthermore, the immigration from New England, already considerable when Kent in 1798 paid his first visit to the new country, was swelling steadily in volume throughout the subsequent years; nor did it cease until the folk of other origins in the western counties had been all but submerged beneath the Yankee tide.[41] Throughout those counties, Canandaigua was reproduced again and again, and the inevitable result was to confirm the conservative interests of society with the powerful aids of New England's peculiar type of religion and of education. It might be urged that even turbulent Tioga succumbed to that all pervading influence; for in 1811 the Chief Justice held the assizes there once again; but if he saw a liberty pole he did not record the fact; if he witnessed assault and battery committed on the person of a gentleman, he made no mention of it. What he did record was that the exercise of the circuit, and the "manly scenes" thereof, elevated his spirits, and sent him home embrowned and hardy.[42]

Indeed, taking the long view of his experiences as a circuit-

[40] *Loc. cit.*, with clipping from *Oswego Gazette*, an issue of April, 1822.
[41] Ruth L. Higgins, *The Expansion of New York*, 101.
[42] *Kent Journal*, 1802–1811 (No. 5), June 9–July 7, 1811.

judge, Kent had little cause to be depressed. His observations made upon the country and the people during the sixteen years that he was going out upon the eyres indicate that both were ready for his ministrations. He beheld a rich land that was rapidly responding to the enterprise of an aggressive race. He discovered that frontier society had its virtues as well as its defects; [43] and that its virtues peculiarly adapted it to receive the law that he came to bring.

A learned modern writer [44] sums up the qualities which that law assumes in the people whom it governs. "It presupposes," says he, "a homogeneous population which is jealous of its rights and in sympathy with the institutions of government. It presupposes a public which is intrinsically law abiding, even if inclined under provocation to vindicate public justice by rough and ready methods. It presupposes a people which for the most part will conform to rules of law when they are ascertained and made known, so that the chief concern of courts and of the state is to settle what is the law. It presupposes a public which in the jury box may be relied upon to enforce law and vindicate justice between man and man intelligently and steadfastly. In other words," declares Dean Pound, "our common-law polity presupposes an American farming community of the first half of the nineteenth century. . . ." Such a community was the New York over which James Kent, now on horseback, now by chaise, travelled yearly for the space of sixteen years, holding the assizes. That the people in general and even the Tiogans in particular were in sympathy with the institutions of government, Kent himself had inadvertently admitted, when sitting on the log of a fallen tree in the woods near Newtown he had scribbled in his Journal: "Oyer and Terminer held and the jurors and other

[43] Kent held 140 courts, tried 1755 cases and had only 8 convictions of murder before him during the 16 years he rode circuit. William Kent, *Memoirs and Letters of James Kent*, 123.

[44] Roscoe Pound, *Spirit of the Common Law*, 123–125.

officers gave a very punctual and decorous attendance."[45] The remark was not consistent with the use of the words fierce and licentious to describe the inhabitants of Tioga; but set down in the journal amid the solemn tranquillity of the forest, where the mind "was drove into itself and became sedate and grave," it probably contained more truth than did epithets hurled in dudgeon.

Whatever the shortcomings of the Tiogans, they were in the main prepared, along with the folk of the other shires, to accept that law which James Kent had made it his life's object to bestow upon them.[46] Their readiness was indeed obscured by all too obvious prejudices. It existed nevertheless; and its roots went deeper than the people themselves may have imagined. For even in the colonial period, the English law, though haltingly and with variations from the original form, had made some progress in New York. At a comparatively early date practitioners had developed the habit of referring to English precedent.[47] While judicial opinions embodying such precedents had as yet been seldom written, more seldom published in official reports, yet neither lawyers nor litigants could have thought very much in terms of law other than English.[48] Nor was this anything but natural. The Dutch,

[45] *Kent Journal*, 1798–1799 (No. 3), July 3, 1798.

[46] The tendency of frontiersmen to cast off the legal restraints of an older society is well-known, but it has perhaps been overdone. Cf. Carroll T. Bond, on early Maryland in his introduction to *Proceedings of the Maryland Court of Appeals, 1695–1729:* "For it seems to be demonstrated that, removed as these people were from the environment of their civilization and relaxed as that civilization must therefore have been . . . they were nevertheless tenacious of regulation by law. . . ." *Vide et* Theodore F. T. Plucknett, "The Laws and Liberties of Massachusetts," (Review), *New England Quart.*, III, 156–159.

[47] Julius Goebel, "The Courts and the Law in Colonial New York," *History of the State of New York,* III, 3–43.

[48] Though the study of natural law was popular, *loc. cit.* For the close approximation of a local American to an English local court, see Richard B. Morris, *Select Cases of the Mayor's Court of New York City 1674–1784, passim.*

superficially at least, had adopted English ways. The State of New York, rejoicing in a name reminiscent of one of the most ancient counties in England, betrayed in matters more significant than name, the fact that its citizens belonged predominantly to the same race as that which inhabited the mother country.[49] In religion, they worshipped according to the varied modes of English Protestantism.[50] So in their institutions of government, save for monarchy and a peerage, they reproduced spontaneously the models existing in the land whence their forefathers had come. They had their shires and their shire towns; sheriffs, constables, justices-of-the-peace and juries of the vicinage they took for granted; while those shires, like their prototypes in England, were connected with government at the capital by the ancient and time-honored device of the judicial circuit. Such a system, inherited rather than borrowed or imposed, assumed as a necessary complement the inheritance of the substantive law with which it had historically developed—the common law which like the speech of England, was the natural expression of the genius of men of English lineage, even though no longer living in subjection to the Crown. The view was officially proclaimed by Kent from the bench a few years later; [51] and in that view, albeit not without some show of reluctance, his fellow citizens seem finally to have acquiesced.

As he moved among them, their confidence in his wisdom increased, and from New York City to the frontier, people

[49] Ruth L. Higgins, *The Expansion of New York,* 101.

[50] Cf. People v. Ruggles, 8 *Johns. Rep.* 290.

[51] Manning v. Manning, 1 *Johns Ch.,* 530–533. English Law, moreover, was somewhat more comprehensive than English *common* law. That is, local courts in England applied law other than the common law as applied in the King's Bench and other royal courts. With this local English law, the Americans were even more familiar than with the common law embodied in the reports and treatises. *Vide* Richard B. Morris, *Select Cases of the Mayor's Court of New York City, 1674–1784; vide et* Julius Goebel, "King's Law and Local Custom in Seventeenth Century New England," *Columbia Law Review,* XXXI, 416 *et seq.*

began to be conscious that a change for the better had befallen the administration of justice. Kent's conduct of the circuit-courts attracted the attention of the press. The Albany *Centinel*, published in a place where tidings from the western counties and from the metropolis were alike of interest, often noticed the favorable impression which the new judge was creating. His charge to the jury showed "great clearness of method and strength of reasoning," remarked that paper upon one occasion; and upon another, when at a term of Court in New York City, he had passed sentence upon certain disturbers of the peace, the same paper praised his observations as "particularly judicious." From Fort Schuyler came the intelligence that his services were appreciated in the west. At a court of Oyer and Terminer held in this county last week, the item read, a man was convicted of murder and "Judge Kent who presided and delivered his sentence explained to him the nature of the crime and of the sentence, in a manner at once plain, full and pathetic. . . . It was calculated," continued the writer, "to show [the spectators] the energy as well as the necessity of the laws by which we are governed." The town of Rome was no less appreciative. "On Friday morning last," as an inhabitant of that place informed the *Centinel*, "the Supreme Circuit Court [held for the county of Oneida] rose after dispatching a great variety of . . . business. . . . The celerity and precision with which the circuit court business is invariably conducted, cannot fail to impress the public mind with the importance of having law characters on the Bench."

Not only the importance, but also the necessity of having trained judges the public was slowly coming to admit. For as Kent passed to and fro among the people, they submitted questions to his determination that necessitated a scrutiny of the books. Not even the learned judge knew offhand all the answers which their litigation required. He was frank in confessing as much, and from the Bench of the Supreme Court he was not unwilling, when better informed upon the doctrines of the English sages, to reverse the decisions which he himself had rendered at the circuit.[52]

To the central curia then we must return, and examine more minutely the nature and the tendency of the opinions which James Kent, as Puisne Judge and Chief Justice over a period of some sixteen years, was handing down.

* * *

Kent's decisions in the Supreme Court derived their significance in large measure from the dominating position which he succeeded in establishing for himself in that tribunal. This was not easily accomplished; for from 1798 to 1814, the period of his tenure, the Democratic party was usually in power, and to that party seven of the eleven men belonged who during those years occupied (from time to time) the New York bench.[53] From 1798 to 1801, the Federalists, as a result of Jay's appointments enjoyed a brief ascendancy; for while Chief Justice Lansing and Puisne Judge Morgan Lewis were Democrats, Benson, Kent and Radcliffe held to the Federalist persuasion. In 1801 Lansing became Chancellor; Lewis was promoted to be Chief Justice, and Brockholst Livingston and Smith Thompson, staunch Democrats, appointed to the places left vacant by Lansing and Benson, reduced Kent and Radcliffe to a minority of two in a court of five. In 1804, Kent succeeded Lewis as the Chief Justice; his friend Jacob Radcliffe resigned, and to fill up the vacancies, Ambrose Spencer and Daniel D. Tompkins were made puisne judges, both

[52] Noble v. Smith, 2 *Johns. Rep.* 54. The quotations in the preceding paragraph are all from the Albany *Centinel,* the issues for August 11, 1801, August 2, 1799, June 30, 1801 and July 4, 1800 respectively.

[53] Kent, Radcliffe, Benson and W. W. Van Ness were Federalists while Lansing, Lewis, B. Livingston, Thompson, Tompkins, Spencer and Yates were Democrats.

Democrats, and Spencer especially zealous, as befitted a convert to the faith. He was, moreover, self-assertive and domineering,[54] and his undoubted abilities added weight to the Democratic majority which for three years, from 1804 to 1807 was four to one. With the election of Tompkins to the governorship, and the appointment of Livingston as Associate Justice of the Supreme Court of the United States, William W. Van Ness and Joseph Yates became puisne judges of New York, and thus from 1807 to 1814 the state court was divided, upon politics at least as three to two, with Thompson, Yates and Spencer Democrats, and Van Ness and the Chief Justice still pledged to a waning Federalism.[55]

Were it not for the fact that a legal issue had become a political one, the preponderance of Democratic judges would not of itself have been especially important. But among the numerous questions on which the parties of the day divided was the extent to which the English law should be received in America. That it had been transplanted, that long before independence it had taken root are facts that have been already noted.[56] It ought also to be observed that the new environment had modified the English law, that in the course of a century and a half before the Revolution, native growths had been so freely engrafted as to make American jurisprudence already distinguishable from the parent stem.[57] To James Kent and his contemporaries, however, the history of this interesting development was but little known; for they

[54] James Kent to Thomas Washington, October 6, 1828. *Kent Papers*, Vol. V.

[55] For the above terms see *Johnson's Cases*, Vols. I–III, and *Johnson's Reports*, Vols. I–XI *passim*.

[56] *Vide supra* in the preceding section of this chapter, and authorities there cited; viz. Goebel, Bond and Plucknett. In Massachusetts, Biblical precedent was influential, yet cases were lost and won on English precedent. *Vide* review in *American Historical Review*, XL, 135–137, *Records of the Suffolk County Court 1671–1680*.

[57] Richard B. Morris, *Studies in the History of American Law, passim.*

had no access to the important legal materials of the period in which it had taken place.[58] As a consequence they regarded American law as still unsettled. Furthermore, from the behavior of the courts, they might well have inferred that it was destined to remain so. Judges were not yet devoting much time to their deliberations. They were, as a rule, rendering their decisions orally; they were publishing few opinions, and like the colonial judges before them, they were making it necessary for their successors to begin anew as though they themselves had never been.[59] What the law was, therefore was uncertain. Upon the necessity of making it certain all were agreed; but whether the law should emphasize English tradition or American originality was an issue in dispute. The Federalists were inclined to favor the first; the second appealed to the Democrats, though they had no objection to the influence of foreign jurists, especially if they happened to be French. Indeed a predilection for French law was noticeable in the New York court.[60]

The Democratic antipathy to the English jurisprudence was in part at least but a phase of that national prejudice which the Revolution had engendered against all things English. Since the Revolution, the relations between the mother country and her lost colonies had been too often strained to cause that prejudice to soften. Moreover, Americans had

[58] Since they had not been made available in print. *Vide* section preceding and Richard B. Morris, *op. cit.*, 95.

[59] James Kent to Thomas Washington, October 6, 1828. *Kent Papers*, Vol. V. James Kent to William Kent, March 7, 1847. *Ibid.*, Vol. XI. Kent speaks as though no native jurisprudence existed. The view is historically unsound; but since colonial decisions were not readily available, few knew of its existence. For practical court purposes, therefore, the view was correct.

[60] Professor Pound says that the Republicans called with some enthusiasm for a reception of French law. Roscoe Pound, *The Spirit of the Common Law*, 116. Kent speaks of the fondness of his judicial brethren for French law. *Vide* James Kent to Thomas Washington, October 6, 1828. *Kent Papers*, Vol. V.

emerged from their dependent status so recently that they were still sensitive about it, still apprehensive of being reduced to colonies again; and this apprehension bore directly upon their attitude toward English law. For surely nothing was more plausible to urge than that the Revolution was still incomplete, if the precepts of Westminster Hall remained binding.[61]

There were other and better reasons for the Democratic position. Many formalities encumbered the English system which were of little use in America. These had already been pruned away in part, and the resulting innovations had been such as to encourage the belief that Americans had enough ingenuity to devise a satisfactory system of their own,[62] if left unhampered by the practices and maxims of another nation. Moreover, since many of the English doctrines derived from the feudal age, it was plausible in a generation which considered that age barbarous, to represent them as impediments to the progress of civilization. How they might thus operate was illustrated by the federal courts during the years when President Washington was striving to maintain American neutrality in the war between France and Great Britain.

That war not a few Democrats affected to regard as a struggle between light and darkness. France they saw surrounded by the foes of liberty and of the rights of man; and such was their zeal in her behalf, that they set out to help her by preying as privateersmen upon the commerce of Britain. This course, endangering the precarious peace between that country and the United States, openly violated the President's proclamation of neutrality, which the courts tried to uphold by instructing juries that such a proclamation had the force of law. The pronouncement aroused Democratic resentment, because it appeared to furnish the Chief Magistrate of a free

[61] This feeling is shown as late as Manning v. Manning, where Kent combats it.

[62] For an account of early innovations, *vide* Richard B. Morris, *Studies in the History of American Law, passim.*

commonwealth with the prerogative power of a British King. Democrats were no better pleased when Congress supplemented the proclamation with a statute which forbade American citizens to embark upon privateering enterprises against either adversary. But Congress reckoned without the zeal of France's friends in America. If they could not aid France as American citizens, they would invoke their natural right of expatriation and become citizens of the French Republic. When, however, they had been overhauled on the high seas, and brought back to their native shores there to confront federal judges, their plea was heard with little patience. The courts informed them that the United States had inherited the common law of England; that the doctrine of that law was that allegiance was inalienable, and that therefore they still remained American citizens and were still subject to the prohibitions of the congressional enactment.

Few doctrines could have served better than this to inflame the indignation of the Democrats. They had long complained of the British practice of impressing American sailors; but the pretext upon which the British had attempted to justify that practice was the same rule as that which the federal judges were now announcing. If American courts regarded an American as incapable of becoming a Frenchman, there was no reason why British courts and British captains should not regard an Englishman as incapable of becoming an American. Thus it appeared that the federal judges had given a convenient handle to the British claims upon the services of naturalized American sailors. That they had done so by declaring the common law a national inheritance was not well calculated to enhance the esteem of that law in the minds of good Democrats.[63]

[63] For the federal courts, and the common law doctrine of inalienable allegiance, *vide* Charles Warren, *The Supreme Court in United States History*, I, 159–164.

Nor was their objection confined to the specific doctrine of inalienable allegiance, oppressive though it was. That, after all, was only a corollary to the proposition that the United States had inherited the English common law in their federal capacity. If that were true, the federal courts possessed a general jurisdiction which exempted them from the limitations of delegated power, and furnished them with an opportunity of steadily encroaching upon the jurisdiction of the state tribunals. The danger of this alarmed the Democrats for the safety of their most distinctive constitutional dogma, the inviolability of states' rights.[64]

As their belief that the federal government lacked sympathy for the ordinary man had been a principal reason why they opposed the growth of federal authority, so too they were hostile to the extension of the common law, because they suspected it of the same undemocratic leanings. The telling arguments which that law had supplied in defense of the rights of Englishmen against the tyrannies of English ministers were no longer so useful as they once had been. But more useful than ever were the means afforded by that law for protecting the rights of property long jeopardized by successful revolution. Such usefulness, however, the Democrats were less prone to appreciate than their opponents; and the innumerable actions of debt which filled the courts and busied the lawyers, could not but intensify their animosity toward the legal system. For a Democratic politician the task must have been simple to distort the law's insistence that debts be paid into a general bias of the law against the common man,[65] whose misfortune it is to fall often into debt.

Had a yet more pertinent instance of oppressiveness been

[64] For this aspect of the matter, *loc. cit.*

[65] Debts, and litigations over debts were causes of Shays's rebellion. *Vide* Joseph Hawley to Ephraim Wright, April 16, 1782, *American Historical Review*, XXXVI, 777. In a week, in one county there had been 221 actions, almost all for the recovery of debt.

sought, judicial disinclination to see workingmen insubordinate to their employers would presently have furnished it. The nineteenth century had little more than opened when artisans began to organize combinations for the purpose of raising wages. Soon, however, they found themselves in court to answer the charge of criminal conspiracy. Whether the charge could be sustained, depended upon whether the common law was in force, for it was thence the doctrine came that an organization to raise wages is a criminal conspiracy. The court, holding that the common law prevailed, confirmed the impression that that law was of little value to the common people. Indeed, a Democratic editor observed that it threatened to reduce them to servitude. "Hitherto," said he, "the people had travelled the level road to equal justice. . . . Of all the barbarous principles of feudalism entailed upon us by England none was left but slavery, and even this would be generally restricted in 1808. Yet would it be believed, at the very time when the state of the negro was about to be improved attempts were being made to reduce the white to slavery? Was there anything," he asked, "in the Constitution of the United States . . . which gave one man a right to say to another what should be the price of labor? There was not. It was by the English common law that such things became possible." [66]

Still another grievance against that law was its doctrine of seditious libel as expounded by contemporary courts.[67] No doubt it was a doctrine that would have been slightly noticed, had it not been for the habit of that generation to abuse in the most violent terms those set in authority. Frequent libel suits resulted; and in these suits defendants were told that they could not give the truth in evidence; and that though they

[66] Quoted by John R. Commons, *History of Labour in the United States*, I, 142–143.

[67] One writer regards this as a chief cause of the dislike of the common law. *Vide* Charles Warren, *History of the American Bar*, 236 *et seq.*

might put themselves upon the country, yet it would avail them little, since the jury could determine only the fact of publication. Whether the publication were libellous was a question of law to be resolved solely by the court. These principles, announced in Pennsylvania by Chief Justice McKean [68] and in Massachusetts by Chief Justice Dana,[69] were destructive to the freedom of the press, and to free speech in general. Indeed they seemed to be formidable to all liberty, since they curtailed the function of the jury and clothed the ministers of government with what well nigh amounted to an immunity from criticism. They were principles, which though sustained, as was supposed, by the authority of Lord Mansfield, exhibited the common law in yet another of its unfavorable aspects and furnished illustrations of what Kent at Columbia had once said about the inequalities that blemished it.

Nevertheless, the common law not only survived; it became more definitely the law of the land than it had been before, even in the days of colonial dependence.[70] This turn of events may be set down, so far as it is assignable to deliberate action, to the blame or credit of the New York Federalists, who revolutionized the bench by elevating James Kent to the judicial dignity. Nothing could have been more appropriate. John Jay, the leader of the conservative group that had designed the constitution and inserted therein the provision for the English law, had appointed the very judge best able and, in spite of his professorial pronouncements, most inclined to protect that provision from hostile attack.

But the accomplishment of such a task would have been impossible unless Kent had contrived to gain an ascendancy over his judicial brethren. In his effort to do so, he relied of

[68] Edward Channing, *History of the United States,* IV, 221–222.
[69] Charles Warren, *op. cit.,* 237.
[70] What is in mind here is of course the judicially determined law.

necessity upon his powers of argument and persuasion, and these he sought continually to enlarge by exhaustive study. Already learned, he yet appears to have been far from satisfied with his acquisitions and his appointment but stimulated his desire to perfect his knowledge.[71] Through all the fields of law he roamed, paying especial attention, however, as became a New York judge, to the admiralty reports and to treatises on shipping and insurance. Mindful of the numerous actions of ejectment which plagued the courts of the justices-in-eyre, he studied afresh the law of landlord and tenant, and returned to deepen his friendship with Sir Edward Coke. The history of legal development continued to attract his interest; and going beyond Coke, he read the treatises of Lord Bacon; while finally, with Glanvil and Bracton,[72] he worked backward to the earliest ages of the common law, studying the feudal *consuetudines* as Doctor Stiles long years before had recommended. It is helpful, observed Kent from the bench, to return to the ancient fountains and drink deep; but as befitted a jurist, he voiced the utterance in Latin, *iuvat accedere fontes atque haurire.*[73]

[71] James Kent to Moss Kent, Jr., August 16, 1802. *Kent Papers,* Vol. III.
[72] *Loc. cit.*
[73] Yates v. Lansing, 5 *Johns. Rep.* 291. In Volume III, *Kent Papers,* is preserved a list of the books which Kent read between 1799 and 1805. The original includes English, French and Latin classics. Only the law titles are listed below, as follows:

1799—2 Dallas
Erskine
Harg. Co. Litt.
Martens

1800—Andrews Rep.
3 Dallas
Washington Rep.
Principia Legis
1 Brown's Civil Law

1801—Robinson's Adm. Rep.
Ward on Neutrality
B. & Fuller vol. i
Wille's Reports
Bacon's Law Tracts
Esp. Cases vol. 2

1802—Esp. Reports
3 Esp. Cases
3 Vesey Jr.
3 Robinson's Adm.
Abbott
(on shipping)
Marshall
(on insurance)
Chitty

That these copious draughts from the sources made his opinions long and somewhat labored, Kent himself admitted.[74] Indeed he was led more than once to devote extraordinary learning to the establishment of rules of no more than ordinary importance.[75] This habit might perhaps be called pedantic, had not Kent found it to be helpful in the most practical way.[76] At first he had no easy time upon the bench where collisions were of frequent occurrence, and where to hold his own he found it necessary to seize upon every legitimate weapon of controversy. Erudition, a weapon in itself, was with Kent therefore, no mere vainglorious display. He made it serve the purpose of subduing his opponents into acquiescence in his own views.[77] Skeptical of the English authorities though the other judges were, they found it increasingly difficult to combat them with success, when in solid phalanx he had marshalled them from Mansfield back to Glanvil, and had corroborated their wisdom, as he was often wont to do, with citations from

---

1803—4 & 5 Vesey Jr.
2 East Rep.

1804—3 East Rep.
2 B. & Fuller
Peake's Evidence
Cranch Rep.

1805—Saunders by Williams
4 East Rep.
3 B. & Fuller
5 Robinson no. 1
1 & 2 Kames
Law Tracts
7 & 8 Vesey Jr.
Pothier on Obligations
Bottomry
Cont. du Vente

[74] James Kent to Thomas Washington, October 6, 1828. *Kent Papers,* Vol. V.

[75] *E.g.,* Cortelyou v. Lansing, 2 *Caines's Cases* 200: If a pledge be deposited and the time of redemption left unlimited, the pawnee should not sell the pledge, and if he did, he should be responsible to the pawnor or his agent for its value. Kent cites cases from the reign of James I, the authority of Glanvil and of the Code and Digest of Justinian.

[76] James Kent to Thomas Washington, October 6, 1828. *Kent Papers,* Vol. V.

[77] James Kent to Thomas Washington, October 6, 1828. *Kent Papers,* Vol. V.

the French jurists for whom it was fashionable to profess warm admiration.[78]

Thus, as the years went by, the Supreme Court of New York tended more and more to become the court of James Kent. Puisne Judge from 1798 to 1804, he was in the latter year promoted to be Chief Justice, and for a decade thereafter, while other judges came and departed, he remained to exercise a continuous influence over the deliberations of the tribunal and to succeed finally in shaping them very much according to his own desire. More frequently than any of his associates, he himself delivered the opinions of the Court; [79] and again and again, opinions which he himself had written, he recorded as *per curiam*, for he was loath to offend his brethren's vanity by allowing the reports to show upon their face the strength of his own influence and domination.[80] But from a shrewd observer, that influence could not be concealed. Joseph Story, visiting

[78] *Loc. cit.*

[79] *Vide Johnson's Reports,* Vols. I–XI *passim.*

[80] *Vide loc. cit.* and James Kent to Thomas Washington, October 6, 1828. *Op. cit.* Kent's assertions there are borne out by an inspection of *Johnson's Reports.* 1 *Johnson* abounds in controversy. It contains only 48 opinions *per curiam.* As to the others, Livingston wrote the most; Thompson the next; Kent's were third in number, followed by Spencer's and Tompkins wrote the fewest. But few of these opinions were signed by the individual judges, the others frequently dissented and where they agreed, they were given to doing so on other grounds. In 2 *Johnson* Kent 23 times delivered the opinion of the court; Livingston twice, Thompson 17 times, Spencer 18 times, Tompkins 6, and there were 74 *per curiam* opinions. The number of concurring and dissenting opinions has decreased sharply. In 3 *Johnson* Kent's opinion 19 times was that of the court, his disciple Van Ness's 15 times, Spencer's 11, Thompson's and Yates's 5 each and there were 87 *per curiam* opinions. And these tendencies became more marked in the later volumes. In 8 *Johnson* Kent's opinion, signed by him, was 9 times the court's opinion too; Spencer's 3, Thompson's 2, Van Ness's 1, Yates's 1. There were 110 *per curiam* opinions; but for the reason stated in the text. In 9 *Johnson,* Kent's opinion, signed by him, was 11 times the opinion of the court, Spencer's twice, Thompson, Van Ness and Yates not once, though Thompson wrote one concurring opinion. There were 145 *per curiam* opinions. 10 and 11 *Johnson* tell the same tale even more strikingly.

in New York during the May term of 1807, attended the Supreme Court then in session at the City Hall, where he remarked of the Chief Justice, that he was acute and prompt, inclined to show too much haste perhaps, and disposed to interrupt counsel somewhat too frequently. He criticized him, also, for his rather careless manner of sitting, but this he interpreted as "the ease of a man who felt adequate to the exigencies of his station"; and he added, "On the whole, if he be not a very great man, I am satisfied he is not humble in his acquirements." As for the other judges, Story dismissed them with the observation that they interfered very little in the business of the court.[81] Had he tarried to watch them through the succeeding years, he would have noted that they relapsed more and more into silence, became more and more acquiescent in the will and opinions of their chief,[82] whose ascendancy, then, was little short of that which John Marshall achieved in his own tribunal. Kent, moreover, enjoyed one advantage which the Chief Justice of the United States was never to have known. Of two of his colleagues he had himself been the preceptor in the early years when as youths they had begun their study of the law.[83]

Nor is it too much to say that he never ceased being their preceptor or the preceptor of their colleagues who had ascended the bench before them. For all, he set the example of diligence and industry, and he taught the whole court the value of minute researches. Never again could it be said of the judges of New York, as he had once said of their predecessors,

[81] Joseph Story to Samuel P. P. Fay, May 18, 1807, W. W. Story, *Life and Letters of Joseph Story,* I, 143 *et seq.* Thompson and Tompkins were present with the Chief Justice at this term.

[82] In 10 *Johns. Rep.*, Kent's opinions over his own name are 26; Thompson's 2; Van Ness's 0; Yates's 0; Spencer 1 and one dissenting opinion; *per curiam* opinions 152. In 11 *Johns. Rep.* to p. 78 where Kent leaves the Supreme Court for chancery, the opinions are all either by Kent or *per curiam.*

[83] Thompson and Van Ness, JJ. *Vide* James Kent to William Kent, March 7, 1847, *Kent Papers,* Vol. XI and William Kent, "Notes on the Life of James Kent" in the same volume.

that their decisions showed no trace of knowledge or investigation. Never again could it be said that those judges were content to deliver their opinions orally. On the morrow of his appointment, Kent had mounted the bench furnished with an opinion written out and bristling with citations; and to his associate's dismay, he had kept up the practice until they too were driven to adopt it in self defense.[84] So the decisions of the court came to be kept in written records, and as a result of Kent's urging, an able reporter was appointed, his friend William Johnson,[85] who proceeded to publish them from time to time for the benefit of the bar, not only of New York, but of the other states as well, where his volumes were not slow in earning reputation and authority.[86] As their number increased, the law

[84] James Kent to Thomas Washington, October 6, 1828. *Kent Papers*, Vol. V.

[85] *Loc. cit.* and James Kent to Elizabeth Kent, May 13, 1804. *Ibid.*, Vol. III. Caines had preceded Johnson as reporter. Apparently Kent did not think well of him. He calls him the "profligate Caines."

[86] *Vide infra* where Kent's growing fame as a jurist is dealt with. In the Convention of 1821 it was stated that Johnson's Reports were authority in every state from Maine to Florida.

For the task before him, Kent was admirably equipped, as admirably in his way as was John Marshall. It well may be that he lacked the strong original genius of the great Virginian, who without precedent to guide him reasoned out from the premises of the Federal Compact an imposing system of rules to control the relations of the coordinate branches of the central government, of private persons with the Union, of the Union with States, and of the States with one another. Such a task was unprecedented in the annals of the law, and it was rendered the more delicate and difficult because the manner in which it should be performed would affect for weal or woe the whole course of the country's political development. But the subjects with which Marshall mainly dealt, formed only a limited chapter of the law; and howsoever minutely he might expound them, he left the broadest areas of jurisprudence still unexplored. Indeed, those areas for the most part lay beyond the limits of his jurisdiction, and if they were to be traversed at all, the task would have to be undertaken by the judges in the several states who, as a general rule, alone were legally competent to touch them. Among such Judges, Kent was preeminent. Of the originality which was Marshall's distinguishing characteristic, he had comparatively little need; for the law, which he was called upon to expound, was rich in precedents, and his duty required him to investigate and apply old principles and doctrines rather than to invent new theories of his own. Yet, though always deferential to gained in certainty and precision, and upon all its topics was cast a new and more revealing light than any which had shone hitherto save that which emanated from the Supreme Court of the United States. And as the volumes of Dallas, Cranch and Wheaton portrayed the rise of the constitutional jurisprudence of the Union, so those of Johnson depicted the growth of the jurisprudence of the State, a jurisprudence far more varied in its titles, and more intimately than constitutional law could ever do, coming home to every man's business and bosom.

* * *

The fabric which Kent thus erected displays in almost every part his admiration for the laws of England. Had the legislature admired those laws as he did, one might safely surmise that the jurisprudence of New York would have fallen only a little short of becoming a transcript of the mother country's. But the legislature, though it had in fact passed many a statute in words identical with those used at Westminster, was by no means unmindful of its power as well to modify as to imitate; and some titles of the law it had altered almost beyond recognition. The new system, however, retained in its modified form the traces of its origin, and required, therefore, in those who administered it, a sound and comprehensive understanding of its antecedents. Thus even where changed, it offered Kent an opportunity to put his common law learning to use.[87] Where

the ancient oracles, he was no mere servile imitator of the past. He could differ in opinion from the most venerable sages; and, upon a nice question of the recent federal jurisprudence, from the most eminent of his contemporaries, including Marshall, concerning whose labors he kept himself constantly and thoroughly informed. Of his own peculiar work, however, the emphasis was indeed upon the old authorities; and the questions that arose before him he settled only after a long, minute and exhaustive examination of the books.

[87] Brant v. Gelston 2 *Johnson's Cases* 384–391, where the New York statute abolishing entailed estates is involved, and it is necessary to determine whether the estate in the case is an estate tail. The decision makes use of the celebrated rule in Shelley's case:

cases arose which illustrated the legislature's disposition to abide by the old law, whether common or statute, that opportunity was enlarged.[88] It was most ample, of course, where statutes gave no guidance, for here the judge was free to indulge to the utmost his inclination to make the common law of England the law of the state of New York.

In using this freedom Kent proceeded too far no doubt to please those who would have preferred to see the native features of our jurisprudence accentuated. Since he was in no position to acquaint himself with the history of legal development in the colonies, he perhaps believed that colonial courts had been as faithful to the precedents of Westminster Hall as their imperfect knowledge had permitted, and that he was but following the example which they would have set, had they possessed his learning.[89] All this, however, is conjecture. The fact is that Kent was so profoundly deferential to English law that he sometimes applied it when he doubted of its justice in the particular case, and that, although he was aware of pertinent precepts from the civil law much more harmonious with his own idea of the right.[90] If he could thus dismiss a Roman maxim for which he had a personal preference, it is not likely that he would have scrupled overmuch, in case of conflict, to

---

When ancestors a freehold take
The words *his heirs* a limitation make.

The action was one of ejectment for certain lands in New York City.

[88] Snider and Van Vechten v. Cray 2 *Johnson's Reports* 227–229, an action of trespass. It was argued that executors could not bring trespass for an injury done to the testator's personal property in his life time. This had once been the law, Kent said, but it has been changed by Parliament *temp.* Edward III, and the English statute had been reenacted by the New York legislature. *Vide et* for other examples of the use of the older common law: Jackson v. Rogers at 1 *Johns. Cases* 34 (What constitutes a disseisin?); Jackson v. Sisson 2 *Johns. Cases* 321; Jackson v. Lunn 3 *Johns. Cases* 109.

[89] "In the early nineteenth century . . . what was thought to be the law of England was employed by the courts in the delusion that the colonists had themselves obediently observed it." Richard B. Morris, *Studies in the History of American Law*, 95.

[90] Thorne and Thorne v. Deas 4 *Johns. Rep.* 97.

lay aside the rulings of native in favor of those of English judges. But as a result of his belief that native jurisprudence was a blank before his time [91] such conflicts could occur only seldom. They would have presupposed an American law more mature than Kent was ready to acknowledge had ever yet existed. For him therefore the principal source of legal wisdom could only have been the English books, although when these were silent or conflicting, he did consent to hearken to those whom he called the foreign jurists.[92] In this manner he enriched our law with the doctrines of Emerigon, Valin and Pothier. Oftener than not, however, these are cited only to confirm what had been decided in England.

When a judge reveals such an attachment for *stare decisis*, one is impelled to ask whether he does not lighten his labors by making them mechanical. In accepting passively the opinions of his predecessors does he not spare himself the necessity of thinking out his own? Does he not reduce his function to one of mere antiquarian research? And does the law which such research establishes have any other advantage than that of being venerable for its antiquity? Be the views upon these matters what they may, one can maintain that unless the judge does elect to follow *stare decisis* and to lay down the law as he finds it, he must take it upon himself to make law on his own initiative, and thus to substitute his own personal and perhaps arbitrary will for that impersonal will of the law which generations have been taught to believe is the embodiment of reason. That belief Kent professed to share with others of his time; and he no doubt subscribed to the saying of Marshall that "judicial power is never exercised for the purpose of giving effect to the

[91] He says "We had no law of our own. . . ." James Kent to Thomas Washington, October 6, 1828. *Kent Papers*, Vol. V, and that "The progress of jurisprudence was nothing in New York prior to 1793." *Vide* letters probably to William Kent under dates of February 17, 1847 and March 7, 1847. *Ibid.*, Vol. XI.

[92] Mumford v. The Commercial Insurance Company 5 *Johns. Rep.* 266.

will of the judge; always for the purpose of giving effect . . . to the will of the law." [93] If that will erred in doing less than justice, it was, said Kent, the province of the legislature, not of the judge, to correct the error.[94] Yet the greatest judges have won fame through their readiness to improve upon the law; and none who is acquainted with the career of Marshall would contend for an instant that he had never done so, or that he had never exercised judicial power for the purpose of giving effect to his own imperious will.[95] Is one justified in asserting that Kent himself never did the same? The question must be answered warily; for surely no judge ever expressed a profounder reverence for authority than he, provided it was the authority of "the generous oracles of the common law" to whose responses, as he said "we listen with delight and instruction." [96]

But would those responses have been so gratifying had they conflicted with Kent's own predilections? It is not to be denied that he could and did sometimes follow English precedent which he frankly disliked. That was not however his consistent habit. If, for example, he thought that a given rule had originated in circumstances peculiar to England, he might refuse altogether to accept it here. An instance of this is his treatment of the old English doctrine of *markets overt*, with which, though urged by eminent counsel,[97] he would have nothing to do. At the same time, he was careful to observe that it was a doctrine which the English courts themselves regarded as exceptional "and restricted . . . with unusual jealousy and vigilance." [98] Thus he appeared to seek the countenance of the

[93] Osborne v. Bank 9 *Wheaton* (U.S.) 738, 866, quoted by Walter Nelles in "Towards Legal Understanding," *Columbia Law Review*, XXXIV, 1050.

[94] As Chancellor in Manning v. Manning 1 *Johns. Ch.*, 533.

[95] Edward S. Corwin, *John Marshall and the Constitution, passim.*

[96] People v. Croswell 3 *Johns. Cases* 386.

[97] Samuel Jones and Josiah Hoffman.

[98] Wheelright v. De Peyster 1 *Johns. Rep.* 470–485.

English judges even when deviating from a rule which they upheld. A better example of deviation is afforded by an insurance case, in which Kent, adopting a principle advanced by Hamilton as counsel, declared that a blockade must be effective in order to be lawful.[99] That decision one might be tempted to interpret as evidence that the judge was overcoming his Anglophile proclivities. Certainly the doctrine there announced was beneficial to American merchantmen as the principal neutrals; certainly it was inauspicious to the success of the operation of the British squadron which the case involved; nor did the court, a fact most interesting of all, pay deference on this point to Sir William Scott, ordinarily much heeded. Yet the decision ought not to be weighed too heavily in the scale against the many others in which Kent so closely followed not only the common law judges, but also those of the admiralty, as to increase the practical advantage of England.[100] At best the case shows that the English jurists' sense of right did not invariably correspond to that of the Chief Justice of New York, who had a will of his own when he deemed it wise to express it.

Fortunately for him, since his ideas of sound policy were not unanimously applauded, that will had already been expressed by what he and his contemporaries imagined to be the impersonal and oracular utterance of the law.[101] If that utterance sometimes dealt with matters too mundane and trivial to conjure up the image of Apollo's priestess sitting among the Delphic vapors, yet it was not for that the less gratefully received. For among other things in which that generation needed guidance were their disputes arising in the course of trade; and to

[99] Williams v. Smith 2 *Caines* 12. Even in 2 *Caines* 12 the rule followed by Kent, would have benefited the English more than it did Napoleon, since with their superior fleet, they could more easily create an effective blockade.

[100] *Vide infra.*

[101] "In his moral sense . . . there was seldom much conflict between justice and English legal usuals." Walter Nelles, *Columbia Law Review*, XXXIV, 876.

this need the oracles responded in plain and satisfactory terms. Kent was consulting them continually, and applying their pronouncements to the relations developed by the expanding commerce of his country.

How widely ramified had grown the enterprise of American merchants, though discoverable from no other source, would yet sufficiently appear from the record of litigations in Kent's own tribunal. Here questions arose with references to voyages from the Caribbean to the China Sea, and they involved all the principal heads and titles of commercial law—[102] bills and notes, charter-parties, bottomry, partnerships, freight, marine insurance. To each question, Kent devoted patient care, and ere he retired from the court a fairly complete code of commercial law had been elaborated. Through this useful achievement the course of trade was smoothed and accelerated as known rules dispelled perplexities and doubts. It was an achievement which won distinction for the Chief Justice and caused his admirers to compare him with Lord Mansfield.[103] The comparison was not altogether inept; though the latter in working the law merchant into the ancient body of the common law, had undoubtedly performed a more creative task than Kent who after all in Mansfield had what Mansfield lacked, an oracle to aid him.[104]

The nature of that aid, and the kind of question where it

[102] *Vide e.g.* Abbot v. Sebor 3 *Johns. Cases* 39. (Shippers' profits anticipated from a voyage are insurable.) *Vide id.* for rule as to when abandonment possible. Other insurance cases cited in text. Negotiable instruments, *e.g.* Jackson v. Richards at 2 *Caines* 343, Furman v. Haskin 2 *Caines* 369, Johnson v. Bloodgood 1 *Johns. Cases* 51, Conroy v. Warren 3 *Johns. Cases* 259 etc., etc. Examples of cases on partnerships: Lansing v. Gaine & Ten-Eyck 2 *Johns. Rep.* 302, Holmes v. United Insurance Co. 2 *Johns. Cases* 329, *et passim.*

[103] Ogden, Duer *et al* to James Kent, July 31, 1843. *Kent Papers,* Vol. X. *Vide et Law Reporter,* VI, 37. For Mansfield *vide American Jurist,* VI, 73.

[104] Unless one considers the merchant juries which Mansfield kept, to be oracles. In his free use of the civil law, he may perhaps be said to have been consulting oracles.

proved most valuable should be more curiously examined; and for the purpose a marine insurance case will serve as an example.[105] The schooner *Sukey and Polly,* owned by the plaintiffs, was by them chartered to a shipper to bear a cargo from New Orleans to Cape Nicolas-Mole, and thence to one other port, be it Port-au-Prince, Cape François or the island of St. Thomas. The insurance on the freight, taken by the owners against sea risks only, amounted to the sum which the schooner was expected to earn in freight if the voyage was performed. Unfortunately, the voyage terminated within a day's sail of Cape Nicolas-Mole, the *Sukey and Polly* being obliged by perils of the sea to take refuge at Kingston in Jamaica, where her cargo was received by the shipper's agent, the schooner herself surveyed, pronounced incapable of repair, was accordingly sold, and the voyage broken up. To her owners' claim for a total loss of freight the insurance company objected; and while granting that loss had been sustained through the perils insured against, contended for a reduction in proportion to the amount of the voyage that had been performed. The question, then, as posed by the court, was whether the owners "were entitled to recover for a total or for a partial loss of freight." It was a question analogous to that determined in Luke v. Lyde by Mansfield in the King's Bench; [106] and the noble lord, now as then, supplied the solution.

"It is now too late," said Kent, "to deny or disregard the rule that freight *pro rata itineris* is due, when a ship, by reason of perils, goes into a port short of her destination, and is unable to prosecute the voyage and the goods are there received by the owner. An implied *assumpsit* to pay for the labor performed and the service rendered is raised by the acceptance of the goods at such intermediate port. The case of Luke v. Lyde is said to have adopted this rule from the marine law [and] the rule ap-

[105] Robinson v. Marine Insurance Co. 2 *Johns. Rep.* 325–326.
[106] 2 *Burr.* 882 (1759).

pears to have been too long and authoritatively settled in the English courts to be now shaken. . . . The plaintiffs, therefore [are] entitled by the acceptance of the cargo at Kingston to a *pro rata* freight. . . . But the great difficulty is to ascertain by some general and sound rule the amount of the freight earned." Ought it to be calculated by ascertaining how much of the voyage had been performed when the ship first encountered the peril which interrupted her course? Or by ascertaining how much had been performed when the goods arrived at the intermediate port? The second rule, Kent noted, appeared to be more nearly just, because the intermediate port marked the extent of the voyage as it respected the shipper's interest; but it was impossible of application in the present instance, since no data were at hand by which to discover the difference of a voyage between the intermediate port and the port of destination on the one hand, and on the other, between the port of destination and the place where the vessel's course had been interrupted. The determination of that difference by geographical distance would be incorrect "for the course of winds and currents, and the season of the year will make a very great variation in the duration and expense of the voyage, over an equal extent of space." The first rule, it was concluded, therefore must apply, the rule adopted in Luke v. Lyde, which "was to calculate how much of the voyage had been performed when the disaster happened." In accordance with this calculation, the plaintiffs were to recover for only a partial loss.[107]

[107] Robinson v. Marine Insurance Co. 2 *Johns. Rep.* 326. The court's calculation of the recoverable sum makes the point clearer. Thus:

From New Orleans to Cape Nicolas-Mole, an ordinary voyage	= 25 days
From Cape Nicolas-Mole to St. Thomas, whither the shipper's charter-party gave him the right to go	= 20 days
Thus the whole duration of the voyage would have been . .	= 45 days
From New Orleans to point where disaster happened . . .	= 24 days

Therefore the vessel had performed 24⁄45 of her voyage, and the court's order was that a sum in the proportion of 24 to 45 should be deducted from the amount of the recovery for a total loss.

The doctrine of freight *pro rata itineris,* and the rule by which it was reckoned may possibly be thought significant only as an illustration of Kent's reliance on the English law to meet the needs of commercial litigation in New York. Many similar examples could be cited as dull in detail as this. Yet their cumulative effect is not without interest, since they witness the advent of a class to such power and importance that the solution of its problems becomes one of the major objects of the law's concern. Furthermore, if the observer is affected with a Marxist squint, he may persuade himself that he discerns how that class makes use of law not only to adjust the rivalries of its own members to their mutual satisfaction, but also to furnish those members as a group with an advantage in their conflicts with an opposing class. Thus, while Kent in an infinite variety of causes was seeking with great pains and scruple to do justice to the men of business, particularly to merchants and the owners of merchant ships, he was frankly less preoccupied with doing justice to those who manned the ships; for while he informed the shipper that his profits anticipated from a given voyage were insurable, he let the mariner know that he could expect no such protection for his wages. Indeed, he told him that unless the vessel earned her freight, he would be entitled to no wages at all. If a vessel sank and the sailor survived and attempted in Kent's court to recover his pay for the part of the voyage already performed, he met with brusque refusal. The learned justice applied the English rule that "freight is the mother of wages and the safety of the ship is the mother of freight." [108] The reason of the rule, more comforting to owner than to crew, was that if mariners depended on the safety of the ship for their wages, they would be more strenuous in striving to save her from the perils of the sea.

The benefit of such a code to the business community is obvious. It was a benefit which one cannot doubt tended to

[108] Dunnett v. Tomhagen, 3 *Johns. Rep.* 156.

confirm the attachment of the Federalists to the common law, since business men and merchants were more numerous and influential in that party than elsewhere. But the Federalists had other than commercial motives for liking the common law; and with those motives Chief Justice Kent heartily sympathized. The attitude of the law and the attitude of the party toward certain large questions of social policy were in well nigh complete accord. For the Federalists, as they often reminded themselves, sprang from the wealthy, the well born and the able, a class which nature destines to remain select and small in any society. Such a class, however, compensates for its good fortune by arousing the envy of the less-favored multitude. The social antagonism thus engendered leads inevitably to political collisions in which wealth, gentility and individual competence incur the danger of being overborne by the oppressive weight of majorities. From so calamitous an issue those ancient English liberties enshrined in the common law, and from that stock engrafted into the American constitutions, seemed to furnish a dependable hope of escape. It was natural therefore that a party always apprehensive of democratic oppression should affect to cherish those liberties with devotion. It was logical that that party should produce a judge, who however much he might admire the foreign jurists, could nevertheless assert that "The English system [has] fostered the soundest and most rational principles of civil liberty" [109] and that the English courts have "protected right to a degree never before witnessed in the history of civil society. . . ." [110] That these observations meant that the peculiar excellence of the common law consisted in its jealousy lest the multitude oppress the minority, a review of the cases will establish.

Of these one of the most pertinent is Dash v. Van Kleeck,[111]

[109] Yates v. People, 6 *Johns. Rep.* 422.

[110] Goix v. Low, 1 *Johns. Cases* 345.

[111] 7 *Johns. Rep.* 477. For an interesting reference to this case, *vide* Edward S. Corwin, *The Twilight of the Supreme Court*, 59–60, who holds

where a sheriff was a defendant in an action for damages for having allowed a debtor to escape from gaol. The sheriff's plea was a *nil debet* on the ground that his prisoner, before the commencement of the suit, had returned into custody and that a recent statute permitted sheriffs in that case to avail themselves of the return as a valid defense. The plaintiff's right to his action against the sheriff collided therefore with the legislative will which Mr. Justice Spencer in a strong opinion was for upholding. The Chief Justice differed; and as usual had his way; showing with some originality how the basic principles of English law furnished vested rights with protection against legislative encroachment.

He began amiably enough by quoting the statute on which the defendant had relied in his plea, that nothing shall be "so construed as to prevent any sheriff, in cases of escape, from availing himself of a defense arising . . . from a returning of the prisoner within the sheriff's custody before an action shall be commenced for the escape." As the prisoner had returned as required, it seemed that the sheriff had made out a good case, but the Chief Justice's keener penetration discovered otherwise. As the statute had been enacted not only after the escape, but also after action brought, it could apply in this case, said he, in but one of two ways: Either as a new rule for the government of a past case, or as a declarative interpretation of former statutes for the guidance of the court in the case at bar.[112] In neither was its application acceptable to Kent.

this to be a very significant case in the process of incorporating the vested rights principle into our constitutional law. He comments upon Kent's original interpretation of retroactivity in the law; but in his notes, observes, as Kent did in the opinion, that there were English precedents for what he was doing. The due process of law idea, which Corwin makes Kent invoke, does not to me seem to be so conspicuous, as his use of the doctrine of the separation of powers; though if a law contrary to due process means simply contrary to common right and reason as understood by the court, we have here a good example of an early use of substantive due process.

[112] Dash v. Van Kleeck, 7 *Johns. Rep.* 500.

He proceeded to elaborate: "The very essence of a new law is a rule for future cases. The construction here contended for on the part of the defendant, would make the statute . . . defeat a suit already commenced upon a right already vested. This would be . . . divesting [the plaintiff] of a right previously acquired under existing law. Nothing could be more alarming than such a subversion of principle." [113] Spencer himself had admitted that the statute was retroactive, but he believed it should be allowed to stand since the constitution forbade retroactive laws only when of a criminal nature, not of a civil nature like the one in question. Kent took a less technical view, saying rather wilfully that civil laws were equally within the principle of the prohibition and that if governments were to be permitted to oppress by retrospective acts in civil cases, experience taught that in criminal cases they would eventually do the same. Furthermore, as he observed, the current of authorities had been strong against the validity of such legislation since the days of Bracton; and he declared it to be a principle of English law as ancient as that law itself that a statute even of its omnipotent Parliament may not thus operate.[114] Coke and Mansfield had proclaimed the doctrine, and Bracton himself, if it required further sanction, had appeared to derive it from the Roman law where we find "the same principle that the lawgiver cannot alter his mind to the prejudice of a vested right. *Nemo potest mutare consilium suum in alterius injuriam.*" [115]

Here then was a maxim of civil liberty which both Roman and English law respected. But in the Roman law, as "the will of the prince was paramount to every obligation," that maxim could be arbitrarily evaded. Not so, however in the English; and herein consisted the distinction between Roman subject and English freeman, that the latter's law protected him even

[113] *Ibid.*, 502.
[114] *Ibid.*, 502–503.
[115] *Ibid.*, 502–503.

against government in his rights of personal liberty, personal security and private property. "These rights," said Kent, "have been better understood and more exalted in public estimation" where the common law prevails; and what is more, they have been better "secured by provisions dictated by the spirit of freedom, and unknown to the civil law." [116] Of these provisions none exceeded in effectiveness the separation of powers which was not "distinctly known or prescribed in imperial times" when "the prince was in the habit of interpreting his own laws for particular occasions." [117]

But was there any essential difference between that practice on the prince's part and that on the part of the legislature, if the statute on which the defendant was relying, was a legislative exposition for the guidance of the court in the case before it? Chief Justice Kent refused to believe that there was; and he did so upon the ground that the legislature would then be taking cognizance of a judicial question, and "This," he affirmed, "could not possibly have been the meaning of the act; for the power that makes is not the power to construe a law. It is a well settled opinion," he continued, "that the union of these two powers is tyranny. Theorists and practical statesmen concur in this opinion. Our government like . . . the only free government at present remaining in Europe, consists of departments, and contains a marked separation of the legislative and judicial powers." [118] To ignore this salutary principle for the sake of extending clemency to a sheriff who had been too lenient with an imprisoned debtor, would have constituted a surrender to sentimentality which Kent could but have regarded with disgust. It would have jeopardized not only the mere right to an action which was here involved; it would have endangered both liberty and property at once by opening to

[116] *Ibid.*, 503–505.
[117] *Ibid.*, 503.
[118] *Ibid.*, 508.

the legislature the opportunity of exercising authority in disregard as well of the restraints of due process [119] as of those of the separation of powers.

Seldom did Kent have occasion, as in Dash v. Van Kleeck, to correct from the bench legislative carelessness of vested right. The constitution provided him with a more direct method of achieving that end.[120] At the same time there are other cases which show as clearly his vigilant guardianship of individual privilege. Where, for example, a certain man owned a close, but with the reservation that the inhabitants of a neighboring village should have "free egress and regress . . . with the liberty of fishing or fowling or any other needful occasion," Kent was urged by one of the most eminent lawyers [121] to consider that usage as evidence of a franchise belonging to the village, and to construe it liberally for the benefit of the inhabitants thereof, for, as counsel argued, the doctrine of prescription "is in favor of common right and is never held in diminution of it." [122] But the Chief Justice spoke out emphatically in favor of the owner's private right, and interpreting the reservation strictly, he declared that it gave no more to the inhabitants than what had been expressed. They could go fowling there, and fishing, but they could take neither wood nor grass nor yet anything else appurtenant to the soil, not even the sea weed which had been washed up, and which they had long been wont to gather for use as a manure. "The rule is," said Kent, referring to the common law, "that if the marine increase be by small and almost imperceptible degrees it goes to the owner of the land. The sea weed must be supposed to have accumulated gradually. The slow increase and its usefulness as a manure and as a protection to the bank, will upon every just and equitable principle vest the property of the weed in the owner of the

[119] Edward S. Corwin, *Twilight of the Supreme Court*, 59–60.
[120] *I.e.* in the Council of Revision *vide infra*.
[121] Egbert Benson, who had resigned from the bench.
[122] Emans v. Turnbull, 2 *Johns. Rep.* 318.

land. It forms a reasonable compensation to him for the gradual encroachment of the sea to which other parts of his estate may be exposed; this is one sound reason for vesting the maritime increments in the proprietor of the shore. The *jus alluvionis* ought in this respect to receive a liberal encouragement in favor of private right."[123]

The most celebrated case exhibiting Kent in the role of champion of proprietary privilege is that in which the Livingston steamboat monopoly was at stake. Of that monopoly the courts themselves had been less tender than the Chief Justice could have wished. In Livingston v. Van Ingen, the Chancellor of New York, John Lansing, had refused to sustain it in an opinion described by the biographer of Marshall as one "of great ability and almost meticulous learning."[124] The Chancellor, however, was reversed by the Court of Errors, where Chief Justice Kent came to the rescue of his victims.

The case[125] had arisen amid interesting circumstances. By a series of statutes extending over a period of years, Robert R. Livingston and Robert Fulton had received the exclusive privilege of running steamboats in the waters of New York. In their early efforts to perfect that mode of navigation both men had encountered only ridicule, but with a result that is a commonplace of history, they had persevered in their experiment. Having borne the burden of expense in perfecting the new method, they naturally desired to enjoy its benefits; and with steady vigilance they attempted, in pursuance of the New York law, to exclude all steamboats from the state, save only those that belonged to them or had been licensed by their authority. This vigilance not only vexed the citizens of their own, it also antagonized those of other states, which proceeded to retaliate

[123] *Ibid.*, 322.
[124] Albert J. Beveridge, *Life of John Marshall*, Vol. IV, 405.
[125] Livingston v. Van Ingen, 9 *Johns. Rep.* 506.

by establishing similar monopolies within their respective boundaries and by punishing with similar penalties the infringement of them by the citizens of New York.[126] The hostile rivalries thus engendered, augured ill for the development of commerce under the new conditions. They augured ill for the peace and security of the Union.[127]

It was inevitable that Fulton and Livingston, surrounded as they were with envious and unfriendly men, should have been more than once openly defied. Steamboats began to navigate Hudson's river without their permission, and to put an end to this violation of their right, the partners sought redress at equity by praying for an injunction against James Van Ingen and some twenty others. This the chancellor refused to grant, and he based his refusal upon doctrine that had wide popular appeal.

Examining the *Institutes* of Justinian, he discovered that it was there laid down that those things which by the law of Nature are bestowed upon mankind in common, are the air, running water and the sea; that all ports and rivers are to be considered public, and that consequently the right of fishing therein is a right that belongs to all.[128] Drawing the obvious corollary, he continued: "When Justinian . . . devised his code of civil law, he acknowledged the source of the right to the common enjoyment of air and water to be paramount to his authority and bestowed as a common boon by the hand of Nature, or as we would express the same sentiment, by *Nature's God*, an acknowledgement, from the situation of the legislator, from the occasion and manner of making it, calculated to im-

[126] Forfeiture of boat and tackle. *Vide* grants to Fulton and Livingston summarized in 9 *Johns. Rep.* 572. The grants were made in 1798, 1807, 1808, and 1811.

[127] Albert J. Beveridge, *Life of John Marshall,* IV, Ch. VIII *passim.*

[128] 9 *Johns. Rep.* 517. Lansing cites *Institutes,* Lib. 3 tit. 1 *de aere et aqua profluente* and Lib. 2 tit. 2 *de Fluminibus et Portubus.*

press the mind with its sincerity and truth, and that it was dictated by the general sense of mankind." [129] While heaping praises on the civil law,[130] the chancellor did not ignore the common law of England, and on the authority of Bracton and Sir Matthew Hale, he tried to show that that law, like the Roman, consecrated the navigable rivers to the common use, established a common right incapable of alienation or restraint, and shielded the public, in the exercise of that right, "from every species of private appropriation." [131]

The chancellor made an ingenious effort to strengthen this argument by reference to the Federal Constitution. That instrument guaranteed to the citizens of each state the privileges of citizens in the several states, in all of which, at the time when the Constitution was adopted, the common law was the basic jurisprudence. As that law, then, conceded a general privilege of using the navigable rivers, the attempt of New York to curtail that privilege by creating a monopoly, could be represented as a violation, not only of an established common law principle, but of the Federal Compact itself.[132]

With the chancellor's conclusion that, in view of all these difficulties, the injunction ought not to be granted, Livingston and Fulton were of course dissatisfied, and they lost little time in taking an appeal to the Court of Errors,[133] where Lansing was speedily reversed. Chief Justice Kent delivered the opinion of the court, an opinion in which his colleagues, both senators and judges concurred by a large majority.[134]

The Chief Justice began by saying that the presumption was in favor of the validity of the grants. Had they been unconstitutional, the numerous statutes, extending from 1798 to

[129] Livingston v. Van Ingen, 9 *Johns. Rep.* 517.
[130] *Loc. cit.*
[131] *Ibid.*, 519.
[132] Livingston v. Van Ingen, 9 *Johns. Rep.* 519–520.
[133] Their lawyers were the best: Hoffman, Colden, Riggs, Emmet. For the respondents: Wells, Henry and Van Vechten.
[134] 9 *Johns. Rep.* 562, 572.

1811, which had established and extended the monopoly, would not have been likely to have withstood so repeatedly the scrutiny of both the legislature and the Council of Revision. Of that latter body Governor Jay had been a member, when the first statute in the series had been submitted, and Jay was distinguished "for the scrupulous care and profound attention with which he examined every question of a constitutional nature." [135] Unless, therefore, the Court of Errors could justify itself by the soundest argument, a decree prostrating all these laws would be ill-advised as tending to enfeeble the sanction of law in general.[136]

"But," said Kent, "we are not to rest upon presumption alone; we must bring these laws to the test of a severer scrutiny." [137] Considering the power to grant such a monopoly, he observed that it appertained to every sovereign authority, and that it had already been exercised in many ways that had not been questioned. Bank charters, he maintained, charters to bridge, canal and turnpike companies, to ferries and to markets, were similar grants of exclusive privileges; [138] and though they might be unwise or inexpedient, such a criticism had nothing to do with the constitutional power of conferring them. That power was limited only by the constitutional provisions, by the fundamental principles of all government, by the unalienable rights of mankind,[139] none of which in the present case was operative; for here, the grant withdrew no preexisting vested privilege, it interfered with no man's preexisting property and it left every citizen "to enjoy all the rights of navigation and all the use of the waters of this State which he before enjoyed. There was then," continued Kent, "no injustice, no violation of first principles in a grant to the

[135] Livingston v. Van Ingen, *Ibid.*, 573.
[136] *Loc. cit.*
[137] *Loc. cit.*
[138] *Loc. cit.*
[139] *Loc. cit.*

appellants, for a limited time, of the exclusive benefit of their own hazardous and expensive experiments. The first impression upon every unprejudiced mind would be that there was justice and policy in the grant. Clearly then it is valid unless the power to make it be taken away by the Constitution of the United States." [140]

Construing the clause of that instrument which declares that the citizens of each state shall be entitled to the privileges and immunities of citizens in the several states,[141] the Chief Justice failed to see how it was violated by the monopoly; for the meaning of that clause was not that other citizens upon entering New York, should carry with them the privileges that they had possessed at home, but rather, that they should enjoy such privileges as the citizens of New York enjoyed. A law of the state that excluded the vast majority of New Yorkers from the business of running steamboats was not the sort of discriminatory law which the Constitution had intended to prevent. Giving but brief consideration to the argument, the Chief Justice hastened on to deal with a more pertinent inquiry.

Though Chancellor Lansing had been silent upon the subject, counsel had contended that the monopoly was in violation of the clause which bestows on Congress the power to regulate commerce among the several states. The ground of this contention was that the power was vested in Congress exclusively. If this was true, the monopoly was void, for the statutes that had created it, having necessarily to do with at least one phase of commerce, had been enacted *ultra vires*.

In discussing the question thus raised, one of the most important in the whole field of constitutional law, Kent proved that his abilities derived from something more than a mere mastery of the books. The problem here posed was a novel one,

[140] *Loc. cit.*
[141] *Constitution of the United States*, Art. IV, Sect. 2–1.

and it required for solution not learning but originality. Thus like most other questions of federal jurisprudence, it was markedly different from those with which James Kent was used to dealing. Nevertheless, in disposing of it, he showed that he was not only a scholar, but an ingenious reasoner as well.

Examining, then, the Constitution, he found that the power to regulate commerce was indeed, as contended, a power conferred on Congress; but that it followed that the states were thereby precluded from exercising a similar power was a conclusion which he refused to admit.[142] Congress could also levy taxes, yet none had ever argued or supposed that states could not do the same. That power, as every citizen was aware, belonged to both sovereignties jointly. The regulation of commerce resembled the levying of taxes in that it was an exercise of authority of which both were concurrently capable. Nowhere did the Constitution prohibit it to the states; and the tenth amendment had emphatically declared that the powers not prohibited still remained.[143]

It could, however, be objected that concurrent possession of authority upon the same subject would lead inevitably to collisions between state and Union. This, Kent was willing to admit, if it were contended that the authority of each was paramount. But such a contention, involving as it did an absurdity, he refrained from advancing; and he readily conceded that where Congress enjoyed a delegated authority and chose to exercise it, the authority of the state was inferior and must give way.[144] So long, however, as Congress abstains from occupying the field, so long the state is free to enter it, nor need it retire until the Congress has advanced to take possession. "We are not always walking *per ignes suppositos cineri doloso,*" said the Chief Justice. "Our safe rule of construction and of action

[142] Livingston v. Van Ingen, 9 *Johns. Rep.* 574.
[143] *Loc. cit.*
[144] *Ibid.*, 574–575.

is this, that if any given power was originally vested in this State, if it has not been exclusively ceded to Congress, or if the exercise of it has not been prohibited to the States, we may then go on in the exercise of the power until it comes practically in collision with the actual exercise of some congressional power." [145] Applying this doctrine to the case at bar, he discovered no act of Congress with which the monopoly in question conflicted; [146] and since in the absence of such a restriction, the states were at liberty to make their own commercial regulations, he concluded that the grant to Livingston and Fulton was valid and ought to be sustained.[147] To do otherwise, on the contingency that that grant might possibly collide with some future act of Congress, was to proceed upon a maxim which the Chief Justice called "a monstrous heresy." [148]

To the argument that the monopoly was incompatible with the power of Congress to grant patents to inventors, Kent paid slight attention; for the question again was one of the concurrent authority of Congress and state legislatures, and that the latter had a perfect right to confer patents, he had not the slightest doubt.[149] Furthermore, in the present case the argument was irrelevant, for the respondents had no patents, nor had Livingston and Fulton obtained their grant as inventors. Their privilege, therefore, was totally unconnected with the patent power.[150]

Having disposed of the constitutional question involved, the Chief Justice finally addressed himself to the task of showing that the common law of England not only tolerated but encouraged monopolies of the sort which had been given to the appellants. "This power to encourage the importation of im-

[145] Livingston v. Van Ingen, 9 *Johns. Rep.* 575.
[146] *Ibid.*, 578.
[147] *Loc. cit.*
[148] *Loc. cit.*
[149] *Ibid.*, 581.
[150] *Ibid.*, 583.

provements by the grant of an exclusive enjoyment for a limited period is," said he, "extremely useful and the English nation have long perceived and felt its beneficial results." [151] Learnedly reviewing the precedents that had been established and the laws that had been enacted on the subject, he emphasized the celebrated statute of King James I's reign which abolished all existing monopolies, save only those especially excepted. These, he remarked, were worthy of consideration, and first among them, were the monopolies granted by Parliament, "For," he declared, "no one ever doubted (unless it be since the origin of this controversy) of the power of the legislature to create an exclusive privilege." [152] Moreover, as he pointed out, the selfsame statute also permitted the King to issue grants, for a limited time, for the sole working or making of any new manufactures not before used in the realm.[153] But this power given to the King by statute, had been exercised before at common law, for there was a case at hand, analogous to the present case, in which during Elizabeth's time, it had been freely admitted that where any man by his own charge or invention, doth bring any new trade into the realm or any engine tending to the furtherance of trade, even the King might grant monopoly patents.[154] In view of this case, the Chief Justice asked the question whether it were possible to suppose that the State of New York were without the power contended for, a power which "if well and judiciously exerted may ameliorate the condition of society by enriching and adorning the country with useful and elegant improvements." [155]

Had the power in the present case been judiciously exerted by the New York Legislature? The Chief Justice was convinced that it had; and though he himself had once been skepti-

[151] *Loc. cit.*
[152] *Loc. cit.*
[153] *Loc. cit.*
[154] *Ibid.*, 584.
[155] *Loc. cit.*

cal of the steamboat experiment,[156] he now made handsome amends for his lack of faith. "I think," he confessed, "the power has been wisely applied, in the instance before us, to the creation of the privilege now in controversy. Under its auspices the experiment of navigating boats by steam has been made, and crowned with triumphant success. Every lover of the arts, every patron of useful improvement, every friend to his country's honor, has beheld this success with pleasure and admiration. . . . It is difficult to consider even the known results of the undertaking without feeling a sentiment of good will and gratitude towards the individuals by whom they have been procured, and who have carried on their experiment with patient industry, at great expense, under repeated disappointments, and while constantly exposed and held up, as dreaming projectors, to *the whips and scorns of time*. So far from charging the authors of this grant with being rash and inconsiderate, or from wishing to curtail the appellants of their liberal recompense, I think the prize has been dearly earned and fairly won and that the statutes bear the stamp of an enlightened and munificent spirit." [157]

Such was the eloquent language of Kent as he made ready to reverse the decision of the chancellor and to order the desired injunction to issue. He was aware that what he was about to do was most unpopular,[158] though he could hardly have known that his act, destined as it was to prolong the life of the envied and burdensome monopoly for some fifteen years, would prove at last to be in vain. Failing to reckon with the astute perceptions of John Marshall, he was himself long years afterward to be overruled,[159] and that by a judge who, however deeply he

[156] He had once referred to the steamboat as useless machinery!

[157] Livingston v. Van Ingen, 9 *Johns. Rep.* 584–585.

[158] *Ibid.*, 589.

[159] In Ogden v. Gibbons, 4 *Johns. Ch.* 150. But the same question was involved. Marshall did not, be it noted, destroy Kent's doctrine of concurrent powers.

respected the rights of property, cherished more dearly still the peace, the prosperity and the power of the Federal Union. Kent prized them too, and with a sincerity that allows of no doubt. But the rights of property he considered sacrosanct; and when they were once ascertained, he deemed it his most solemn duty as judge to protect them at whatever cost.

Holding that the legal right was in favor of the appellants, he therefore concluded that the remedy prayed for by their bill was a matter of course. "If we refuse the injunction," said he, "it ought to be for some substantial reason. We must not put it upon the mere *hoc volo, sic jubeo, sit pro ratione voluntas.* . . .[160] If the laws are valid, it would be of pernicious consequence not to arrest their further violation . . . ,"[161] though failure to do so might win popular applause.

"I am sensible," said the Chief Justice, "that the case is likely to excite sympathy (I feel it with others). . . . [But] if we were to suffer the plighted faith of [these statutes] to be broken, upon a mere pretext, we should become a reproach and a bye-word throughout the Union. It was a saying of Euripides and often repeated by Caesar that if right was ever to be violated, it was for the sake of power. We follow a purer and a nobler system of morals, and one which teaches us that right is never to be violated. This principle ought to be kept steadfast in every man's breast; and above all it ought to find an asylum in the sanctuary of justice."[162]

The sanctuary of justice in which the Livingstons thus found refuge from community discontents, sometimes sheltered a freedom that meant something more than the exemption of vested privilege from external interference. That fact spares Kent the ungenerous imputation of being interested in liberty only to make it serve the ends of property, though the

160 Livingston v. Van Ingen, 9 *Johns. Rep.* 587.
161 *Ibid.*, 589.
162 *Loc. cit.*

twain were indeed linked fast in his philosophy. Nor was the union so artificial as that of liberty and equality whose praises were glibly sung by Jacobins in France and reechoed by Democrats in America. For surely an invasion of the rights of property in the name of equality would destroy freedom by presupposing, as Kent believed, a capricious and arbitrary government, unrestrained by check or balance, unmindful of minorities; and to him such a government was tyranny whether its authority reposed in prince or people. He had watched with fascination the developments in France where liberty and equality had been exalted together only to be together sacrificed under the despotism of Napoleon which he execrated from the bench.[163] Disgusted, then, with French doctrine, he viewed its progress in America with apprehension; and presently in his own court his apprehension was confirmed, for he was there confronted with a case which proved that the American Jacobins were as menacing to freedom as to property. To save freedom the Chief Justice put forth the greatest effort of his career.

The case of the People v. Croswell,[164] arising in Jefferson's first administration, involved the Federalist editor of the *Wasp*, who had published an attack on the President, declaring that he had paid one Callendar to call Washington a traitor, a robber and a perjurer, and John Adams "an hoary-headed incendiary." For this publication, Croswell was tried for libel at the circuit by the then Chief Justice Lewis, to whom he applied to postpone the trial that time might be given to produce Callendar as witness who could prove the truth of the charge against the President. This the Chief Justice had refused to do; and holding that the truth could not be given in evidence, he instructed the jury to that effect, and charged them in addition to confine

[163] Craig v. United Insurance Co., 6 *Johns. Rep.* 255.

[164] 3 *Johns. Cases* 336 *et seq.* There is a MS. of this opinion, in Kent's own handwriting, in the MSS. Division of the New York Public Library.

themselves to the fact of publication; that whether it were a libellous publication or published with libellous intent, were questions for the sole concern of the court. To support his view, he read the opinions of Lord Mansfield in the Dean of St. Asaph's case, and declared that the law there laid down was the law of New York.

Thus it appeared that that state was following the example of Massachusetts and Pennsylvania in adopting the unpopular English law of seditious libel. That a judge should have been responsible for this, who like Lewis, belonged to the party of Thomas Jefferson was inconsistent at the least; though the inconsistency was one which could be regarded as venial, even convenient, since Jefferson himself had been the victim of the vilifier now to be punished. To Croswell's aid, however, came Alexander Hamilton and James Kent, the one as advocate, the other as judge, and between them they effected his rescue. At the same time they contributed somewhat to make the common law more popular by demonstrating that it was less harsh than had been hitherto supposed.[165] In his own effort toward the accomplishment of that task Kent proved that despite his esteem for the English sages, he could yet be critical of them even to impugning the authority of the most famous; but it required both boldness and agility in a judge who was never wearied of citing Mansfield now to repudiate his Lordship and to decide that the law laid down in the case of the Dean of St. Asaph was not after all such law as the State of New York should elect to follow. But if Kent delivered an opinion which better accorded with his own idea of the right than did Mansfield's, it was an opinion which nevertheless derived from English sources; nor did he venture to pronounce it until after a prolonged consultation of oracles even more venerable than the

[165] Kent's opportunity of passing upon this question arose when Hamilton as Croswell's counsel moved for a new trial in the Supreme Court. Kent's opinion was delivered when that court was debating whether the new trial should be awarded.

Lord Chief Justice. Since, however, the result of that consultation was to reestablish the law that once had been, rather than obediently and without self-will to announce the law that was, Kent's labors resulted in a greater act of creation than he perhaps would have thought it expedient to acknowledge.

At any rate, he was at the greatest pains to find a warrant for his views in the ancient books; and that, in spite of the fact that he had reached those views by means of reasoning which for lucidity and force would have done credit to Marshall. He had begun with the axiom that a crime consists in the intent with which a given deed is perpetrated, and he embellished this beginning with a Roman maxim to the same effect: *Actus non facit reum nisi mens sit rea.* Now it is the province of the jury, he continued, to determine whether a crime has been committed, and on the basis of that determination, to return their general verdict. But since the crime itself consists in the malice of the intent, the jury cannot properly say whether it has been committed, unless they can arrive at a prior decision concerning the intent, whether it was good or evil. To preclude them from judging of the intent, would be, therefore, seriously to restrict their power, impair their function and render their role in courts of justice all but negligible. Such was the general tenor of the judge's reasoning. Applying it more specifically to the case before him, he held that the rule laid down by the Chief Justice would prevent the jury from bringing in, as they ought, a general verdict of innocence or guilt, and he expressed anxiety lest its effect would be to "transfer the exclusive cognizance of crimes from the Jury to the Court and to give the Judges the absolute control of the press." [166]

The grounds for such anxiety were substantial. The fact of publication, which was all that Lewis would have left for the jury to decide, was in itself indifferent. But, said Kent, "It is the application to times, persons and circumstances, it is the

[166] People v. Croswell, 3 *Johns. Cases* 364.

particular intent and tendency that constitutes the libel," [167] and if these were to abide the sole and exclusive determination of the judge, his discretion in establishing the crime would be unbounded. The rule upon which Lewis had depended in his charge, that the libellous intent was an inference of law, and that the court determines law, the jury fact, Kent brushed aside with telling strokes. The maxim, he said, was to be taken literally only when law and fact could be separated. But a libel being a compound of both, was a case to which the general rule could not apply; for, said he, "This application to circumstances and this particular intent are as much *matters of fact* as the printing and publishing. When an act innocent in itself becomes criminal when done with a particular intent, that intent is the material fact to constitute the crime." [168] It may be an inference of law as well, but if so "The law and fact are so involved that the jury are under an indispensable necessity to decide both unless they separate them by a special verdict." [169]

Such was the position which Kent assumed in the case of Croswell. It was a reasonable position and it could indeed be considered as a liberal one. Kent himself no doubt considered it so, and there have been modern writers who have accepted his appraisal of it.[170] But, however reasonable or liberal he may have regarded it, the judge was not satisfied until he found Littleton reporting that the inquest may give a verdict as general as the charge, if they will take upon themselves the knowledge of the law. Coke and Hobart reenforced the view of Littleton, and Sir Matthew Hale's observation that "as the Jury assists the Judge in determining matter of fact, so the Judge

[167] *Ibid.*, 363.

[168] People v. Croswell, 3 *Johns. Cases* 363.

[169] *Ibid.*, 367.

[170] Thomas R. Powell, "James Kent's Contributions to Constitutional Law," *Columbia Alumni News*, XIV, 372–73; Charles Warren, *History of the American Bar*, 238–239.

assists the Jury in determining the point of law" [171] implied a similar doctrine. "To meet and resist directly this stream of authorities is impossible," asserted Kent, but he added that while the power was admitted, there might be a disposition to deny that it could rightfully be used. To show that such an assumption was ill founded he examined minutely some of the most celebrated causes in the legal history of England, and announced with satisfaction that Jeffries had denied but Holt had affirmed the jury's right to use its power.[172]

The "free, full and diligent" investigation which Kent gave to the first question presented by Croswell's case, was equalled if not surpassed by that which he gave to the second. Hamilton had objected to Lewis's decision at the circuit not only because it had excluded the jury from any determination of the law. He had asserted that an equally grave error had been committed in the refusal to give the defendant time to produce his witness; and to the reason of the refusal, that in a libel case the truth cannot be given in evidence, he had taken prompt exception. Here also he was sustained by Kent who again had recourse to the old authorities.

Unfortunately, now as before, they answered in equivocations, though the tendency of their earlier utterances seemed to be to establish the doctrine that in a public libel falsehood is a material ingredient.[173] Such was the meaning to be gathered from divers statutes of the reigns of Edward I and Richard II,[174] statutes so ancient that they could be considered as blended into the body of the common law. Such too, at a much later date, was the clear and emphatic import of the words of the Lord Chief Justice Holt, when in Fuller's case, turning to the defendant, he had asked: "Can you make it appear that

[171] People v. Croswell, *ibid.*, 367.

[172] *Ibid.*, 368–371.

[173] *Ibid.*, 378, 382.

[174] *Ibid.*, 382 *et seq.* The statutes are Westminster, 1 Edward I, C. 34; 2 Richard II, C. 5; 12 Richard II, C. 11; 2 Phil. & Mary, C. 3.

these books are true. If you take it on you to write such things as you are charged with, it lies upon you to prove them at your peril. These persons are scandalized if you can produce no proof of what you charge them with. If you can offer any matter to prove what you have written, let us hear it. If you have any witnesses, produce them." [175] It was, perhaps thought Kent, a blighting commentary on the wisdom of Chief Justice Lewis, that with the words of a sage like Holt recorded in the books, he had had the rashness to rule dogmatically that the truth could not be given in evidence.

However, the admission was necessary that Holt's doctrine had not been consistently affirmed in the Courts of Westminster Hall where in Franklin's case, decided in 1731, Lord Raymond had so boldly departed from it as to provoke the indignant comment of counsel: "Then I submit whether this will not tend to the utter suppression of the liberty of the press which has been so beneficial to the nation." [176] His Lordship's ruling Kent refused to accept as good law, and to explain his reason, he quoted again the comment of counsel: "I should be glad to have one instance of authority for this, where a publisher of news is not allowed to say this piece of news is true. Is there no distinction to be made between false news and true news, and cannot we now animadvert or take notice of public affairs as well as formerly?" [177] Significant it was, urged Kent, that in the same case, when the attorney-general had been pressed for authorities to uphold the view which he had persuaded his Lordship to adopt, he produced only an irrelevant and dubious dictum of Coke that a printer could print what belonged to his trade, but must publish nothing that might reflect upon His Majesty or His Majesty's ministers. This dictum Kent brushed impatiently aside as even more dangerous to

[175] People v. Croswell, 3 *Johns. Cases* 386.
[176] *Ibid.*, 387.
[177] *Loc. cit.*

the freedom of the press than Lord Raymond's original ruling,[178] the root of which he demonstrated as deriving, not from the generous principles cherished by the Courts of Common Law, but from the maxims of arbitrary and despotic power dear to the manipulators of that engine of Tudor and of Stuart tyranny, the Court of Star Chamber.[179] It was a rule stigmatized by its very origin; nor had the stigma been wholly erased even after Lord Raymond's decision, which itself had not indeed been more consistently followed than had Holt's. Lord Mansfield had departed from it; [180] the bar had withstood it; and amid so resounding a conflict of authorities, Mr. Justice Kent bravely declared, "I feel myself, therefore at full liberty to examine this question on principle and to lay the doctrine aside, if it shall appear unjust in itself or incompatible with public liberty and the rights of the press." [181]

That it appeared unjust in itself was no difficult proposition to establish; for to exclude inquiry as to the truth, was obviously to abridge the means of defense.[182] It was also to curtail the rights of the jury. For, since it had been settled that the crime of libel consists in a malicious intent, and that it is the province of the jury to determine of that intent, if the truth cannot be given in evidence, the jury is impeded in arriving at that very determination to which it may frequently be most material to consider of the truth or falsehood of the charge.[183] "What," asked Kent, "can be a more pertinent circumstance than the truth of the charge to determine the goodness of the motive in making it . . . ?" [184] The answer was obvious, and it conduced persuasively to the conclusion that the doctrine of

[178] People v. Croswell, 3 *Johns. Cases* 387.
[179] *Ibid.*, 380–382.
[180] *Ibid.*, 389; case of John Horne, 11 *St. Tr.* 283.
[181] *Ibid.*, 389–390.
[182] *Ibid.*, 377.
[183] *Loc. cit.*
[184] *Loc. cit.*

Lord Raymond as unsupported by reason or by justice, should be abandoned.

Nor was it more difficult to demonstrate that that doctrine imperilled the public liberty and the rights of the press. Kent was cautious, as usual, in guarding against possible abuse. He wanted it plainly understood that he was not contending for a press beyond the reach of law, for that, said he, "would be emphatically Pandora's box, the source of every evil." [185] Upon false and malicious publications, proved to be so, and upon the view that to prevent or punish them constitutes an interference with freedom, he pronounced a lively condemnation.[186] Such publications were the evidence of license, not of liberty, and the doctrine advanced by Hamilton and approved by Kent, afforded them no protection. That doctrine, as quoted by the judge, was to the effect "that the liberty of the press consists in the right to publish with impunity, truth, with good motives and for justifiable ends, whether it respects government, magistracy or individuals." [187] This was the liberty, well defined and rational, which Lord Raymond's arbitrary ruling had imperilled.

It was a liberty beneficial to the public as well as to the press. The Continental Congress had declared it to be so. The Constitutional Convention of 1787 had spoken in the same sense. The New York Convention which had approved their handiwork had reechoed the identical sentiment.[188] It was, moreover, a just inference to be drawn from the decision of Lord Mansfield in the case of Rex v. Bailley where His Lordship had held that to treat with asperity the officers of Greenwich Hospital was no libel, when the publication had been circulated among the governors of the institution, since the governors were those who from their situation were called upon to redress

[185] People v. Croswell, 3 *Johns. Cases* 392.
[186] *Loc. cit.*
[187] *Ibid.*, 393–394.
[188] *Ibid.*, 390.

the grievance, and had the power to do it.[189] "It might be easily perceived," said Kent, "that according to the same doctrine, it ought not to be a libel to publish generally a true account of the character and conduct of public rulers, because it is of vast importance that their character and actions should be accurately understood, and especially by the public to whom alone they are responsible." [190]

Kent's exposition of the law of libel was at once so generous and masterly that it was received with applause and enacted into statute. The opinion was the most effective witness that he ever bore in behalf of liberty; and it constitutes a worthy and an enduring monument to his fame. Nevertheless, one is tempted to ask whether politics had not lent zest to legal researches, and whether the learned judge's investigations would have produced the same conclusion had the political circumstances of the case been altered. Had it been a Federalist administration that was in power, would Kent have manifested the same eagerness to augment the opportunity for hostile criticism? It is possible seriously to doubt it.

In the eventful year 1798, when he was riding his first western circuit, he had not shown himself particularly jealous of the public's privilege to criticize officialdom. The liberty poles which he repeatedly saw erected in protest against the Federalist administration had only provoked him to anger; and he had attributed them, not to the freedom-loving instincts of a vigilant and high-spirited people, but rather to the corrosive influence of demagogues whom he called contemptible and vile.[191] Nor was this unflattering view of the leaders of the opposition to Federalist government entertained by him alone. His

[189] People v. Croswell, 3 *Johns. Cases* 379.

[190] *Loc. cit.*

[191] *Vide supra* where Kent's experience at Newtown is mentioned. Elsewhere too, as in the Mohawk valley he had exclaimed against the demagogues responsible for these poles. His remarks there may be contrasted with his praise of the Federalists, who during the controversy over the Otsego returns, had erected a liberty pole at Cooperstown.

partisans, in both the state and nation shared it with him, and becoming more and more sensitive to the attacks upon them in the opposition press, they resolved to silence those demagogues by abridging the opportunities for the free discussion of public affairs. They procured, therefore, the passage of the notorious Sedition Act of 1798 which made it a crime to write, print, utter or publish anything tending to bring government into disrepute. Such general language could be construed, in fact it was construed, as discountenancing even so ordinary an observation as that the President was incompetent.[192] To fine and imprison an editor for that remark, a far less caustic one than that attributed to Croswell, may well have appeared to unprejudiced minds as a deprivation of that freedom of the press which the Constitution was supposed to have guaranteed against congressional encroachment. Mr. Justice Chase, however, held otherwise; and staunch defender of the Federalist regime that he was, he had the temerity to declare "that freedom of the press and of speech is not abridged when criticisms of government are punished." [193] Acting upon that maxim, he enforced the Sedition Law with a rigor that won him an unenviable renown, and contributed more than the newspapers ever did to bring the Federalist administration into disrepute. But if James Kent disapproved of Chase's high-handed behavior, it was in secret that he did so. Neither in his letters to friends nor in his journal, nor yet in his opinion in the case of Croswell, did he betray any sign that that attack upon liberty, an attack as bold and brazen as any of which "Jacobinical" Democrats were ever guilty, had given him serious concern, or

[192] As in Cooper's case *vide* John S. Bassett, *A Short History of the United States*, 284.

[193] Charles K. Burdick, *Law of the American Constitution*, 360. It ought to be stated that some of the terms of the Sedition Act of 1798 were liberal enough and anticipated Kent's opinion in the Croswell Case. The act provided that the truth could be given in evidence and the jury could be judge of law as well as of fact. Chase, however, so browbeat the juries that apparently the latter provision was of little avail. *Vide* Burdick, *op. cit.*, 360–361.

enfeebled in any way his conviction that of the country's freedom the Federalists were more reliable custodians than their opponents.

Whether in fact they were so will remain a moot question; though in their efforts to preserve freedom, they may have used more precaution than did Democrats to prevent it from degenerating into license. Even the Sedition Act could be charitably explained as an attempt, not to impair the right of free speech, but as one designed to save it from abuse; and Kent himself was emphatic on the point that newspapers should be within the reach of law. Nor was he less conscientious in throwing safeguards about other liberties equally dear to people and politicians as the freedom of the press. In the Yates-Lansing litigation he was just as emphatic in refusing to tolerate what he believed to be an abuse of the privilege of *habeas corpus*.[194]

Yates, a lawyer, for a contempt consisting of malpractice in chancery, was sent to gaol by Chancellor Lansing, was set at large on an *habeas corpus* by Judge Spencer, and was again committed by the chancery court. At this juncture, Yates succeeded in bringing his case to the attention of the Supreme Court with the purpose of testing the Chancellor's power to reimprison him after his release. Kent, in impressive language, defended the power of courts to punish for contempts, and decided that Lansing had been within his rights when he had remanded Yates to gaol, albeit it was upon an *habeas corpus* that the latter had been at large. But the prisoner refused to abide the decision of the Supreme Court, appealed to the Court of Errors, where he was sustained in spite of the Chief Justice,[195] who demonstrated in a long and learned opinion that that appeal could not lie in the present case. His effort served only to lay him open to the charge of exalting judicial

[194] In the case of J. V. N. Yates, 4 *Johns. Rep.* 314.
[195] Yates v. People, 6 *Johns. Rep.* 335.

authority at the expense of personal freedom; for if the writ of *habeas corpus* was a principal protection of that freedom, and the erroneous commitment of a prisoner could not be corrected by the tribunal established for the very purpose of correcting errors, the argument might be then advanced that a prisoner could be subjected to arbitrary durance, and that the citizen enjoyed his freedom at the precarious pleasure of the judges. This danger was apprehended and voiced by no less a Democrat than Senator De Witt Clinton when a short time later the Court of Errors affirmed Kent's decision refusing Yates the right to sue Chancellor Lansing for having sent him illegally to gaol.[196] "We are told with judicial solemnity," remarked Clinton, "that a judge of the Supreme Court or the Chancellor acting as such, are beyond reach of prosecution or indictment, whether they act with or without jurisdiction, and be their conduct ever so illegal or oppressive. To these doctrines I can never subscribe. And I consider the decision this day [*i.e* of the Court of Errors] as extending beyond the remuneration or punishment of individuals; that it will in all its bearings and aspects, decide whether the law shall bend to the judge or the judge bend to the majesty of the law." [197] The Senator's criticism had no effect upon his colleagues who were satisfied with the grounds upon which the Chief Justice had rested his final decision against Yates. "No man," he had said, "can foresee the disastrous consequences of a precedent in favor of such a suit. Whenever we subject the established courts of the land to the degradation of private prosecution, we subdue their independence and destroy their authority. Instead of being venerable before the public, they become contemptible; and we thereby embolden the licentious to trample upon everything sacred in society and to overturn those institutions which

[196] Yates v. Lansing, 5 *Johns. Rep.* 283.

[197] Opinion of Senator Clinton in the Court of Errors, Yates v. Lansing, 9 *Johns. Rep.* 441.

have hitherto been deemed the best guardians of civil liberty." [198]

Kent's several opinions delivered in the course of this litigation are not the only monuments to his solicitude lest a liberty constitutionally recognized should be perverted into license. A more striking example of this concern is seen in his defense of religion against blasphemy seeking to excuse itself as an exercise of freedom of conscience. The case, which came before him on appeal from a decision of his colleague, Spencer, at a court of Oyer and Terminer, involved one Ruggles, fined heavily for assailing in public the characters of Christ and the Virgin. The Chief Justice not only affirmed the decision of the court below, but proceeded to deliver a long opinion on the legal status of Christianity in New York.[199]

The single question, in the courts' opinion, was whether the language of Ruggles were a public offense by the law of the land. That the language was blasphemous admitted of no doubt; and though blasphemy was prohibited by no statute of the state, the common law forbade it in emphatic terms. Indeed the Court of King's Bench had refused even to allow it to be debated whether the defaming of Christianity was not an offense at common law, and the ground of the refusal had been the doctrine that whatever strikes at the roots of Christianity tends manifestly to the dissolution of civil government. The same view had been advanced in the case of Rex v. Williams, involving the publication of Paine's *Age of Reason,* and tried in 1797 before Lord Kenyon. The tendency of all the authorities, including Blackstone, was to establish beyond all doubt that profane ridicule and contumelious reproaches of Christ and of the Holy Scriptures were offenses at common law, whether uttered in words or writings.

[198] Yates v. Lansing, 5 *Johns. Rep.* 298.

[199] People v. Ruggles, 8 *Johns. Rep.* 290. Ruggles was indicted for calling Jesus Christ a *bastard* and His Mother a *whore.*

"And why," queried Kent, "should not the language contained in the indictment be still an offense with us? There is nothing in our manners or institutions which has prevented the application or the necessity of this part of the common law. We stand equally in need, now as formerly of all that moral discipline and of those principles of virtue which help bind society together. The people of this State," continued he, "in common with the people of this country, profess the general doctrines of Christianity as the rule of their faith and practice; and to scandalize the author of these doctrines is not only, in a religious point of view extremely impious, but even in respect to the obligations due to Society, is a gross violation of decency and good order." [200] The Chief Justice paused to quote Lord Bacon to the effect that "profane scoffing doth by little and little deface the reverence for religion" and noting his further observation, "Two principal causes have I ever known of atheism—curious controversies and profane scoffing," he resumed: "Things which corrupt moral sentiment have been held indictable, and shall we form an exception in these particulars to the rest of the civilized world. No government among the polished nations of antiquity—and none of the institutions of modern Europe (*a single and monitory case excepted*) [201] ever hazarded such a bold experiment upon the solidity of the public morals as to permit, with impunity and under the sanction of their tribunals the general religion of the country to be openly insulted and defamed. The very idea of jurisprudence with the ancient law givers and philosophers embraced the religion of the country;—*Jurisprudentia est divinarum atque humanarum rerum notitia.*" [202] The *Digest* of Justinian lent weight to the conclusion that an offense against religion is an offense also against the law.

[200] People v. Ruggles, 8 *Johns. Rep.* 293.
[201] Italics are the writer's, not Kent's.
[202] People v. Ruggles, *ibid.*, 294.

It had been objected that such a view was untenable in a state where religious establishments had been discarded by the Constitution itself. The Chief Justice, however, held his ground inflexibly and succeeded ultimately in showing that he was sustained by the instrument in question. "The free, equal and undisturbed enjoyment of religious opinion," he conceded, "and free and decent discussion on any religious subject, is granted and secured"; but he hastened to add that "to revile with malicious and blasphemous contempt the religion professed by almost the whole community is an abuse of that right." [203] He was willing to admit that religious establishments had been discarded by the Constitution; yet he qualified his admission by announcing that that Constitution "does not forbid judicial cognizance of those offenses against religion and morality which have no reference to any such establishment but are punishable because they strike at the root of moral obligation and weaken the security of the social ties." [204] The instrument was never meant to withdraw religion in general, and with it the best sanctions of moral and social obligation from all consideration and notice of law, he declared, and he considered that its terms would be fully satisfied "by a free and universal toleration without any of the tests, disabilities, or discriminations incident to a religious establishment." To explain it as breaking down the common law barriers against licentious, wanton and impious attacks on Christianity itself would be an enormous perversion of its meaning; [205] for as the Chief Justice, with telling effect remarked, that grant of toleration carried with it a proviso that "The liberty of conscience hereby granted shall not be construed to excuse acts of licentiousness or justify practices inconsistent with the peace or

[203] People v. Ruggles, 8 *Johns. Rep.* 294.
[204] *Ibid.*, 296.
[205] *Loc. cit.*

safety of the State." [206] Obviously then, this proviso covered the case of Ruggles, and precluded his being excused by the courts. If the religion of Jesus Christ was necessary to the public peace and safety, as the common law declared, to seek to enfeeble that religion by public blasphemies was tantamount to an attempt to undermine society itself. It was a crime the more grievous in that it scandalized the religion of the people—a religion to which the legislature had, though without creating any particular establishment, given its official sanction by making the Christian Sabbath a legal holy day and by prescribing for trials in the courts of justice the kissing of the gospels and the taking upon them of the most solemn oaths. The legislative exposition of the Constitution coincided, therefore, exactly with that which was placed upon it by the Chief Justice—that by forbidding any given establishment with its attendant tests and disabilities, the instrument had yet never intended to deny that Christianity was an essential ingredient of the law to be defended, not only by the pulpit, but also by the bench.[207]

This opinion was not in keeping with the spirit of the times. It could be interpreted as a rebuke to the skepticism which Voltaire and Gibbon, to name but two, had stimulated in their treatment of Christianity. While these authors had addressed themselves to men of cultivation, and had expressed their subversive sentiments with all the wit and elegance of which their respective tongues were capable, others had spoken to simple folk in plainer but equally seductive terms. Among the best known of such popular writers was Tom Paine whose *Age of Reason* had found many readers in both England and America. The result had been the spread of a facile irreligion

[206] People v. Ruggles, 8 *Johns. Rep. 296*; *vide et Constitution of New York* (1777) Art. xxxviii.
[207] *Loc. cit.*

which, as Kent noticed on his circuits, had penetrated to the frontier.

The propagation of such ideas scandalized the orthodox whose apprehensions were far from being allayed by Jefferson's accession to the Presidency. The leader of the triumphant Democracy was supposed by some to be an atheist; others believed that if he worshipped any Divinity at all it was the Goddess of Reason set up by his Jacobinical friends in Paris. If Jefferson was no more an atheist than Paine, certainly he was no more conventional than he in his theological views; nor with those who maintained the conventional position did he have much patience. In particular he disliked and distrusted the clergy of New England both for their Federalist influence and for the priestly superstitions which he thought they harbored. They, in turn, detested him; and upon his alleged apostasy from Christian standards they harped with such insistence that they hardly knew whether to be gratified or shocked at the proof of their charges when he put a vessel of the United States at Paine's disposal to fetch him from Europe to America with honor.[208] At a time when the President thus officially countenanced infidelity, clergymen may well have rejoiced that the Chief Justice of New York officially upheld the faith.

Unofficially, the Chief Justice's views upon religion may not have differed widely from the President's own. He despised Popery; scorned the fanaticism of certain of the Protestant sects; and once, in the privacy of his club, had spoken of Christianity itself as a vulgar superstition from which cultivated men were free.[209] If he still held that opinion, then his

[208] Henry Adams, *History of the United States,* I, 316.

[209] When visiting French Canada, Kent made caustic comments on the Catholic religion. He called the "naked" image of Christ on the cross "disgusting." Once, in describing an enthusiastic Protestant parson, he called him "a pale, distressed looking zealot." For his remark about Christianity

comments on religion from the bench were sincere only as they expressed an aristocratic conviction that religious faith is useful as a buttress to the social order. To that theory of the case his hatred of Jefferson and his constant fear of Jacobinical commotion lend support. Be his private beliefs what they may, whether he was at heart a child of the Enlightenment or not, as a judge he reverenced the Virgin and valued so highly the religion of her Son as to write it into the law of the land.

He thus evinced once more his admiration for "the approved wisdom and sober sense of the English common law" from which, as he had said in another case "our fathers . . . had imbibed . . . that lively sense of order, of decency, of moderation and of right which is inculcated by its generous institutions." [210] That they had engrafted it into our system he pronounced providential; and he could only hope [211] that their descendants, living amidst "the revolutionary novelties and madness of a subsequent period," [212] would be worthy of their birthright. Surely the temptations to sell it for a mess of pottage were powerful and alluring. Kent both in public and private never ceased to warn his countrymen against them by extolling the example of England and animadverting upon that of France, whence Democrats appeared to draw such heady inspiration. But though the Chief Justice might pontificate as he would, his efforts edified those who needed them the least, his Federalist countrymen. It was enough perhaps that he could count on their applause when he derided the novel notions as mere sophistries,[213] when he branded them again and again as Jacobinical and sounded the alarm that all

---

as a vulgar superstition, see William Dunlap's *Diary*, September 30, 1797 *supra cit.*

[210] Yates v. People, 6 *Johns. Rep.* 422.

[211] *Loc. cit.*

[212] *Loc. cit.*

[213] James Kent to Moss Kent, Jr., May 21, 1799. *Kent Papers*, Vol. III.

good men should be upon their guard against the tyranny which Democratic license was certain to produce.[214]

Meanwhile as the star of Napoleon climbed higher, Kent but for England would have despaired. It was always "the glorious English nation" to him; [215] and so steadfastly did he consider Britain as of all countries "the most consoling to mankind" that he sometimes seemed desirous of lending her judicial aid. Thus, where a Frenchman naturalized as an American during the Napoleonic wars, had lost his cargo as prize to the British and had sought to recover insurance on the ground that he was a neutral, Kent disallowed the plea. The subject of a belligerent, he said, who *flagrante bello* is naturalized in a neutral nation, retains his native character with respect to the belligerents, and his naturalization therefore will not support a warranty of neutral property.[216] This decision the Court of Errors reversed, being somewhat more jealous than the Chief Justice of the rights of naturalized Americans. There were other decisions conspicuous for their British bias. In Ludlow v. Bowne and Eddy,[217] a cargo directed by an American to a French firm had been intercepted by a British man-of-war; and though warranted American and so insured, had been condemned by the Admiralty as French. Upon the reluctance of the insurance company to cover the loss, a suit occurred in which it was necessary to inquire whether when a cargo is consigned it retains the character of the consignor until delivery or assumes forthwith the character of the consignee. To decide in the company's favor by holding that the cargo became French upon consignment so that the warranty of neutral property could not be sustained, might well be understood as a surrender of a neutral's right into British hands; and thus did Judge Spencer

[214] *Loc. cit.*

[215] James Kent to Moss Kent, Jr., February 7, 1812. *Kent Papers,* Vol. IV.

[216] Duguet v. Rhinelander, 1 *Johns. Cases* 360; Jackson v. New York Insurance Co., 2 *Johns. Cases* 191. Reversed, 2 *Johns. Cases* 476.

[217] 1 *Johns. Rep.* 1 *et seq.*

construe it, reflecting in his vigorous way upon the practices of Admiralty: "It appears to me that the English courts of Admiralty . . . are governed more by ideas of political expediency and of the necessity of destroying any commerce with their enemy, than by the law of nations. . . . I do not feel myself bound by their precedents nor required to justify their solicitude to condemn from motives of policy." [218] Kent, unperturbed by these remarks, concluded that the law regarded the American warranty as false, the cargo as French and the legitimate prize of the British captors. Nor does that decision mark the limit of his English leanings. Where an underwriter was again being sued, this time for the amount of insurance on a vessel warranted American, but, like the cargo in the former case, condemned as French by an Admiralty judge, the question arose whether the findings of that judge should conclude the New York court, and Kent decided that they should.[219] Apparently not all his brethren were satisfied with the ruling, for in a short time when a similar case confronted them, a fuller discussion ensued, and though Kent again prevailed, he was reversed by the Court of Errors. The principle for which he was contending was the common law principle that where a fact has been litigated and determined in courts of competent jurisdiction that fact becomes *res adjudicata*, no longer open to question by another court. During argument counsel had maintained that this doctrine had been adopted by the English judges in furtherance of Great Britain's maritime power. Kent repelled the suggestion as an unworthy aspersion on the "dignified character" of the British courts.[220]

But it was more than the character of the British courts that was at stake; it was the existence of Britain herself. The Chief Justice's dismay, then, may be imagined, as Jefferson's suc-

[218] Ludlow v. Bowne and Eddy, 1 *Johns. Rep.* 6.
[219] Ludlow v. Dale, 1 *Johns. Cases* 16.
[220] Goix v. Low, 1 *Johns. Cases* 341—Reversed, 2 *Johns. Cases* 480.

cessor added America's weight in the scales against her. It cannot cause much surprise that during the War of 1812 the sentiments which Kent harbored were all but treasonable. Considering that war both contemptible and wicked,[221] he viewed with complacency the failure of the American arms in Canada,[222] and he prayed devoutly: "May God in his infinite mercy grant speedy and rapid success to the arms of the allies in every direction." [223]

This perfervid admiration for the English was hardly becoming to the Chief Justice of a state threatened and afflicted with English invasion. It helps, however, to explain the progress which the English law was making there even during the course of hostilities. At no time did the Chief Justice enjoy a more marked ascendancy over his brethren than during those eventful years; and of that ascendancy he took full advantage. Though the guns along Niagara might boom their defiance of England, they failed to drown the voices of the English judges who from Bracton to Mansfield were speaking all the while through the mouth of Kent, and from his judgement-seat giving law to the country of Leatherstocking.

[221] James Kent to Moss Kent, Jr., July 14, 1813. *Kent Papers*, Vol. IV.

[222] James Kent to Moss Kent, Jr., December 24, 1813. *Kent Papers*, Vol. IV.

[223] *Loc. cit.* Cf. also Kent's letter to Timothy Pickering under date of April 26, 1814, in the Pickering MSS. in the library of the Massachusetts Historical Society: ". . . I always was of opinion that the *orders in council* of November, 1807, were under the then existing circumstances of Europe, justifiable on Principles of Public law. They resulted from necessary self-defense, and as against the extraordinary Domination of France were a just weapon of retaliation and resistance. The speeches of Mr. Percival and Mr. Canning in Parliament on this point I always believed to be solid."

V

The Woolsack

I may safely apply to the English rules of practice the observation of Montesquieu in respect to the Roman law: *Je me trouve fort dans mes maximes lorsque j'ai pour moi les Romains.*

Chancellor Kent, 4 *Johns. Ch.* 186

. . . it has been said of [Kent] . . . with respect to the Court of Chancery, as was said of Augustus with respect to the city of Rome, *lateritiam invenit, marmoream reliquit.*

London Law Magazine, VI, 132

You was spoken of in as high terms of respect as if you had been another Hardwicke.

Moss Kent, Jr. to James Kent, February 1, 1817

* * *

JAMES KENT, arrived now at middle age, may well have considered himself one of the most fortunate of men. The recognition earned through his public labors, his private situation gave him ample opportunity to enjoy. He was not rich, but his stipend, increased in 1812 [1] to three thousand a year, enabled him, prudent man that he was,[2] to support his family as their station demanded; and the care that he gave them, they requited with the warmest affection. The coming of middle age had not lessened his youthful love for his wife Elizabeth, now a vigorous matron, and invariably his "intrepid companion," as

[1] Alfred B. Street, *Council of Revision*, 57–58. In 1797 the stipend was $2000; in 1812 it was raised to $3000 and in 1816 to $4500 *per annum*. Later, for what causes will appear, it was reduced.

[2] Note by William Kent on this subject, *Kent Papers*, Vol. XI near the end.

he called her, on the numerous jaunts that made his vacations memorable.[3] In their children this congenial and contented pair had no reason to be disappointed. Their elder daughter, Bess, an attractive young gentlewoman already sought by eligible suitors, was soon to make a good marriage into the wealthy family of the Hones.[4] Their son William had grown into a promising youth almost ready for entrance into the college at Schenectady whence he would graduate in due time,[5] a classicist like his father, and fired, as his father had been, with an ambition to succeed at the bar. As their elder children grew, and prepared to go out from the paternal roof, the Kents found added comfort in their daughter Mary, happily for them still but a little girl. Among James Kent, Moss and their sister, Hannah Platt, now the mother of a flourishing little family of Platts, relations remained as cordial as ever. When holding the northern circuit, the Chief Justice seems frequently to have made his sister's house his headquarters where apparently he proved himself as successful in the avuncular role as had his bachelor brother, to whom he wrote one midsummer day that he had been in the meadow picking strawberries with their sister's children.[6]

This idyllic pastime served no doubt as a welcome diversion from official duties; though these, even as Kent's career in the Supreme Court drew near its end, were still performed with a zest and energy that left no doubt but that he continued to find them thoroughly to his liking. For in the full maturity of his intellectual powers, he was now, at fifty years of age, equally well endowed with physical vigor, a man whose robust constitution supplied him with buoyant spirits which naught,

[3] *Kent Journals, passim.*

[4] Elizabeth, daughter of James Kent and Elizabeth Bailey, married Isaac, nephew of Philip Hone.

[5] William Kent A. B. Union College, 1820.

[6] James Kent to Moss Kent, Jr., July 17, 1806. *Kent Papers,* Vol. III.

except the ascendancy of Democrats, could long depress. His appearance was less august than might have been expected in a Chief Justice. He was too short to be majestic, too alert and quick in his actions to be stately, yet his carriage was graceful, his manners urbane, and his face, effectively set off by the high, white stock, was keen, genial and expressive.[7]

Such was the man whom the Council of Appointment raised in February, 1814, to the dignity of chancellor.[8] There had been chancellors of New York before James Kent. In colonial days the royal governors had performed the office, and since independence, two eminent citizens, Robert R. Livingston and John Lansing, had held it in turn. But if Kent was not the first of the line, he was certainly the most famous. Indeed, he was the most famous of all the American jurists who have ever been adorned with that ancient and distinguished title.

The reason for this may be easily assigned. That peculiar jurisprudence which it is the function of a chancellor to expound, had been, like the common law, developed in England over a succession of ages into a complex system that required for mastery as long and as assiduous study as the law itself. The system had been in theory translated to America during the period of colonial dependence, and, in theory at least, it had been inherited by the states which arose out of the Revolutionary conflict. But the closing years of the eighteenth, the opening decade of the nineteenth century, found chancery doctrines but little understood, the remedies of chancery but infrequently resorted to, and the decisions in chancery causes

[7] *Vide* various portraits, especially that painted by Rembrandt Peale.

[8] 1 *Johns. Ch.* where occurs a notice thereof at beginning of volume. Kent was appointed by the unanimous vote of the Council. *Vide, New York Evening Post,* February 26, 1814, which comments thus: "The super-eminent talents, the indefatigable industry and stern impartiality which for so many years have distinguished the presiding judge, will continue to exhibit themselves with equal lustre in the Chancellor."

usually delivered, as those in law had once been delivered, orally and upon the basis of casual and imperfect investigations.[9] The appointment of Kent as chancellor changed all this, as his appointment to the Supreme Court had changed the similar situation in the law. From the days when as an obscure attorney in Poughkeepsie he had begun to read Peere Williams, he had shown a perennial interest in the principles of equity. Livingston had been aware of his proficiency in this branch of jurisprudence and had admitted him to practice without examination. Jay had appointed him a master in chancery, and during his incumbency of that office, Kent had enriched his knowledge with practical experience.[10] Thus he brought to his new duties, as head of the equity system of the state, a mind already well informed concerning their nature. He threw open his court, and the suitors, discovering to their gratification that chancery business could be promptly dispatched,[11] entered in constantly increasing numbers.[12] Each succeeding week brought fresh cases to be studied, elaborate opinions to be written until the new chancellor found himself more continuously occupied than in the busy days when as Chief Justice he had presided over the administration of the law.[13] Nor were the results of these labors ephemeral, for into chancery Kent had brought his good friend Johnson to report the decisions there with the same fidelity that he reported causes in the Supreme Court. Thus by the joint efforts of these indus-

[9] For the conditions in chancery, James Kent to Thomas Washington, October 6, 1828, *Kent Papers*, Vol. V. It is possible that Kent exaggerated the chaos of chancery conditions. *Vide* Professor Goebel's article "The Courts and the Law in Colonial New York" in Alexander Flick's *History of the State of New York*, III, *supra cit.*

[10] *Vide supra*, chapter III.

[11] James Kent to Moss Kent, Jr., October 17, 1814. *Kent Papers*, Vol. IV. *Vide et* Resolutions of the Bar on Kent's retirement, 7 *Johns. Ch.* 348 *et seq.*

[12] James Kent to Thomas Washington, October 6, 1828. *Kent Papers*, Vol. V.

[13] James Kent to William Johnson, April 8, 1815; to Moss Kent, Jr., January 8, 1816. *Ibid.*, Vol. IV.

trious jurists, the fabric of American equity began to rise [14] over against that of the law to which they had both already made such notable and enduring contributions.[15]

The difference between these types of jurisprudence had developed at a distant age in the annals of England, where the remedies at law, confined to the recovery of land, of chattels or of money, had become fixed in number, rigid in form and quite inadequate to the needs of justice. To invent novel remedies the judges had displayed a curious reluctance, so that suitors, often failing to obtain satisfaction in their tribunals, had had but one remaining hope for redress, a recourse to the King himself. His Majesty adopted the convenient practice of turning over their causes to the scrutiny and determination of his chancellor. That dignitary, in the Middle Ages invariably a churchman, was the more willing to assume the task inasmuch as he discerned in it the means of making himself useful as well to the church as to his sovereign. Had it not been for him, the statute of mortmain might well have prevented ecclesiastics from receiving further donations of landed property. Such indeed had been its purpose; but the piety and cunning of divers wealthy Christians had attempted to defeat that purpose by a conveyance of lands, not to the church itself to be sure, but to some third person for the church's use. This use, however, the judges had refused to sustain as a legal right. In consequence the indignant clergy appealed to the chancellor, and in his court they were presently consoled. That official was disposed to consider their cause upon its merits, and to decide it in accordance with the precepts of substantial justice, laying thereby the foundation of the doctrine of trusts, destined to remain thereafter one of the principal grounds of equitable jurisdiction. But it was not only the clergy who discovered the

[14] Resolutions of the Bar, 7 *Johns. Ch.* 348 *et seq.*

[15] *Loc. cit.* Johnson was taken to task for reporting too much, *United States Law Journal I*, 210–215.

generous impulses of the early chancellors to be convenient and beneficial to their litigations. Laymen had the same experience; and as the number of suitors increased, the Court of Equity began to develop into one of the most powerful tribunals in the Kingdom. From the liberal disposition of the court in its earlier history, the impression had got abroad that its proceedings were untrammelled by precedent, that its system, if system there were, was fluid and that each succeeding decision rested with the conscience and good judgement of him who for the time being chanced to be sitting on the woolsack.

The notion, though originally sound, became erroneous in subsequent ages, as equity began to imitate the habit of the law in regarding precedent with reverence; and after the labors of the celebrated chancellor, Sir Heneage Finch, in the seventeenth century, it lost its original fluidity to receive instead a definite form, a firm consistency, fixed doctrine and stable usages. Nevertheless, it remained sufficiently distinct from the law to warrant its being administered by a separate tribunal, while the advantages which its methods had over legal methods were solid and conspicuous. Its mode of proof was more expeditious, for it accepted as evidence the disclosure upon oath of facts known only to the litigant himself; and the comparative freedom from technical restraints in this respect adapted it especially to deal with cases involving intricate accounts, debts, legacies and the administration of estates. Its method of trial was less public and less formal, for it proceeded without jury and it dispensed with the requirement that witnesses should be brought before the court, since at equity, their testimony could be taken at a distance by a master, and the depositions thus produced were sufficient to enable the cause to be continued. Its comparative privacy and its use of written depositions as well as of oral and public testimony made equity more suitable than law to take cognizance of domestic controversies; and the relations between *baron* and *feme* constituted an important title of its jurisdiction. Most significant of all was the difference between the remedies which the two systems afforded. While law still permitted only a recovery of land, of chattels or of money damages, equity scrutinized the individual cases with more searching care, fitted its relief more precisely to their needs and where the legal remedies fell short, held out its own, by compelling a specific performance or imposing by means of the injunction its brusque and peremptory restraint.

Thus equity was furnished with more flexible methods of administering justice than was law, though it had long since, at least in England, transcended its original state when decisions in its courts rested in the discretion of the chancellor. That fact had been pointed out by Sir William Blackstone in his familiar treatise,[16] but it nevertheless appears to have been imperfectly apprehended in America not only by the bar but also by the bench. The result of this misapprehension was described by Mr. Justice Story some seven years after Kent had become Chancellor of New York, but ere his opinions, not yet completely published up to date, had gained their widest influence.[17] "If I were obliged to speak from my own very imperfect knowledge and experience," said Story with his usual modesty, "I should be compelled to declare that deviations in America from the established principles of equity were far more considerable than those of the common law. A more broad and undefined discretion has been assumed and a less stringent obedience to the dictates of authority. Much is left," continued he, "to the habits of thinking of the particular judge and more to that undefined notion of right and wrong,

[16] Sir William Blackstone, *Commentaries*, Book III, Ch. xxvii "Of Proceedings in the Courts of Equity," *passim*, from which the above summary.

[17] Nor do Kent's opinions seem to have circulated, when published, as rapidly as the bar could have desired. The reason was the high price charged for his reports by Johnson who had the copyright. The high price seems to have caused one of the adverse criticisms of the reports. *Vide American Jurist*, XV, 249.

of hardship and inconvenience, which popular opinions alternately create and justify." [18] It therefore appeared that under the guidance of ordinary judges, English equity in America was about to revert to that originally amorphous condition from which in England it had long before been rescued by Sir Heneage Finch. There were indeed, as Story took pains to admit, a few exceptional judges who did cherish a due respect for precedents in chancery; but who they were, he deemed it invidious to point out, though he declared it to be of great importance that their example should be followed.[19]

There can be no question but that Chancellor Kent was the jurist whom Story, in this last remark, had particularly in mind.[20] For Kent, as seldom in equity as in law, allowed his course to be deflected from the beaten English paths. A few occasions did of course arise where English precedents were found to be inapplicable. A statute of the reign of James I recognized a process of the peace from chancery; but when a wife, made anxious for her safety by the return of her quarrelsome husband, besought the chancellor to hold him to bail to keep the peace, Kent refused on the ground that the statute relied upon had not been reenacted in New York.[21] Nor is this the only example of Kent's departure from the practices of chancery in England. The rule there obtained that if a man took a mortgage, and left the title-deeds with the mortgagor, he was to be postponed to a subsequent mortgagee who had taken the precaution to get possession of the deeds. The reason of the rule was that by leaving the deeds, he enabled the mortgagor to impose upon others by representing his estate as free from the encumbrance; and this the mortgagor could the

[18] Joseph Story, "An Address Delivered Before the Members of the Suffolk Bar at their Anniversary," September 4, 1821. *Ibid.*, I, 22.

[19] *Loc. cit.*

[20] *Vide infra.*

[21] Codd v. Codd, 2 *Johns. Ch.* 143. The statute referred to here is 21 *Jac.* I ch. 8.

more readily do, since in England there were no registry acts except for Yorkshire and Middlesex. But since in New York the opportunities for registry were ample, the reason for the rule failed; and as a consequence, Kent refused to postpone the first to the second mortgagee, even though the first had been so lax as to leave the deeds with the mortgagor.[22]

Perhaps Kent's most noticeable deviations from English precedent occurred in connection with proceedings in lunacy; for whereas in England, as he observed, the custody of lunatics was committed not to chancery, but generally to the person who happened to be chancellor, in New York on the other hand it was expressly to chancery that that custody was given; [23] and Kent, leaving the limits marked out by his English predecessors, extended it to embrace not only lunatics but also the feebleminded. "Mere imbecility of mind not amounting to idiocy or lunacy has not (prior to our Revolution) been considered in the English Court of Chancery as sufficient to interfere with the liberty of the subject over his person and property," said he, adding however, "yet it is certain that when a person becomes mentally disabled, from whatever cause the disability may arise . . . he is equally a fit and necessary object of guardianship and protection. The Court of Chancery is the constitutional and appropriate tribunal to take care of those who are incapable to take care of themselves. There would be a deplorable failure of justice without such a power." [24] Thus Kent, as English chancellors had seldom done,[25] asserted his right to augment his jurisdiction over *personae miserabiles* and, where a person from old age or other cause becomes incapacitated, to award a commission in the nature of a writ *de lunatico inquirendo*. Indeed, his conception of the

[22] Berry v. Mutual Insurance Company, 2 *Johns. Ch.* 608–613.

[23] Brasher v. Van Cortlandt, 2 *Johns. Ch.* 246.

[24] In the matter of James Barker, 2 *Johns. Ch.* 234.

[25] Though as he takes pains in Barker's case to point out, English chancellors began to do it *after* the Revolution.

numbers of those who require the solicitude of chancery was extremely generous, for on at least one occasion he went so far as to intimate that not only persons incompetent from age or weakness of mind, but also "from some religious delusion or fanaticism, *quem urget fanaticus error vel iracunda Diana,* ought to come under the protection of the court." [26] At the same time, he refused to exercise the English chancery's power of visitation of charitable corporations.[27] It was, held he, a power bestowed upon the chancellor by the King in his character of *pater patriae,* and while suitable enough in a monarchy, inappropriate, except by statutory grant, to a chancellor in a republic.

Such are the sparse examples of Kent's deviation from the doctrines of equity in England. Others might be cited,[28] but they are insufficient whether in numbers or importance to shake the conclusion that in equity as well as in law he followed

[26] Malin v. Malin, 2 *Johns. Ch.* 240. It is not pretended that Kent intended this rather whimsical dictum to be taken seriously. He seems to have uttered it with his tongue in his cheek. The case involved Jemima Wilkinson whom Kent had encountered near the Crooked Lake in his circuit-riding days.

[27] Attorney-General v. Utica Insurance Company, 2 *Johns. Ch.* 390–391.

[28] There are some other cases, but they seem to be of no greater importance than these. The seven volumes of Johnson's Chancery Reports have been searched for instances of deviation, but have yielded only the following:

Codd v. Codd, 2 *Johns. Ch.* 143 *vide supra.*

Attorney-General v. Utica Insurance Co., 1 *Johns. Ch.* 375 *vide supra.*

In the matter of Wendell, a lunatic 1 *Johns. Ch.* 599: The issue whether A be insane is in *New York* to be made up and prepared for trial under the direction of chancery. In England the practice is to deliver the record and traverse to a Court of Law after the Attorney-General has gained issue thereon.

In the matter of James Barker, 2 *Johns. Ch.* 234 *vide supra.*

Berry v. Mutual Insurance Co., 2 *Johns. Ch.*, 607 *vide supra.*

Williamson v. Dale, 3 *Johns. Ch.* 292. The English practice of open bidding at the sale conducted by a Master in Chancery does not obtain in New York.

Titus v. Neilson, 5 *Johns. Ch.* 453. In New York a principle is established not admitted in the English courts, viz. that a wife could be endowed of an equity of redemption arising upon a mortgage in fee.

the rule *stare decisis* with fidelity. If he abandoned it now and then, it was usually in matters of detail that he did so. Far more characteristic it was for him not only to apply the English rule, but to praise it also; and as he had done in the Supreme Court, he sometimes applied it even when he doubted of its justice.[29]

This respect for chancery precedents is nowhere more aptly illustrated than in a case which arose but a short time after Kent had assumed his new office. It is a case the more interesting, inasmuch as during the course of argument, he was reminded by counsel of the obsolete notion that equity, as contradistinguished from the law, addresses itself alone to the merits of the question, unimpeded by what has been determined hitherto. The executors of Manning having been required by the heirs to give an account of the estate, contended that they should have a recompense for the pains to which they had been put in managing it, though no sum for that purpose was given by the will or provided for in any contract. It was argued, nevertheless, that a reward was only just, and the chancellor was urged to allow it in the exercise of that discretion with which his office was supposed to have invested him. Such a power Kent lost no time in disclaiming.[30]

"It would, no doubt," said he, "be at times very convenient

[29] Sterry v. Arden, 1 *Johns. Ch.* 266. The question was whether a deed of conveyance to a daughter as a settlement, when the conveyance was voluntary, was good as against a purchaser. The chancellor said no, and in defending his position, declared, "In short, the principle set up in favor of the purchaser has been so long and so well established by a series of authoritative decisions, supplied by the most eminent judges, that I feel bound by them whatever doubts I might have had . . . if I had been at liberty to follow my own reflections. When a principle has taken such deep root and received such uniform support, it belongs . . . not to the courts of justice to suppress or destroy it." *Ibid.*, 269. *Vide et* Murray v. Ballou, 1 *Johns. Ch.* 565 establishing the rule that if a purchaser for a valuable consideration, has notice of a trust, he buys at his peril. Though the justice of the rule is questioned by considerations addressed to the feelings, says Kent, he cannot dispense with the rule. *Ibid.*, 576, 580.

[30] Manning v. Manning, 1 *Johns. Ch.* 527 *et seq.*

and perhaps a cover for ignorance, or indolence or prejudice to disregard all English decisions as of no authority, and set up as a standard my own notions of right and wrong. But I can do no such thing. I am called to the severer and more humble duty of laborious examination and study. . . . Though proceedings in equity are said to be *secundum discretionem boni viri*, when it is asked *Vir bonus est quis?* The answer is *Qui consulta Patrum, qui leges juraque servat. . . .*" Remarking that equity, like law, is a science that has resulted from the labors of jurists over a long period of time, he maintained that for the adoption of its system, along with that of the law, the constitution of the state had clearly provided and that the provision imposed upon him as chancellor the solemn duty of ascertaining what the system was and of incorporating it by a series of decisions "into the body of our own judicial annals." With the justice or injustice of its rules he confessed that he was but little concerned, for it was his task only to declare them as he discovered them to be; and though a given rule might appear "monstrous" as one of the southern chancery causes had stigmatized it, "I should not," said Kent, "feel myself at liberty to say, as that case does 'so far as I can go, I shall blot it out forever.' It is the province of the legislative and not of the judicial power to change the law."

This announcement must have astonished many; and more than a few may well have been disquieted by the course of action which it portended. But the chancellor had in store a surprise even more startling. It was one thing to affirm a resolution to abide by the precedents established before the separation from England: to announce that respect should be paid to the decisions handed down since that event, was quite another; and indeed in some states, the mere mention of such authorities was forbidden. It was not so, however, in New York; nor had Kent been chancellor for long ere the names of Wedderburne,

Thurlow and Eldon began to resound in his court along with those of Nottingham and Hardwicke.

An opportunity apt for invoking these recent authorities was furnished by a case in which no less a personage than the Duke of Cumberland was a suitor in the New York court of equity.[31] The noble lord, who was an heir-at-law of the Countess of Bath to lands in the central part of the state,[32] was contending with the heirs of the Countess's personal property whether they or he should be held responsible for a certain mortgage debt with which those lands had been encumbered by the original owner some years before. It was the Duke's opinion that he should be exempt; and this he based upon the rule of law that where a person dies and leaves a debt, that debt becomes a prior charge upon the personal property. The rule was not popular in New York, and counsel for the Duke's opponents suggested that it ought not to be heeded, since it was designed to protect the interests of a landed aristocracy.[33] This contention, however, would have weighed but little with Kent, who was to accept the broad principle of the Duke's argument and to announce it officially more than once.[34] But in this particular case, he decided against the Duke, on the ground that a valid distinction existed between a debt which a man had personally and directly incurred, and one which came to

[31] Cumberland v. Codrington, 3 *Johns. Ch.* 229 *et seq.*

[32] Henrietta Pulteney, Countess of Bath, daughter of Sir William Pulteney, had inherited the Pulteney estates in central New York. Sir William, though he had paid a large sum for those lands, could not at first hold them, since a law of the state prohibited aliens from holding real property. In this exigency, Captain Charles Williamson, as Pulteney's agent, had become naturalized, and so had got possession of the lands in his own right, though in fact, as Pulteney's agent.

[33] Cumberland v. Codrington, 3 *Johns. Ch.* 238.

[34] Livingston v. Newkirk, 3 *Johns. Ch.* 319: Personal estate to be first applied to the payment of debts and legacies. Thompson v. Brown, 4 *Johns. Ch.* 619: Real estate will not be directed to be sold, until the deficiencies of the personal estate have been ascertained.

him indirectly in the form of an encumbrance upon a purchased estate. Such a case made an exception to the general rule and rendered the land the primary fund to pay the debt. This conclusion the chancellor was the more disposed to accept because he found that for the last forty years it had been favored in England.[35]

"But we are told," he said, anticipating the amazement with which his pronouncement would be heard, "that no English authorities since 1775 are of binding authority, and that our courts are not to vary with the opinions or perhaps caprice of English tribunals. It is true," he conceded, "that we are not bound by their errors nor do we feel subdued by their authority, but we can listen with instruction to their illustration and application of the principles of the science. 'Far from me and from my friends, be such frigid philosophy' or such unreasonable pride, as may turn us with indifference or disdain from the decisions and the wisdom of other nations." Remarking upon the state of equity in America, he continued, "It is to be recollected that we have very little domestic precedent . . . to guide us. A question of this kind has probably never before arisen in our courts. We *must* resort for information to the courts of that nation from which our jurisprudence, as well as the best of our institutions, are derived, and we can do it with uncommon advantage." That advantage, he declared, was bestowed, not only by the sages of the ancient law, but also by those distinguished jurists who had been cultivating the field since the Revolution, and he went on to praise in stately periods

[35] When the New York law was changed so as to permit aliens to hold land, Sir William Pulteney applied to Williamson to convey the estates to him. Williamson would do this only on condition that Sir William take the conveyance subject to the mortgage-debt in dispute; and Sir William complied with the condition; and had already paid off part of the mortgage when he died. He did not mean to make the debt his own so as to render his personal assets the primary fund to pay it. So held the chancellor. See narration of facts, Cumberland v. Codrington, 3 *Johns. Ch.* 251 *et seq.*

Lord Eldon's "vast labors and eminent discretion," to extol "the enlightened judgement of Sir William Grant," and to laud in Gibbon's phrase, "the majestic sense of Thurlow and the skilful eloquence of Wedderburne." [36] Indeed with such animation did the chancellor depict the merits of the English judges who had flourished since '75, that his audience may well have wondered whether he had not persuaded himself that the Revolution was a mistake.

It would have been hardly surprising if this deference to English standards had engendered a wide-spread antipathy to the chancellor's decrees; and his course did breed among the populace a vague resentment. Among the profession, however, it produced an almost universal respect; [37] and as the volumes of Johnson's *Reports* succeeded one another, the Courts of Equity in other states began to imitate the New York chancellor by bringing their decisions more and more into harmony with the English jurisprudence.[38] As a result, it was to come about in less than a generation that what Story had said about the wide divergence of American chancery from its English model was no longer true; and it was to Kent that the credit for this unexpected development was everywhere given. "The chancery law of the United States may be said to have com-

[36] Cumberland v. Codrington, 3 *Johns. Ch.* 262–263. He proceeds to show, however, that the recent decisions had only amplified and applied principles "long antecedently known" and he cites Hardwicke and Nottingham at length to prove his point. *Ibid.*, 264 *et seq.*

[37] "Prior to your appointment, to a vast majority of lawyers of the state, the principles and the practice of the Court of Chancery were alike unknown, and by the mass of the community, its proceedings were regarded . . . with suspicion and dread. You dispelled the ignorance of the Bar and the fears of the public. . . ." Address of the New York Bar to Chancellor Kent, July 31, 1843, *vide Law Reporter,* VI, 293. It is to be doubted whether Kent *wholly* dispelled the *public* fears.

[38] *E.g.* ". . . no English books of chancery decisions are more frequently or more respectfully cited in the courts of South Carolina than the seven volumes of Mr. Johnson's reports of Kent's decisions." *London Law Magazine,* VI, 132. But to cite Kent was to cite Hardwicke.

menced with [him]," declared the *American Quarterly Review* in an article that was read and quoted in England.[39] The observation was confirmed by Story, who writing of Kent in the *North American Review* asserted that "it required such a man with such a mind . . . always reverencing authorities and bound by decisions . . . to unfold the doctrines of chancery in our country, and to settle them upon immoveable foundations." [40]

Especially gratified were the English in remarking the new tendency which had been imparted to the evolution of this branch of their jurisprudence in America. With them,[41] as well as with the jurists of Massachusetts [42] and South Carolina, the reputation of Chancellor Kent was firmly established; and the effect which his decisions had exerted upon American equity they pointed to with no little complacency. When Story had finished his treatise upon chancery pleading in the United States, the work was favorably reviewed in London,[43] and the reviewer confessed a curiosity to see how far the English doctrines were in harmony with those of America. "That there should be a difference upon essential principles we did not expect," said he, "but we have certainly been much surprised to find that all our doctrines, with, we believe, scarcely any ex-

[39] *Loc. cit.* quoting the *American Quarterly Review* number 10, 367.

[40] "Equity Jurisdiction in the State of New York," *United States Law Journal,* I, 47 quoting Story in the *North American Review,* vol. XI, new series vol. II.

[41] *London Law Magazine,* VI, 127–132; *United States Law Journal,* I, 43.

[42] "The Bench of New York, ever since we have been able to judge of its character by the masterly reports of Mr. Johnson has been distinguished by great learning and uncommon legal acumen," per Parker, Ch. J. in Packard v. Richardson, 17 *Mass. Rep.* 136 quoted *American Jurist,* XII, 39. The case cited, however, does not follow Kent; but says, "If anything could cause us to hesitate in pronouncing an opinion, which we have arrived at after mature deliberation, it would be to find that opinion contradicted by a deliberate decision of a court we so highly respect." 17 *Mass. Rep.* 136.

[43] "English Equity in America," a review of Story's treatise on equity pleading, published in the *London Law Magazine,* May, 1839, and quoted *in extenso* in *American Jurist,* XXII, 232 *et seq.*

ceptions, are approved of and adopted in daily practice in the American Courts of Equity." He continued: "A half century has elapsed since the two countries were separated. During that period the courts of America have been wholly independent of the courts of England. American advocates have been allowed to argue, and judges to decide, without any other deference to the decisions and principles of the English courts, than that which good sense and pure morality will always retain over enlightened and correct understandings. Yet we find that the sway of our equitable principles is as firmly established in American courts, as if they still owed allegiance to the house of lords as to the Supreme Court of appeal. This result appears to us most satisfactory; a result, in which this country may find abundant cause for self-congratulation. . . . The dynasty of Napoleon has passed away, but his code still asserts for his memory abundant claims upon the gratitude of France; and now that England has lost political dominion over her colony, she still maintains with every judgement that issues from her courts a judicial authority over her independent ally." [44]

Thus it appeared that Chancellor Kent's insistence upon abiding by the wisdom of the English chancellors had been by no means vain. He had set a contagious example, which if English jurists criticized, they criticized because it seemed almost to go too far. "We confess," said the London reviewer, commenting upon the habits of the American equity tribunals, "that we did not wish to find the homage to English authority carried to so great an extent." [45]

* * *

Had Chancellor Kent not succeeded in discovering in English equity doctrines useful at once to the individual and to

[44] *American Jurist,* XXII, 233.
[45] *Ibid.,* XXII, 233–234.

society, it is improbable that his deference to the Lords Nottingham and Hardwicke would have been long endured. For the people of New York, like most of their compatriots, were somewhat reluctant to admit the value of learning and researches unless they could be persuaded that practical advantages would derive from them; and against English learning in particular, New York more than other states had cause to be prejudiced, since she had but recently experienced the discomforts of an English invasion. That in Kent she tolerated a court of chancery, frankly patterned after the court of Lord Nottingham, is not so much a tribute to her forbearance as it is to the usefulness of the system which she consented to receive.

How the chancellor demonstrated that usefulness may be explained by describing the manner in which he employed the injunction, the most familiar and characteristic of the equitable remedies. In his hands it proved an effective instrument for protecting private right against the aggressions not only of individuals but also of the state. Yet not without discrimination did he use it; nor did he lose sight of the fact, as judges sometimes do, that it is an extraordinary remedy designed to supplement, not to supplant, the remedies of law.

That principle Kent illustrated at the time when New York, stimulated by De Witt Clinton's leadership, was bending her best energies to the task of digging the Erie Canal. In furtherance of that object a lock and a dam were being constructed near the town of Troy where one of the engineers, acting under the authority of the canal commissioners, had set men and teams to work taking out quantities of rock with which he proposed to fill in the projected dam. The labor was one of great public utility, but unfortunately, it constituted a trespass upon the lands of the farmer where the rock lay; and the farmer, loath to be a martyr to the public good, prayed the chancellor to prohibit any further excavation.[46] To that prayer, however, Kent turned a deaf ear, though he gave the cause careful consideration. The question, said he, is "whether a Court of Equity ought to interpose, by injunction, to restrain a trespass when the injury does not appear to be irremediable and destructive to the estate, and when the ordinary legal remedies can afford adequate satisfaction." [47] In this case, he held, they were sufficient; and in effect, he bade the irate farmer begone and prosecute, if prosecute he must, in a court of law; since the rocks which the engineer was carting off, were proved to be valueless for any other purpose, even for one merely esthetic.[48] At the same time, the chancellor intimated that "where the mischief reaches to the very substance and value of the estate and goes to the destruction of it in the character in which it is enjoyed," there the injunction may be properly invoked.[49]

That in such an exigency he was willing to grant it, he proved more than once, even though in so doing he might find it necessary to set aside a statute. The legislature had passed a law which authorized the trustees of Newburgh to supply the town with water, and for that purpose to divert the springs upon the lands of private persons. For indemnifying the owners the law had carefully provided, but it had omitted to in-

[46] Jerome v. Ross, 7 *Johns. Ch.* 315. *Vide History of the Bench and Bar of New York,* I, 385 which regards Jerome v. Ross as Kent's greatest decision in equity.

[47] *Ibid.*, 331.

[48] So the record states, and so apparently thought the jury, for when Ross submitted his case to the law, the jury gave him only nominal damages. I have not dealt with the second part of Kent's opinion, where he considers the great need which the engineer had of the rocks for filling in the dam. Kent observes that the statutes under which the canal commissioners operated, bade them to do no needless damage to private property. If there was damage here—and Kent thought not—it was indispensable to the needs of construction. Furthermore, he noted with approval that the statutes provided a compensation.

[49] Jerome v. Ross, 7 *Johns. Ch.* 331–332.

demnify those through whose fields and pastures the springs discharged their beneficial streams. As a result of this omission, one enterprising freeholder found himself threatened with a great loss. His brick-yard and distillery would cease to operate, his fields would fade, his cattle thirst; nor would any compensation be forthcoming. In dread of this calamity he requested the chancellor to enjoin the trustees of the village from proceeding with their plans.[50] The case, Kent held, showed clearly the need of a preventive remedy, for it was one where a great and immediate mischief was impending. "A right to a stream of water," he announced, "is part of the freehold, of which no man can be disseised 'but by the legal judgement of his peers and the law of the land' "; [51] and if the maxim was true in general, in this particular instance, where more than ordinary enterprise depended, its truth coming home with more than ordinary persuasiveness, ought to be especially respected. He therefore ordered that the injunction issue, and that it remain in force until the legislature should so amend the law as to meet the requirements of due process by furnishing an adequate indemnity.[52]

The mischief prevented had not, in this case, been deliberately planned. There were cases, however, where there was no doubt but that it had been so. Though the public authority seldom offended thus, individuals often did; and their contrivances the chancellor was always alert to circumvent. It mattered nothing to him that the right encroached upon was

[50] Gardner v. Newburgh, 2 *Johns. Ch.* 162. *United States Law Intelligencer and Review,* I, 94 notices with approbation Gardner v. Newburgh in an article entitled "Restrictions upon the state power in relation to private property."

[51] Gardner v. Newburgh, 2 *Johns. Ch.* 165–166. A good example of an early case on due process of law.

[52] *Ibid.*, 168. For a case involving a similar situation and principle *vide* Belknap v. Belknap, 2 *Johns. Ch.* 463, others are cited in Jerome v. Ross, *supra cit.*

sometimes unpopular, or that those who invaded it could plausibly represent their invasion as in the interest of the general convenience. Such a consideration Kent never allowed to tip the scales. If the right had been established, and if the mischief that was threatened reached to its substance, he could be counted upon to envelop that right with the protection of equity. For those, therefore, who had a stake in the existing arrangements, the system, as administered by him, revealed a particular value.

The observation is borne out by the readiness with which he used the injunction to safeguard the Fulton-Livingston steamboat monopoly. That monopoly, as might have been predicted, came into increasing disfavor as the years went by, and the attacks upon it, begun when Lansing was chancellor, continued during the incumbency of Kent, despite the elaborate opinion in Livingston v. Van Ingen. But these attacks Kent steadily repelled,[53] although it was now contended that a federal coastwise-shipping law constituted that exertion of the paramount congressional power over interstate commerce before which the state, according to the doctrine of Livingston v. Van Ingen, was now bound to retire. The validity of the contention the chancellor refused to admit, for the congressional act in question had been passed without reference to the New York statutes which invested Livingston and Fulton with their monopoly. "We must be permitted to require," said Chancellor Kent, "at least the presence and clear manifestation of some constitutional law, or some judicial decision of the supreme power of the Union, acting upon those laws in direct collision and conflict, before we can retire from the support and defense of them. We must be satisfied that

[53] Livingston v. Ogden and Gibbons, 4 *Johns. Ch.* 48.
North River Steamboat Company v. Hoffman, 5 *Johns. Ch.* 299.
Ogden v. Gibbons, 4 *Johns. Ch.* 150.
Gibbons v. Ogden, 17 *Johns. Rep.* 448.

'Neptunus muros magnoque emota tridenti
Fundamenta quatit.' " [54]

The steamboat monopoly was not the only form of privilege to which the chancellor extended the benefits of equity. The owners of toll roads and of toll bridges found in him a reliable defender; and their franchises became more lucrative as a result of the construction which he put upon them. For Kent laid down the doctrine that a corporation takes not only what is expressly conceded by its grant, but also whatever may be, by implication, necessary or convenient to the exercise of the rights which the grant bestows. Thus, where the legislature has given to a bridge company or a turnpike company the privilege of levying tolls, that privilege must be viewed as carrying with it the power to prevent others from opening roads or bridges in such proximity as to destroy the value of the original franchise by diverting traffic. In accordance with this doctrine, Kent consistently enjoined prospective competitors from executing their plans; [55] and in so doing he admitted that he put aside as irrelevant any consideration of the fact that new roads and new bridges might promote the convenience of the community.[56] Such a view, far from conducive to popularity, was to be repudiated before many years by both the state and federal courts; [57] but Chancellor Kent even then seems never

[54] Gibbons v. Ogden, 17 *Johns. Rep.* 495.

[55] Croton Turnpike Road Company v. Ryder, 1 *Johns. Ch.* 610.
Newburgh Turnpike Company v. Miller, 5 *Johns. Ch.* 101.

[56] *Loc. cit.*

[57] The remarks of Selden, J., in Auburn and Cato Plank Road Company v. Douglass, reported at 9 *New York Rep.* 444 *et seq.*, are illuminating: "There is not a word in the plank road law giving them [*i.e.* the company] any exclusive privilege whatever; or any rights as against adjoining proprietors. Do they take such rights by implication? This presents . . . the only debatable question in the case. It is . . . [a question] which has received the most elaborate discussion. It involves the great question whether acts of the legislative power, conferring special privileges . . . are to be construed strictly according to their terms, or liberally with a view to make the grant as beneficial as possible to the grantee. . . . The question has

to have harbored much doubt of its substantial justice.[58]

For such intransigence one might be tempted to blame him; and beyond doubt those who profess a hatred of special privilege, would succumb to that temptation with feelings of pleasure. Yet in fairness to the chancellor, it must be admitted that he decided as he did because he sincerely believed that the best interest of the community was thereby promoted. In his view that interest consisted in an impartial administration of justice, by which is meant, in the traditional language of the law, the meting out to every litigant his due. But where the litigant is a corporation possessing a franchise, it would be rather to deprive him of his due, were the franchise so to be construed as to destroy the very value which had induced him to seek it and to risk his resources in the investment. Furthermore, the fact ought not be lost sight of that the state in granting the disputed privilege, had entered into a contractual relation with the grantee, and should, therefore, abide equally with him by the

---

been repeatedly before our courts, *and our judges have divided upon it according to the natural bias and tendency of their minds. Chancellor Kent . . . adopted the latitudinarian view of corporate rights.*" Here Selden quotes the two cases just cited, and a note in the *Commentaries*, Vol. III, 459, as exhibiting Kent's view. Then he shows that other judges disagreed. Tuckahoe Canal Co. v. Tuckahoe Rail Road Co., 11 *Leigh* 42; Enfield Toll Bridge Co. v. Hartford and New Haven Rail Road, 17 *Conn.* 454; Thompson v. New York and Harlem Rail Road, 3 *Sanford Ch.* 625; and of course, the celebrated Charles River Bridge case. *Vide et* Oswego Falls Bridge Co. v. Fish, 1 *Barbour Ch.* 547 (1846); Mohawk Bridge Co. v. Utica and Schenectady Rail Road, 6 *Paige Ch.* 554 (1837). It is apparent that Kent's doctrine was beginning to be doubted before the Charles River Bridge case dealt it a knock-out blow, for at 1 *Barbour Ch.* 549, Walworth, Chancellor, says that 6 *Paige Ch.* 554 was decided by him before the Charles River Bridge case was reported. The new doctrine was that the grant to a corporation of the right to erect a toll-bridge does not deprive a future legislature of the power to authorize the erection of a free bridge over the same river, so near as to divert part of the travel which would otherwise have crossed the first bridge. 1 *Barbour Ch.* 547, 6 *Paige Ch.* 554.

[58] Though in his *Commentaries* of a later edition, as noted by Selden, J., he admits that his "latitudinarian view" in this respect no longer prevails. But *vide infra* in Chapter VII, where in his correspondence with Story he deplores the new doctrine.

obligation which the contract, whether expressly or by implication imposed. If the courts should release the state from that obligation on the facile plea of inconvenience, the question might well be asked, what then of the covenants of individuals with one another? If society itself repudiates an obligation merely because it is irksome, why should not individuals be allowed to do the same? The chancellor could apparently see no reason to prevent them once the state had set the example; [59] and such an example, threatening to make all contracts meaningless, was not, according to his quaint, old-fashioned view, the most rational mode of promoting the public advantage.

Nevertheless, when all has been said which fairness to the chancellor requires, the fact remains that the tendency of his latitudinarian view of corporate rights as applied to the bridge and turnpike cases, was to lay the whole community under an inescapable tribute to special privilege.[60] In his want of concern lest that tendency accentuate inequalities of wealth, he displayed only the attitude which might have been expected of a judge whose political philosophy was fashioned upon the maxims of Blackstone and the *Federalist.* Such inequalities he may have regarded as beneficial to society.[61] Certainly he contributed in chancery less to diminish than to augment them; though it is not by any means implied that the rank or riches of a litigant ever swayed his considerations,[62] or that the conse-

[59] See Kent's letter to Joseph Story, on the Charles River Bridge case, June 23, 1837, Story Papers. Kent there expresses the idea, as was his frequent habit, in a Latin verse: *Quicquid delirant reges plectuntur Achivi.* The letter is quoted below in Chapter VII. See also Kent's opinions in the Council of Revision, discussed below in Chapter VI.

[60] See the comment of Selden, J., in Auburn and Cato Plank Road Company v. Douglass, 9 *New York* 444 *et seq.*, on Croton Turnpike Company v. Ryder, 1 *Johns. Ch.* 610 and Newburgh Turnpike Company v. Miller, 5 *Johns. Ch.* 101.

[61] In the *Commentaries* he expresses this belief; though it has not been found expressly stated in the opinions.

[62] Cumberland v. Codrington *supra cit.* where he decided against the Duke.

quence of his decrees was an invariable boon to the moneyed classes. Indeed, where the oppressed and unfortunate appeared before him, he was disposed to relieve them, and more than once he proved that equity could mitigate even the embarrassments of a debtor.

It was under that head of his jurisdiction which had to do with trusts that Kent sometimes revealed what popular opinion may well have considered the more benevolent side of his judicial character. For he was never more vigilant in detecting or more severe in punishing abuses than when they were practiced upon widows or minors or the feeble-minded by those who, for the better protection of such persons, had been invested with the powers and responsibilities of trustees. Nor were his labors in this field limited to the meting out of punishment for frauds already practiced. They resulted in a body of doctrine designed to be preventive by forbidding the trustee to demand compensation for his services beyond a positive agreement,[63] by prohibiting him from realizing personal gain from the use of trust funds [64] or from acting in any way for his own benefit upon any subject connected with the trust.[65] His negligence, too, was as effectually discouraged as was a fraudulent design, for should he allow the funds in his charge to be idle, he could be required to pay interest upon them; [66] should he lend the money of the *cestui que trust* without security, he would be responsible if the borrower became insolvent; [67] and if he so confounded the trust property with his own that his own could not be distinguished, he thereby rendered himself liable to lose it.[68] Such are the specimens of rules which Chancellor Kent laid down upon the subject of the duties of trustees. That he suc-

[63] Green v. Winter, 1 *Johns. Ch.* 27.
[64] Schieffelin v. Stewart, 1 *Johns. Ch.* 620.
[65] Davoue v. Fanning, 2 *Johns. Ch.* 252.
[66] Schieffelin v. Stewart, *supra cit.*
[67] Smith v. Smith, 4 *Johns. Ch.* 281.
[68] Hart v. Ten Eyck, 2 *Johns. Ch.* 62.

ceeded in making those duties more onerous and delicate, as well as more explicit, than they had hitherto been,[69] there is no doubt. That he devised them to protect those who most needed his protection, is evidence that the widow and the orphan often found in him as intrepid a champion as did the turnpike companies and the owners of the monopoly of steamboat navigation.

Debtors also discovered that he had a decent sympathy for their distress; and that while he would never encourage the evasion of a just debt, he could yet be counted upon to prevent the debtor from being exploited. The relation of debtor and creditor caused him deep concern which he expressed in his decisions. It is, as he observed, a relation "which has, in all ages of the world produced fearful consequences; and to preserve the laws of justice in that relation, has hitherto required the utmost sagacity on the part of government and the greatest wisdom and firmness in the administration of justice." [70] His own wisdom and firmness in this respect he had occasion to display in the frequent cases which were before him involving the discovery of accounts; and again and again, to the advantage of the debtor, he resisted the fashionable current of Benthamite teaching by sternly enforcing the law against usury.[71]

But Kent's reluctance to see debtors oppressed should not be taken to mean that he regarded them with sentimental pity or that he was in the least inclined to turn equity into an instrument for defeating the just claims of creditors. If he refused

[69] *I.e.* in America.

[70] Thompson v. Berry, 3 *Johns. Ch.* 399, where he prevents usurious exaction.

[71] Among other cases: Hine v. Handy, 1 *Johns. Ch.* 5.
Connecticut v. Jackson, 1 *Johns. Ch.* 13.
Fanning v. Dunham, 5 *Johns. Ch.* 122.

Kent's views on the necessity and wisdom of a law against usury are favorably contrasted with Bentham's views on the subject in *United States Law Journal*, II, 71.

to tolerate usurious exactions on the part of the one group, so with equal steadfastness he refused to tolerate evasion and subterfuge on the part of the other; and if he conceded the wisdom of a law forbidding usury, a bankruptcy law, upon the other hand, he condemned as not only unwise, but pernicious, since it constituted a standing temptation to the debtor to avoid the fair meeting of his obligations.[72] Kent himself was always at pains to require that they be fairly met; and occasionally the rules which he laid down for that purpose appeared excessively strict.

Thus, for example, where in the presence of debts, a voluntary settlement of landed property had been made upon a child, the chancellor would not sustain it, lest it defeat the creditor's right, though the settlement in dispute had not apparently been made with any such object in view.[73] This mitigating circumstance, however, Kent deemed it inexpedient to allow much weight. "The inclination of my mind," he said, "is strongly in favor of the policy and wisdom of the rule which absolutely disables a man from preferring, by any arrangement whatever, and with whatever intention, by gifts of his property, his children to his creditors." [74] Admitting that "hard cases may arise in which we should wish the rule to be otherwise," he was yet convinced that "more good will ensue to families and to the public at large, by a strict adherence to the rule than by rendering it subservient to circumstances." [75] His attitude upon the subject is more strikingly shown in the case of Bayard v. Hoffman [76] decided a few years later, when it was contended that a voluntary settlement of certain kinds of personal property was good against creditors, even if made by

[72] For Kent's views on bankruptcy laws see the *obiter dicta* in 7 *Johns. Ch.* 307, Hicks v. Hotchkiss.

[73] Reade v. Livingston, 3 *Johns. Ch.* 495.

[74] *Ibid.*, 505.

[75] *Loc. cit.*

[76] Bayard v. Hoffman, 4 *Johns. Ch.* 450.

an insolvent debtor. The reason of the contention was that the settlement of such property, choses in action like stock or money in the funds, did not impair the creditor's right, since according to Queen Elizabeth's statute of frauds that species of property, even where no settlement had been made, could not be reached by process of execution. For support of this view, counsel relied upon a pronouncement of Lord Thurlow which had been followed consistently in England since his time. Chancellor Kent, notwithstanding his respect for Thurlow, chose to regard his pronouncement in this case as a mere dictum, declaring that he would "be sorry to find it to be the settled doctrine of the court. . . ." [77] Recurring, as his habit was, to the older authorities, he discovered that the great Hardwicke had held otherwise and that both Fortescue, Master of the Rolls and Northington, Lord Keeper, had done the same. "Here," exclaimed Kent with satisfaction, "is a succession of three solemn adjudications which establish that property, not tangible by *fieri facias* at law will be reached by this court, and that too, whether such property does or does not rest upon a voluntary settlement fraudulent and void under the statute of Elizabeth." [78] The reason of his preference of the older to the novel doctrine, which Thurlow had advanced, was that Thurlow's doctrine opened to the debtor a too easy avenue of escape. "A debtor, under shelter of it," said Kent, "might convert all his property into stock, and settle it upon his family, in defiance of his creditors, and to the utter subversion of justice." [79] The chancellor's dread of such an issue was not unanimously shared either by the bench or the profession, and not long after his retirement, his successor, Sanford, was to repudi-

[77] Bayard v. Hoffman, 4 *Johns. Ch.* 453.

[78] *Ibid.*, 455. The statute in question is 13 *Elizabeth*, c. 5. See Bayard v. Hoffman, *ibid.*, 450. The statute had been reenacted in New York *loc. cit.*

[79] *Ibid.*, 453.

ate the doctrine, and to return, with the applause of respectable lawyers, to the dictum of Thurlow.[80]

* * *

The repudiation of the doctrine of Bayard v. Hoffman was perhaps the less difficult to acquiesce in, since it occurred after Kent had withdrawn to private life where he was agreeably occupied with new activities. There were reversals of his decisions, however, while he sat on the bench and to these he strenuously objected, for they were the results of the deliberations of a tribunal which he regarded as of inferior ability. Where a formal marriage settlement had been agreed upon by which the husband had disclaimed every right to his wife's property, but then had used it albeit with her oral consent, such consent as weighed against the formal contract the chancellor held to be of no effect. Hence he required the husband, now become a widower, to make good to the estate the sums which he had disbursed under the parole sanction of his defunct spouse.[81] The widower, whose affliction this ruling no doubt contributed to make even more severe, took an appeal to the Court of Errors, which, speaking principally through Chief Justice Spencer, assuaged his melancholy by reversing the chancellor's decision.[82] A merchant trading to the Orient had given notes for considerable sums charged with the heavy interest rate of twelve *per cent.* The contract had been made in China, but was to be executed in New York where seven *per cent* was the maximum interest permissible. The question that arose was whether the foreign or the domestic rate should pre-

[80] Donovan v. Finn, *Hopk. Ch.* 59. Chancellor Sanford's position, as contrasted with Kent's, is applauded in *United States Law Journal*, II, 286. *Vide et* Jackson v. Town, 4 *Cow.* 599; Verplanck v. Sterry, 12 *Johns. Rep.* 536; Harper v. Clayton, 84 Maryland 346.

[81] Methodist Episcopal Church v. Jaques, 3 *Johns. Ch.* 77.

[82] 17 *Johns. Rep.* 548.

vail, and the chancellor declared in favor of the twelve *per cent;* supporting, with his usual array of citations, the rule that interest is payable according to the laws of the country where the contract has been made.[83] The Court of Errors holding that the law of that country governs where the contract is to be executed, reversed him,[84] and added thereby to his growing disgust, which was aggravated by further reversals.

Kent's concern for the rights of creditors may have seemed exaggerated to the court, and it would appear that on one occasion they went out of their way to tell him so. If a man for the sake of evading his debts should convey his property to another, the transaction would be obviously dishonest. But if the property thus conveyed were purchased in good faith by a third person, what right against him the creditor should have would be a question of greater difficulty. Would the fraud of the first transaction taint the second also, defeating thereby the title of the purchaser in good faith? Kent contended that it did, and he perpetually enjoined such purchaser from advancing any claim to the land in question. Again, however, he was reversed by the Court of Errors; [85] whereupon his disgust began to deepen into dudgeon, intensified by what appeared to be the disposition of the court to interfere unseasonably in chancery proceedings. The case was one where a reference had been made to a master to investigate an account, and in the order to that effect, both litigants had acquiesced until the case was almost ripe for final hearing when the defendant carried an appeal before the Court of Errors. That step the chancellor instructed the master to ignore as irregular, and, as though nothing had happened, to proceed with the finishing and filing

[83] Consequa v. Fanning, 3 *Johns. Ch.* 587.

[84] Reversed, 17 *Johns. Rep.* 511.

[85] Roberts v. Boyd and Anderson, 3 *Johns. Ch.* 371, reversed at 18 *Johns. Rep.* 515.

of his report. To his great chagrin, the appeal was entertained, although no final chancery decree had as yet issued.[86]

This series of reversals quite subdued for the time being Kent's natural buoyancy of disposition; and to his friend Johnson he confessed himself discouraged and heart-broken.[87] "The judges," he wrote, "have prevailed upon the Court of Errors to reverse all my best decisions. . . . After such devastation what courage ought I to have to study and write elaborate opinions? There are but two sides to every case and I am so unfortunate as to take the wrong side. . . . I never felt so disgusted with the judges in all my life." [88]

It was not only the judges who aroused his indignation. The legislators were even more objectionable, even though they had once won his regard by raising his stipend. In 1816 they had added liberally to the remuneration of all the higher dignitaries of the state, and the chancellor had rejoiced in the increased security for the future offered by the handsome salary of four thousand five hundred a year. Such generous conduct he warmly approved, praising the legislature as having "acted worthy of the great and rich community which they represent." [89] Nevertheless he generally adopted toward the legislative branch an attitude of suspicion and dislike. He called it the political nuisance.[90] He longed for the coming of spring when it would adjourn; [91] and he congratulated Johnson upon

[86] Prior v. Rhinelander, 3 *Johns. Ch.* 120, reversed at 17 *Johns. Rep.* 538. One can hardly escape the conclusion that the Court of Errors was more interested in embarrassing Kent than in establishing good law. That court, made up largely of senators, had a political bias, and may have sensed that Kent was not popular. The *History of the Bench and Bar of New York,* I, 127–128 speaks of a growing but vague popular discontent with chancery as an undemocratic institution.

[87] James Kent to William Johnson, April 4, 1820. *Kent Papers,* Vol. IV.

[88] *Loc. cit.* The cases he refers to are those cited immediately above.

[89] James Kent to Moss Kent, Jr., April 18, 1816. *Ibid.*

[90] James Kent to William Johnson, April 8, 1815. *Ibid.*

[91] *Loc. cit.*

its having risen without enacting any laws detrimental to the judiciary and the administration of justice.[92] For his apprehensions there were solid grounds. The legislature, if still far from democratic in its constitution, was becoming each year more democratic in sentiment; and sensitive to popular opinion, it was exhibiting an increased dissatisfaction with the form of government established in 1777 by John Jay and his aristocratic colleagues. The time was rapidly approaching when the demand for change would prove irresistible. Nor did the growing restiveness arise from causes wholly unconnected with the chancellor's own career. The very office which he held was regarded as contrary to the genius of democratic institutions; [93] and his rigor [94] in administering a system of which the one advantage was commonly supposed to consist in a want of rigor, was not calculated to increase his popularity or to endear him to a legislature growing more sensitive to popular praise and blame.

Yet it was an undertaking of difficulty to attack him directly. He had few, if any, personal enemies. His private life was above reproach. Hints of corruption had never so much as been whispered against him; and he had never sullied his ermine by descending into the dust of the political arena. Moreover, though his dominant position in the affairs of his state might be challenged, his fame throughout the Union was so bright and so secure that open attack upon him was bound to be interpreted as having been prompted by something less generous than a concern for the public advantage. Had Kent been so inclined, he may well have flattered himself that he had gone far toward realizing his youthful ambition "to

[92] James Kent to William Johnson, April 14, 1819. *Ibid.*

[93] *History of the Bench and Bar of New York*, I, 127–128.

[94] *E.g.* even Story criticized one of Kent's opinions where he had refused to allow a party to offer a defense which in a prior case he had forgone an opportunity to make. Moss Kent, Jr., to James Kent, February 1, 1817. *Kent Papers*, Vol. IV.

put in a claim for some of those honors that imprint immortality on characters."

For his fame was confined to no section, nor was it limited exclusively to the legal profession. The University of Pennsylvania, Dartmouth and Harvard had ratified the judgement of Columbia, paying him the highest tribute of the academicians in the doctorate of laws.[95] From South Carolina, Chancellor De Saussure apprised him of the renown which he enjoyed to the southward, and sending several volumes of his opinions, invited the Chancellor of New York to offer his criticism upon them.[96] High-toned, old-fashioned Federalist though he was, Kent had his admirers in the opposite camp, of whom curiously enough, the aging radical, Marinus Willett was one. This venerable fomenter of seditions even urged upon President Monroe the appointment of Kent to the Supreme Court of the United States.[97] There was little likelihood of this, for the chancellor's antipathy to all that savored of the Jeffersonian Democracy was too well known to make him, from the administration's point of view, an acceptable addition to the federal bench. Yet his name was familiar in Washington, and as Moss Kent learned to his pleasure, it was, among those who followed the law, a name to conjure with. Congressman Kent informed his brother that he sat next to a prominent member from New Hampshire named Daniel Webster who had mentioned to him that he had dreamed a singular dream the night before. He thought he was discussing a law question with the Chancellor of New York. "I took the opportunity," wrote Moss, "to ask him if he thought much of said chancellor as a lawyer. He said that he considered him the greatest lawyer in the United States; that

[95] Franklin B. Dexter, *Biographical Sketches of the Graduates of Yale College*, IV, 190.

[96] Henry W. De Saussure to James Kent, March 31, 1819. *Kent Papers*, Vol. IV.

[97] Letter undated, *Kent Papers*, Vol. V. William Wirt also urged the appointment of Kent to the Supreme Court.

he had studied his opinions in Johnson's reports till he had them nearly by heart and that he meant to return to Portsmouth by the way of Albany for the express purpose of becoming acquainted with the great personage whom he saw and conversed with in a dream." [98] If the honorable member from New Hampshire had been induced to flattery by the hope of gaining a colleague's vote, now and then praise was bestowed by other eminent men which certainly could not have been open to the same construction. Mr. Justice Story, reported Moss, had been asked whether he read the New York chancery reports and his reply had been "that he had read every word of them, as he had everything from Chancellor Kent, that he considered them equal to any of the English chancery reports . . . [and] that they would be of great use to him in his circuit." [99] To James Kent, confident of his abilities though he was, such praise from such a man must indeed have seemed a rich reward for his labors, but his brother summed it up in a way to make it still more gratifying. "You was spoken of," concluded Moss, "in as high terms of respect as if you had been another Hardwicke." [100]

But sad to relate, neither a Hardwicke nor a Nottingham, with howsoever much of dignity he may have borne his office, was the sort of hero that appealed to the ordinary citizen. It was the misfortune of Kent that as their successor he was required by his duties to apply their maxims in a democratic community. He had consistently disdained to make use of his long dominant position in the judicial hierarchy as a means of currying popular favor. That scrupulous adherence of his to English principles, while it pleased the profession and gratified the great, was not calculated to draw approval from the

[98] Moss Kent, Jr., to James Kent, March 5, 1816. *Ibid.*, Vol. IV.

[99] Moss Kent, Jr., to James Kent, February 1, 1817. *Ibid.* Story had said of Kent's labors as chancellor: *exegit monumentum aere perennius.*

[100] Moss Kent, Jr., to James Kent, February 1, 1817. *Kent Papers*, Vol. IV.

masses, even though their descent and character predisposed them to acquiesce, as the constitution required, in the precepts of the English jurisprudence. And it may be argued that Kent both as chief justice and as chancellor could have succeeded in bringing in a substantial body of that law without having shown himself so steadfast in applying at their full strength the English doctrines. In this he was disposed to go to extremes. Though the rule be monstrous, he had said, "I should not feel myself at liberty to say 'so far as I can go, I shall blot it out forever.' It is the province of the legislative and not of the judicial power to change the law."

Chancellor Kent, however, had little desire to see the law changed even by the legislature. Upon legislative acts his position in the Council of Revision gave him an opportunity to exercise a veto power; and of that opportunity he was led to avail himself by interposing first one and then another obstacle to the legislative will. "Democracy is raging in all its fury in the Capitol," he informed his brother; [101] and that conflagration illumined clearly the chancellor's path of duty. He must quench these mad passions before they should consume the fabric of society. "At home here," he wrote again, "I am now occupied in the council, and shall enter my feeble protest against several violent bills coming from our Jacobin legislature and governor." [102] The chancellor entered his protest, but in vain; and it served, in the long run, only to jeopardize his security in office.

[101] James Kent to Moss Kent, Jr., February 8, 1811. *Kent Papers,* Vol. IV.
[102] James Kent to Moss Kent, Jr., October 17, 1814. *Ibid.*

VI

Jacobinical Winds

It has hitherto been supposed that this institution [*i.e.* the Council of Revision] was one of the wisest in our state constitution, and certainly it has often been the means of arresting great unconstitutional measures. But if we look at the proceedings which lately took place in that body . . . we shall see that in times of turbulence and difficulty, when its salutary restraint is most necessary, it is, like all other provisions upon paper . . . utterly nugatory. The people cannot be too grateful to the great and learned Mr. Chancellor Kent for the bold and noble stand he made and stood alone, while he made it against the late attacks upon their rights in the shape of laws. Behold 'the man who dare be honest in the worst of times.'

The New York Herald, November 2, 1814

Let the whole government go into the hands of the people; there is no danger that they will commit political suicide. . . . Do not let us deceive ourselves with the idea that our ancestors knew almost everything . . . it is no fiction to say that they lived in ages comparatively dark . . . had too much of the prejudice derived from the musty schools of feudalism, monarchy and despotism.

The Albany Register, November 7, 1821

* * *

ONE summer's day after court had risen, James Kent sat under the shade of a tree talking politics with a group of lawyers. When the group broke up and all had gone except Kent and one other, the judge impatiently exclaimed, "Oh! These politicians! What trouble and vexation do they not cause! For myself I have been content to eat my cake in peace," and tapping his hearer on the shoulder, he asked, "don't you think that is the wisest course, young man?" What answer his companion made to this query has not been recorded, though he may well have thought that the wisest course for a judge was not necessarily the best for himself. Such a view would have been reasonable enough. The young man was Martin Van Buren upon whom politics would soon be exerting an irresistible and fortunate fascination.[1]

James Kent, upon the other hand, found politics repellent. Since the day when his brother-in-law, Theodorus Bailey, had defeated him in the congressional contest, he had entered the political arena but seldom, and then only in the minor capacity of an assemblyman from New York City. Thereafter he prided himself upon keeping aloof from what he chose to call "polluted factions," and he professed to devote his energies to study and the business of the courts.[2] Unfortunately, his judicial duties themselves imposed upon him a task essentially political by requiring his attendance in the Council of Revision. The power of that body, though not absolute, since its effect could be overcome by a two thirds majority in the houses,[3] did nevertheless constitute an effective check upon legislative authority; and it resulted in the failure of legislative bills in no less than one hundred and eighteen instances in a space of some forty years.[4] Such a power, lodged in a little group of seven men, of whom none but the governor owed his office to popular vote, was well calculated to preserve the aristocratic principle in the constitution of a republic. It was well calculated, as the aversion to aristocracy increased, to engender suspicion and animosity.

The hostile feelings which the council provoked were not wholly unjustifiable; for it sometimes disposed of bills in a manner which showed a concern rather for partisan than public advantage. The legislature, for example, attempted to

[1] For this incident, Martin Van Buren, *Autobiography*, 62–63.
[2] James Kent to Elizabeth Kent, April 20, 1804. *Kent Papers*, Vol. III.
[3] *Constitution of New York*, 1777, Art. III.
[4] Alfred B. Street, *Council of Revision*, 7.

equalize the senatorial districts. The council, speaking through Kent, forbade the measure on the pretext that a new modelling of the districts would involve a reapportionment of senators which could properly be made only upon the return of the census.[5] The imposition of this unprecedented [6] curb on legislative power, while it pleased the Federalists who found the existing arrangement satisfactory, stimulated a less agreeable emotion in the bosoms of good Democrats; and Democratic leaders nursed remembrance of the veto as a grievance to be avenged whenever the opportunity should arise.[7] By further manifestations of partisanship the council added to the sense of injury. A coterie of influential Federalist financiers, in seeking a charter for a new bank, resorted to practices so brazenly corrupt that Governor Tompkins prorogued the legislature in disgust; but his action proved insufficient to avert the passage of the bill, which in the subsequent spring when the houses reassembled, became law with the approval of the Council of Revision. Here had occurred an opportunity for that body to demonstrate its worth as the guardians of the public good. The opportunity, however, was permitted to slip by, and neither rebuke nor remonstrance was forthcoming.[8]

These were not the only instances of the peculiar manner in which the council sometimes exercised its power. While the bank bill was yet pending, Governor Tompkins, fearing that

[5] *Ibid.*, 353–354.

[6] Nathaniel H. Carter and William L. Stone, *Reports of the Proceedings and Debates of the Convention of 1821*, 80. Hereafter cited as Carter's *Convention of 1821*.

[7] Carter's *Convention of 1821*, 80. While Governor De Witt Clinton was nominally a Democrat, he was not well liked by other Democratic leaders or by the rank and file of the party. As will appear below, he was on too good terms with the Federalists for his sincerity as a Democrat to be above suspicion. It was partly due to Clinton, that the Council had become conservative.

[8] Alfred B. Street, *Council of Revision*, 432; Carter, *op. cit.*, 80, 82; DeAlva S. Alexander, *Political History of the State of New York*, I, 191–197.

his colleagues would approve it, had tried to circumvent them. He had procured an act which authorized him to pack the council by appointing two more judges to the Supreme Court. He was apprised that the number of judges could not be increased. The reason that supported this conclusion was as singular as the conclusion itself. The constitution, it was said, had patterned the Supreme Court after the King's Bench, the Common Pleas and the Exchequer in England, in each of which tribunals the maximum number of judges had been fixed at five by immemorial usage. That usage ought not to be flouted here. It had become a part of the constitutional system; and if it was abandoned, the state would lose the protection which the council as traditionally constituted was designed to furnish against inexpedient and unconstitutional bills.[9]

By bills of that description, the council often meant measures injurious to the rights, and especially the property rights, of individuals. Such measures it was always on the alert to detect and disallow. Speaking through Kent, it vetoed a proposal to abridge the dower-rights of the widows of men who had been convicted of loyalty to the Crown during the Revolution.[10] By the same spokesman it rejected with less reason a bill to incorporate an aqueduct association and to authorize it to seize land by eminent domain. Though the act provided for compensation to the individuals affected, the council contended that it conferred a power too extraordinary to be justified except "on the principle of some important public object." [11] How important such an object had to be before it could justify an infringement of the rights of property, Kent did not precisely say. He was to show, however, by his behavior during the conflict with Great Britain that he was reluctant to

[9] Alfred B. Street, *Council of Revision,* 370–371.
[10] *Ibid.,* 333.
[11] *Ibid.,* 336.

admit that even the necessities of war furnished an adequate occasion.[12]

In time of peace it was obvious that the occasion, seldom, if ever, should occur. The legislature, entertaining a contrary view, gave the highway commissioners power to decide, in their own unlimited discretion, that the toll roads of their respective counties were out of repair; and to order the proprietors of such roads to mend and open them to the public forthwith. Unless the proprietors should comply, they were liable to heavy penalties. The council vetoed the measure because, as Kent said, it "vests in these commissioners an arbitrary power over the interests and property of individuals which is unknown to the constitution, and if carried into effect would become in a high degree injurious and alarming; for the rights vested in the stockholders of a turnpike company, incorporated by law, are as sacred and as much entitled to protection as any other private rights. . . ." [13] Unimpressed by this pronouncement, the legislature mustered the required majority and reenacted the bill.[14]

The next object of attack was not a commercial, but an educational corporation. Columbia College possessed a charter which empowered the trustees to fill up the vacancies from time to time occurring in their body, an aristocratic little company of Federalists and Episcopalians. The politicians sought to deprive them of their power by transferring the choice of trustees to the Regents of the University of the State of New York. This attack, however, failed. The council's veto was not overridden. Once more it had been pronounced by Kent who declared it to be "a sound principle in free governments that the charters of corporations cannot be affected without due process of law." [15] But for this service, Columbia may well

[12] *Vide infra* in this same section.
[13] Alfred B. Street, *Council of Revision*, 338–339.
[14] *Loc. cit.*
[15] *Ibid.*, 345.

have anticipated the experience of Dartmouth. Had that happened, there can be no doubt how Kent would have acted in the matter; for like Marshall, he regarded a charter as a contract the obligation of which the federal constitution prohibited the state from impairing.[16] This doctrine gave comfort, not only to colleges, but to corporations in general, and it furnished federal protection to those interests which Kent had always believed the states incapable of guarding securely.[17]

This conviction was strengthened by his experiences during the War of 1812. New York, lying in an exposed and vulnerable situation, suffered more than the other states from the attacks of the enemy. But her misfortunes neither aroused the sympathies of James Kent nor won his approval of the vigorous measures which Governor Tompkins and his Democratic followers concerted for the common defense. On the contrary, like the Federalists in the legislature,[18] he did what he could to obstruct them; and his position was more strategic than theirs, as he belonged to a body which had power to veto legislative proposals. In Kent's opinion the war itself was execrable enough. When Democrats made it the excuse for egalitarian legislation it became insupportable.

That such was their intention, the governor's address to the houses in January, 1814, gave proof. After describing the horrors of invasion on the Niagara frontier, Tompkins took official notice of the need "of some legal provision whereby the burden of defense may be more equitably diffused, and the less wealthy part of the community be relieved from the disproportionate share of actual service to which they are subject by existing laws. . . ." [19] In September of the same year he again took up the theme: [20] "I have . . . submitted to the consideration of

[16] *Vide infra* where the *Commentaries* are dealt with.
[17] Kent expressed this belief in the convention of 1821.
[18] Martin Van Buren, *Autobiography,* 43–44.
[19] *Public Papers of Daniel D. Tompkins* (Military) III, 429.
[20] *Ibid.,* III, 538–539.

the legislature," said he, "the propriety of relieving the poorer classes of the community from bearing that unreasonable proportion of the burden of militia duty. . . . The experience of this campaign has furnished abundant evidence of the unequal operation of the present system, and has shown the indispensable necessity of substituting property as the criterion of contribution to the public defense." With an alacrity that excited disgust among the wealthy classes,[21] the legislature, now Democratic in both houses, set about the task of translating the governor's proposal into an elaborate bill which before the middle of October was ready to be presented to the Council of Revision. It bore the title, *An Act to Authorize the Raising of Troops for the Defense of this State*,[22] but those innocuous words did not conceal the legislature's purpose of imposing upon wealthy Federalist gentlemen the burden of a war which they detested.

The act authorized the governor to call twelve thousand men to arms, and the troops thus raised were to be placed at the disposal of the President of the United States. This alone was enough to make the measure unpalatable to Federalists. But it was the method of raising the troops that provoked their liveliest objection. All the male inhabitants of the state, being free, white and between the ages of eighteen and forty-five, were divided into classes and charged with the responsibility of furnishing for each class one able-bodied soldier to the ranks, and of paying him a suitable bounty not to exceed two hundred dollars. Should a given class be unable to agree upon the amounts which the members thereof should respectively contribute, it became the duty of the town assessors where the class resided, to apportion the sum and to assess the various members agreeably to their individual estates and circumstances. The

[21] Martin Van Buren, *op. cit.*, 56.
[22] *Laws of the State of New York,* Vol. III, Ses. 38, c. xvi.

assessments thus levied were made recoverable on suit before any justice of the peace within the county.

The act contained other provisions more objectionable than these. It required each class to supply the assessors with a list of the amounts paid in, and the assessors then were to make out the aggregate sum contributed by all the classes in their respective towns, and to lay the same before the board of supervisors who thereupon would proceed to levy a tax on the non-resident property, not included in the classes, to the end, as the act recited, that that property might bear a just proportion of the bounties. Here was a provision obviously designed to ensnare the Federalists who were not only the largest land owners in the state, but were also absentee landlords more frequently than any other group of citizens. Their indignation was therefore comprehensible; and it was little wonder that James Kent, their most distinguished spokesman in the government, should raise the old, familiar cry, "Jacobinical." [23]

But his protest fell upon deaf ears even in the Council of Revision. Nor does it seem to have deserved a better fate, for the objections on which it was based were specious at the best. Kent found a discrepancy between the title and the body of the act. While the one alleged a purpose to raise troops for the defense of New York, the other evinced the true object which was to place those troops at the disposal of the United States, an exercise of power beyond the competence of the legislature, inasmuch as the whole authority for conducting war was vested in the Federal government,—except when an emergency required the state to exercise it in self-defense. In making this exception as he did, the chancellor, in effect, asked his colleagues to believe that the act in question had no bearing upon such an emergency; that it must be held unconstitutional because it was intended to aid the Union to wage war against an enemy from

[23] James Kent to Moss Kent, Jr., October 17, 1814. *Kent Papers*, Vol. IV.

whose ravages the state itself had been a principal sufferer.[24]

Unwilling to stake his reputation upon this argument alone, the chancellor produced others. Beset with the continuing danger of invasion, the country had immediate and urgent need of armies. This fact, however, Kent chose to ignore by protesting against the bill as an oppressive scheme to transform forcibly citizens into soldiers for a long national service. Such a measure was superfluous, for, said he, "It is hardly to be supposed that the government of the United States, if it really deserves and retains the affection and confidence of the nation, cannot raise by voluntary enlistments and on reasonable terms a force adequate to all the just purposes of national defense." [25] Kent knew full well the embarrassments which that government had encountered in its efforts to raise sufficient forces; and the knowledge afforded him lively satisfaction. His Federalist partisans could rely upon him to do all that lay within his power to prevent those embarrassments from ceasing.

That the bill proposed to furnish unconstitutional aid to the Union was not the most compelling reason for disallowance. That reason was to be found in the plan whereby property was to assume the burden of military expenditure. As the chancellor took unnecessary pains to point out, the bill was so drawn that a person would be liable to assessments for bounties, not only in the county where he lived, but also in any other county where he might own property. This provision, amounting to a scheme of double taxation,[26] vitiated the whole measure; and, if Kent had prevailed, would have alone sufficed to condemn it.

If he had prevailed, other important war bills would have been rejected. The legislature proposed to raise two regiments of negroes, to establish a corps of sea-fencibles, and, by means of associations endowed with corporate powers, to encourage

[24] Alfred B. Street, *Council of Revision*, 443–444.
[25] *Loc. cit.*
[26] Alfred B. Street, *Council of Revision*, 445.

privateering ventures against the enemy's commerce on the high seas.[27] Kent urged that all these proposals be vetoed; [28] but, except for incurring an unfavorable notoriety,[29] he was disregarded. They received the assent of a majority in the council and became law.[30]

In resorting at such a time to the tactics of obstruction, Kent laid himself liable to censure. Yet the course that he followed, if hardly politic, was courageous in a stubborn sort of way; nor was it entirely without benefit to the state. It prevented the enactment of at least one law which, prompted by the passions of war, would have been undoubtedly oppressive. Recalled by the chancellor's protest to sober second consideration, the legislature dropped the bill in spite of the fact that it had been made part of the general programme for a more vigorous prosecution of hostilities.

The measure was intended to aid in apprehending deserters from the army and navy of the United States; and Kent, who now for once was heeded, objected to it upon several grounds.[31] The bill made it lawful for any person, on the mere suspicion that another might be a deserter, to apprehend him without warrant, and take him before a justice-of-the-peace. This, said the chancellor, is an arbitrary power "in direct violation of all the rights of personal liberty which we inherited from our ancestors and which have been secured to us by the constitution and the law of the land." When the person thus arrested made his appearance before the justice, that official, again upon mere suspicion and probability was empowered to deliver him to gaol or to the nearest military post, a proceeding, which as Kent observed, would "render travelling insecure beyond the extent of a man's immediate neighbors." Furthermore, upon

[27] Martin Van Buren, *Autobiography*, 57.
[28] Alfred B. Street, *op. cit.*, 440, 446.
[29] Martin Van Buren, *op. cit.*, 57–58.
[30] *Laws of New York*, Vol. III, Ses. 38, c. xii, xvii, xviii.
[31] Alfred B. Street, *Council of Revision*, 377 *et seq.*

all sheriffs, deputy-sheriffs, constables and militia officers was imposed the duty of arresting every person "who shall from his appearance, dress, conversation or otherwise" give cause to suspect him of desertion; and for neglect of this duty, all such officers, both civil and military, were declared guilty of a misdemeanor and punishable by fine and imprisonment. Of this provision the chancellor remarked: "To punish an officer thus criminally for refusing to invade the sanctity of personal liberty upon a suspicion of which he must be the judge . . . is giving to our criminal code a severity beyond example." This objection was followed by another of equal weight. The bill enacted that all non-commissioned officers and privates should be bound to obey the orders of their superiors in the making of these arbitrary arrests. "By this means," said Kent, "all the militia . . . are made instruments in hunting down any citizen whomsoever who may have the misfortune 'from his appearance, conversation or otherwise' to fall under suspicion. . . ."

Had such a bill passed, freedom in New York would have become a mockery. That it failed may be attributed to the courage and vigilance of the chancellor, who, speaking in behalf of the council, demonstrated for once how salutary an influence that body upon occasion could be made to exercise. Nevertheless, its popularity was rapidly waning, and to that tendency Kent's fulminations against the military programme materially contributed.[32] Before the War of 1812 was over, the impression was confirmed that the council, and especially the most eminent member of the council, were swayed by partisan motives;[33] and that the political role in which the judges were there cast tended to involve the judiciary itself in politics, and deprive it of the necessary impartiality.[34]

[32] Carter's *Convention of 1821*, 72.
[33] *Ibid.*, 71–72.
[34] *Loc. cit.*

Thus was stimulated the desire to have the council abolished. But that body, after all, was only one of many features of the constitution which the democracy found increasingly repugnant to its ambitions. The whole instrument, though devised in the midst of a revolution, was nevertheless conservative and aristocratic; and demand that it be radically altered, if not altogether abandoned, was yearly becoming more insistent. The Council of Revision did what it could to defer the change, and its effort received fortuitous support as a result of strife within the Democratic party. That party had not responded to the leadership of Governor De Witt Clinton with the same enthusiasm which it had shown for the great war-governor, Daniel Tompkins. Schism was the consequence.

For this there were reasons both personal and political.[35] Clinton was imperious and abrupt; Tompkins insinuating and suave. Tompkins was a self-made man who had risen from the people. Clinton was born into an established family which had little in common with the plain folk whom it led; and as Clinton by a natural instinct courted the company of Federalists such as the chancellor, so too he sought to turn that social intercourse to account by attracting them into a political alliance with himself if not with his party. In this he partially succeeded.[36] The Federalists admired him personally for his liberal tastes and esteemed him politically for his efforts in promoting the project of the Erie Canal, a scheme which promised incalculable benefit to their landed interest throughout the newer regions of the state. As a consequence they became Clintonian in considerable numbers, to the scandal of the regular democracy whose suspicion of Clinton's political sincerity developed apace. That suspicion was confirmed, when in the late autumn of 1820, the governor agreed with the Council of Revision in

[35] *Vide* DeAlva S. Alexander, *Political History of the State of New York*, I and Dorothie Bobbé, *De Witt Clinton*.

[36] Kent voted for Clinton, and in the council supported his canal project.

rejecting a popular bill calling for a constitutional convention.

In assenting to that veto, De Witt Clinton stepped forth upon the side of the conservatives in company with the arch-conservative, Chancellor Kent, who expressed the council's objections to the bill.[37] The chancellor began by paying his respects to the dogma that just governments derive their power from the consent of the governed. But regard for that truth, he maintained, could conduce to no other conclusion than that the bill in question should be disallowed, as it lacked the previous and formal sanction of the electorate. A change in the fundamental law was so grave a thing to contemplate that the legislature alone was incompetent even to summon a constitutional convention without first ascertaining whether the people themselves desired it. That it was widely known, in an informal fashion, that they did, mattered but little to the council, who were bent upon delaying the evil day as long as possible. Their effort, temporarily successful, deferred the calamity until the following spring, when a bill, so drawn as to put the question *convention or no convention* [38] squarely before the people, was submitted. The council with reluctance allowed it to pass, and waited anxiously to learn the results.

Their fears proved to have been justified. The people demanded a convention. What it would be like, gentlemen predicted with misgivings; since, according to law [39] the commonest sort of persons were to take part in electing it. All free males of twenty-one years and upward who were freeholders, or had paid any taxes, or had worked on the roads or seen service in the militia were given the right of voting for convention members. The law was so liberal as to include almost everybody, being male and twenty-one. Fearful indeed to anticipate was the effect of this heterogeneous mass upon the symmetrical

[37] Alfred B. Street, *Council of Revision,* 390 *et seq.*
[38] *Laws of New York,* Vol. IV, Ses. 44, c. xc.
[39] *Loc. cit.*

fabric designed by John Jay long ago, and defended by James Kent for now almost a quarter of a century.

* * *

The convention assembled at the end of August, 1821, in the City of Albany. It was a distinguished body, boasting among its members so many men of wealth, of social eminence and of talent that the apprehensions of the conservatives seemed to have been needlessly aroused. It was certain that if any Jacobinical proposals were to be advanced, they would meet with spirited resistance from a formidable phalanx of defenders of the old regime.

Among these, fittingly enough, appeared Peter Augustus Jay,[40] the son of the chief architect of the constitutional fabric which it was now proposed to renovate. With Jay stood the great patroon, Stephen Van Rensselaer, and though social respectability required no more, professional distinction reinforced it with the presence of leaders of the bar like Elisha Williams and Abraham Van Vechten. The bench was represented by Chief Justice Spencer of the Supreme Court and by two of the puisne justices, Jonas Platt and William W. Van Ness, while at the head of the judicial delegation, stood Chancellor Kent, the very embodiment of the law's hostility to change.

Yet change was in the air that the convention breathed. A large majority of the members belonged to the Democratic party,[41] and that party was inexorably committed to change. Nor were the Democrats a rabble that were likely to forfeit for the want of leadership the advantage they derived from superior numbers. Among their ranks were men of experience

[40] A list of all members occurs in Carter's *Convention of 1821; vide et* Jabez D. Hammond, *The History of Political Parties in New York,* II, chap. i.

[41] Jabez D. Hammond, *The History of Political Parties in New York,* II, 2.

and tried ability. The war governor, Daniel D. Tompkins, was there; and they made him president of the convention. Influential on the floor and in committee was the affable and astute Van Buren; while more intensely, more radically democratic than either, was Erastus Root, aggressive, ambitious, plausible, a master of sarcastic abuse, and hailing appropriately from the county of Delaware, of whose inhabitants Kent had once observed that they principally consisted of "raftsmen, squatters, insolvent emigrants and demagogues." But the party was not entirely devoid of the support of gentlemen of birth and fortune. By an anomaly, Rufus King was counted as a Democratic member,[42] while Peter R. Livingston, that scion of aristocracy, proved himself quite as susceptible to the seductions of democratic dogma as did Erastus Root. Indeed, to those seductions the convention as a whole succumbed; and one after another the aristocratic features of the old instrument were brought under hostile scrutiny, and one after another they were condemned either to radical change or outright abolition.

The judiciary was a favorite subject for debate. All agreed that it required some alterations to make it more efficient in conducting its increased business, and a moderate proposal was made to that effect. The committee in charge of the matter, believing it wise "to preserve the present system as entire as possible," [43] proceeded with caution. On the law side, they advocated the retention of the Supreme Court as at present constituted, and, to relieve that tribunal of the press of litigation, recommended the establishment of a Superior Court of Common Pleas with an almost concurrent jurisdiction.[44] For equity, it was considered best that the chancellor should remain, and that to aid him in the discharge of his duties, a vice-chancellor should be appointed from whom he would reserve

[42] *Ibid.*, 3.
[43] Carter's *Convention of 1821*, 500.
[44] *Ibid.*, 232.

the right to hear causes on appeal. The committee paid their respects to Kent. No other man in the state, it was said, could perform the duties of the office as he performed them, and it was asserted that he had reduced them to a system which did honor both to the state and to himself.[45] These observations were as true as they were seemly, but the report which embodied them was rejected, and with the offering of a substitute proposal by Erastus Root, the tone of praise changed sharply to one of bitterness and suspicion.

Root hated not so much the judiciary itself as the jurists who presided there; and had his scheme been followed in its entirety, they all would have been thrust from office. He wished to create a new Supreme Court of three judges to be newly appointed; and these were to be relieved of their circuit duties by the establishment of a series of permanent circuit courts. Most drastic of all, he would have abolished a separate chancery and committed its peculiar powers to the tribunals of the common law.[46] In speaking of the bench, Root showed himself to be no respecter of persons. "It is the fashion," said he,[47] "to laud the chancellor and judges and to set them forth as the most perfect patterns of piety and legal learning in the world. How often have we been told that Johnson's reports are quoted not only from Maine to New Orleans but that the decisions they contain are regarded with reverence in the legal sanctuary of Westminster Hall? The chancellor too has been described as a branching oak, whose roots penetrate the Union while its branches afford shelter to all those who are fortunate enough to obtain access to its shade . . . although it has been admitted

[45] *Ibid.*, 232, 500–501.

[46] *Ibid.*, 502; *vide et* Jabez D. Hammond, *The History of Political Parties in New York*, II, 55.

[47] Carter's *Convention of 1821, 616*. For a severe criticism of the convention's attitude toward the judiciary *vide United States Law Journal*, I, 35–40, in article "Equity Jurisdiction in the State of New York," highly laudatory of Kent and of all that he stood for.

that it casts a baneful political pestilence around it, and that like the Bohon-Upas of Java it carries death and desolation to the extent of its atmosphere." This Bohon-Upas tree Erastus Root would have hewn down with mighty strokes. The motives that prompted him to undertake the arduous labor he did not make entirely clear.

Though he denounced the chancellor's political activities, he did it in such vague and general terms as to be unconvincing. Though he asserted that chancery powers were too extensive to be vested in one person,[48] he failed to prove that they had been either abused or inadequately exerted. Though he ranted continually against the whole judiciary, of specific criticism of decisions there was little; except that he accused Kent of having attempted in the case of Ruggles to establish a state religion,[49] and that he charged the judges generally with useless refinements that tended to diminish the liberty of the citizens.[50] An example of this, he asserted, occurred in their handling of libel cases, where contrary to the doctrine laid down in the Croswell trial, they had usurped the right of the jury to determine concerning the worthiness of the motive with which the libel had been published.[51] These criticisms, Kent, aided by Jay,[52] repelled without rancor. He was especially concerned, however, to demonstrate the impropriety of merging the administration of law with that of equity.

"The Court of Chancery," said Kent, "has become too deeply incorporated in our institutions and jurisprudence to be now destroyed as an independent jurisdiction without the utmost inconvenience and hazard. It is wisest and safest to have the systems of law and equity deposited in separate and distinct courts. The systems are essentially different in their character,

[48] Carter, *op. cit.*, 505; also 518–519, 532.
[49] *Ibid.*, 462–463.
[50] *Ibid.*, 519.
[51] *Ibid.*, 491–493.
[52] *Ibid.*, 463, 488, 620.

relations and objects."[53] The member from Delaware had asserted that the powers of chancery were too extensive to be vested in one person; that thus lodged they tended to make his office dangerous to liberty. On the contrary, maintained Kent, "It would be dangerous, and contrary to the cautious policy of a free government to accumulate all the powers of each system in one tribunal—we should then," he prophesied, "run the hazard of having equity so intermixed with law, and law so intermixed with equity as to lose the certainty and distinct character of each."[54] To illustrate the impropriety of the project, he sketched the outlines of chancery jurisdiction, maintaining that trusts, accounts, the administration of estates, presented too technical and too intricate questions to be conveniently submitted to the determination of a jury; and he seemed to imply that it would be difficult, if not impossible, for a law court to resolve itself into an equity tribunal without relying upon juries as well in the second capacity as in the first.[55] Though in less than a generation experience was to prove that such a contention was ill-founded, Kent carried his colleagues with him, and to his great relief, saw Root's proposal to abolish an independent chancery voted down.[56]

Unpopular though he was in many quarters, Kent thus fared decidedly better than his brethren of the Supreme Court. Changed but in detail to lighten his load of business, his office retained all its dignity and power; and the consensus of opinion was that however hostile to democracy he himself might be, he should continue as chancellor until he should have reached the constitutional limit of sixty years. To this decision no doubt his fame as a jurist contributed. No doubt

[53] *Ibid.*, 506; *vide et United States Law Journal*, I, 40, which holds the same language.

[54] Carter, *op. cit.*, 506.

[55] *Loc. cit.*

[56] *Ibid.*, 523. In the third constitution, 1847, law and equity were merged into one set of courts.

his advancing age added a more powerful reason. As he had but two more years to go before his term would constitutionally expire, it may well have appeared like a needless indignity to cast him out before that time. Kent, however, seems to have expected the convention to treat him still more liberally.[57] It was a fact well known that John Jay and his colleagues in 1777 had prescribed an age limit for judicial tenure in order to avoid the vexations they had once experienced from the senile infirmities of Chief Justice Horsmanden.[58] To penalize Kent for the shortcomings of that ancient worthy, long since defunct, seemed to be both unjust and inexpedient, and the chancellor and his friends had hoped that the convention would amend the constitution in such a manner as to permit him to remain on the bench indefinitely. In this they were disappointed. The majority of the convention were quite ready to see the day arrive when James Kent, though capable as ever, would be required by law to retire into the obscurity of private life. For the departure of the Chief Justice and of his associates, Platt and Van Ness, they were more impatient; and by providing for the creation of a new Supreme Court to consist of three new judges, the convention deftly manoeuvred them from the bench.[59] To the objection that three were insufficient to carry on the business of the court, Erastus Root replied that their ability could be magically and economically increased by decking them out in the trappings of the British judges. "A ponderous wig," said he, "a black gown and a band are placed upon the judge, thereby making him appear artificially wise. Now if we could do with a less number of judges by placing on their heads these wise wigs, it would be a great relief to our treasury and perhaps law and equity would be full as well administered

[57] *Vide infra.*
[58] 7 *Johns. Ch.* 346.
[59] Jabez D. Hammond, *The History of Political Parties in New York.* II, 61, 137.

as with the present number."[60] Thus amidst derision, Chief Justice Spencer and his colleagues, William Van Ness and Jonas Platt, were driven from the bench. Kent should have deemed himself fortunate that he was permitted to remain at all.

For the animosities which had been excited against the courts the judges had principally themselves to chide. While it is true that they expounded a system of law which was not especially democratic, yet it was not in the purely judicial aspect of their careers that they evoked the liveliest criticism. What did arouse intense hostility was their proneness to engage in politics. Chief Justice Spencer was an avowed partisan who did not hesitate to descend from the bench to take part in the tumults of a campaign. Justices Platt and Van Ness displayed an almost equal zeal. The chancellor had a nicer sense of judicial propriety; yet in the Council of Revision even he exhibited a political bias; and it was that as much as anything else which led to the downfall of the institution. "I object to the council," said Martin Van Buren on the floor of the convention, "because . . . it tends to make our judges politicians"; and in support of the charge he cited the chancellor's fulminations against the Democratic programme for the conduct of the War of 1812. "Beyond all doubt," said he, "at that moment was produced the sentiment which has led to the unanimous vote to abolish the council."[61]

That reform had been accomplished[62] without meeting much opposition even in debate, though the tone of the Democrats in urging it had called forth some remonstrance. Peter Livingston asserted that the council had alarmed the people

[60] Carter's *Convention of 1821*, 617. "Pains have been taken to create and diffuse prejudices against the higher courts of the state; and we regret to say that this temper was openly manifested on the very floor of the convention." *United States Law Journal*, I, 35.

[61] Carter's *Convention of 1821*, 71–72.

[62] *Ibid.*, 44 *et seq.*

by deciding the expediency as well as the constitutionality of laws.[63] Erastus Root assailed it as an aristocratic anomaly,[64] and found fault with its disallowance of the act passed during the War of 1812 for the apprehension of deserters.[65] The council had still other sins to answer for. As Van Buren observed, it had approved a bank bill so notorious that the governor had prorogued the legislature for passing it.[66] That governor was now the president of the convention; and, coming down from the chair, he added his voice to the chorus of recrimination. He pointed out the council's refusal to approve the bills for altering the senatorial districts and empowering the governor to appoint additional judges.[67] The council's insistence that the common law forbade additional appointments to the Supreme Court he branded as an insult to the intelligence. With growing uneasiness the conservatives, fearful of the effect which these criticisms might have upon the judiciary, made ready to answer them as best they could, though their effort was enfeebled by their admission that the council had outlived its usefulness. Nevertheless, Chief Justice Spencer and Judge Platt tried to justify it,[68] and the chancellor, in a rather half-hearted way, came to their support by insisting that he had endeavored "to discharge his trust without regard to party influence and with a single reference to the intrinsic merits of the bills that have been submitted. . . ."[69] Needless to say, this claim of impartiality carried no conviction to any but the chancellor's own friends.

Having done away with the Council of Revision, the convention discussed the wisdom of providing some new check

[63] *Ibid.*, 51.
[64] *Ibid.*, 61.
[65] *Ibid.*, 98–99.
[66] *Ibid.*, 71.
[67] *Ibid.*, 80.
[68] *Ibid.*, 54, 113–114.
[69] *Ibid.*, 88.

upon the legislature. Peter Livingston proposed that the governor alone should exercise the veto power, subject always to the right of the houses to over-rule him by a bare majority.[70] At this suggestion, Kent took alarm. "I apprehend," said he, "that the sober-minded people of this state would not be satisfied to see this column of the constitution destroyed [*i.e.* the Council of Revision] without having it replaced by something efficient"; [71] and he emphasized the necessity of restraining the legislature from enacting laws in haste and passion.[72] "Better no veto at all," maintained the chancellor, "than one so weak as here proposed." [73] The convention in general agreed with him, and imitating the Federal constitution, gave a veto power to the governor and authorized the legislature to nullify it only by a majority of two-thirds.[74] The chancellor was satisfied with this; and to reassure those who feared that the provision would make the executive too powerful, he prophesied that the governor would exercise the veto power but seldom, and then only on constitutional grounds when the rights of individuals and of property were assailed.[75]

Under the new constitution that was in the making there was little danger that the executive would be vested with too much authority. Indeed, so strongly did the old jealousies of the governor's prerogative still operate, that the Democrats argued for a reduction of his term to a single year.[76] In vain did the chancellor and the conservatives attempt to retain it at three.[77] A two year term was at last agreed upon as a reasonable compromise.[78] In this brief period it was not likely that the

[70] Carter's *Convention of 1821*, 48.
[71] *Ibid.*, 63–64.
[72] *Loc. cit.*
[73] *Loc. cit.*
[74] *Constitution of New York*, 1821, Art. I, Sec. xii.
[75] Carter, *op. cit.*, 63.
[76] *Ibid.*, 137.
[77] *Ibid.*, 148.
[78] *Ibid.*, 158.

governor would find an opportunity to make himself a tyrant, especially since he was to be deprived of the power of controlling appointments. That power had hitherto been shared with a special Council of Appointment which during the course of its history had incurred almost as much hostility as the Council of Revision. It was, like that body, abolished by unanimous vote.[79] The substitute provisions were hardly more wise but certainly more democratic; for the appointing power was broken up and distributed piece-meal, in small part to the governor alone, in part to the two houses of the legislature to whom henceforth the chief administrative officers such as the Secretary of State, the Comptroller and the Attorney-General were to be beholden for their dignities.[80] Such was the manner in which responsibility was to be diffused in the future discharge of executive functions.

But the most striking innovations of all were those which related to the suffrage franchise. Upon that head the old constitution had been conservative, prescribing the possession of a £20 freehold or the payment of a yearly rent of 40s. as the qualifications of voters for assemblymen. A still larger property was necessary to qualify for taking part in the elections of governor and senators, who, as the constitution declared, were to be chosen "by the freeholders of this state, possessed of freeholds of the value of £100 over and above all debts charged thereon." [81] To Chancellor Kent's dismay, the Democratic majority in the convention proposed to abolish these restrictions and to substitute others that would permit the prospective voter to qualify more easily, whether by an established residence, by the payment of taxes, by work on the roads or by service in the militia.[82] Such limitations the chancellor con-

[79] Carter's *Convention of 1821*, 296.

[80] Jabez D. Hammond, *History of Political Parties in New York,* II, 78.

[81] *Constitution of New York*, 1777, Arts. X and XVII.

[82] Carter, *op. cit.*, 178 *et seq.* The £100 qualification for electors of Senators meant a freehold estate worth about $250. The £20 qualification

sidered as amounting to universal manhood suffrage in disguise; [83] and he made a strenuous effort to retain the old qualifications at least for electors of the senate. His exertions were futile. The Democrats paid no heed to his warnings, though they complimented him upon having composed "an elegant epitaph" for the old constitution.[84]

"I cannot but think," said the chancellor as he began his address on the subject of the franchise,[85] "that the considerate men who have studied the history of republics or are read in the lessons of experience, must look with concern upon our apparent disposition to vibrate from a well-balanced government to the extremes of the democratic doctrines. Such a broad proposition as that contained in the report, at the distance of ten years past, would have struck the public mind with astonishment and terror. So rapid has been the career of our vibration." Reviewing the advantages which had accumulated under the old regime, the chancellor warned his hearers against the sin of ingratitude. Our lives, he said, our property and our privileges had been protected; there had been a succession of wise legislatures; the administration of justice had been honest, prompt and regular; industry had increased, education flourished, science advanced, population trebled; and now, as a climax to all these accomplishments "we are successfully engaged in connecting the Great Lakes with the ocean by stupendous canals." Under the old constitution these blessings had been attained, a fact which ought always to be borne gratefully in mind. "When the husbandman," said Kent, "has gathered in his harvest and has filled his barns and his granaries with the fruits of his industry, if he should then become discontented and unthankful, would he not have reason to ap-

---

for an elector for assemblyman meant a freehold worth about $50; the 40s. rent was reckoned at about $5. *Vide* Carter *op. cit.* 220.

[83] Carter's *Convention of 1821*, 220 *et seq.*

[84] *Ibid.*, 237.

[85] *Ibid.*, 219 *et seq.*, for the chancellor's address.

prehend that the Lord of the Harvest might come in his wrath and with his lightning destroy them?"

This apparently was the punishment in store for the people of New York if they dispensed with the requirement that senators should be chosen only by the freeholders. "The senate," continued the chancellor, "has hitherto been elected by the farmers of the state . . . by the free and independent lords of the soil. . . . The governor has been chosen by the same electors, and we have hitherto elected citizens of elevated rank and character. Our assembly has also been chosen by freeholders. . . . We propose now to annihilate at one stroke all these property distinctions and to bow before the idol of universal suffrage." The danger to which the commonwealth would be exposed by this change Kent set forth in solemn periods. "That extreme democratic principle," said he, "when applied to the legislative and executive departments of government, has been regarded with terror by the wise men of every age, because in every European republic, ancient and modern, in which it has been tried, it has terminated disastrously, and been productive of corruption, injustice, violence and tyranny. And dare we," queried the orator, "flatter ourselves that we are a peculiar people who can run the career of history, exempted from the passions which have disturbed and corrupted the rest of mankind? If we are like other races of men, with similar follies and vices, then I greatly fear that our posterity will have reason to deplore in sack-cloth and ashes the delusion of the day."

Conceding that the old qualifications for electors of the assembly would have to be discarded, Kent announced that he would be grateful, "if we may be permitted to retain the stability and security of the senate bottomed upon the freehold property of the state. Such a body, so constituted," he prophesied, "may prove a sheet anchor amidst the future factions and storms of the republic." Reiterating his desire to preserve the senate as the representative of the landed interest, he foretold the dismal time to come when, "the men of no property, together with the crowds of dependants connected with the great manufacturing and commercial establishments, and the motley and undefinable population of the crowded ports may predominate in the assembly." Such an event would be sad to contemplate, and yet, as the chancellor reassured his audience, "We should be perfectly safe if no laws could pass without the free consent of the owners of the soil. That security we at present enjoy; and it is that security which I wish to retain."

Trying to show that the dangers of universal suffrage were no figments of the imagination, Kent asserted that such an experiment was "too mighty an excitement for the moral constitution of men to endure. The tendency of universal suffrage is to jeopardize the rights of property and the principles of liberty. There is," said he, "a constant tendency in human society (and the history of every age proves it), there is a tendency in the poor to covet and to share the plunder of the rich; in the debtor to relax or avoid the obligation of contracts; in the majority to tyrannize over the minority, and to trample down their rights; in the indolent and profligate to cast the whole burden of society upon the industrious and virtuous, and *there is a tendency in ambitious and wicked men to inflame these combustible materials.*" [86] That tendency the chancellor perceived at work in the affairs of America and he feared that its consummation might occur at no distant day "The disproportion," he said, "between the men of property and the men of no property will be in every society in a ratio to its commerce, wealth and population." In view of this disturbing fact, the removal of constitutional safeguards for the propertied classes seemed to Kent little short of suicidal. "The notion that every man that works a day on the road, or serves

[86] Carter's *Convention of 1821*, 221.

an idle hour in the militia, is entitled as of right to an equal participation in the whole power of the government is," asserted he, "most unreasonable, and has no foundation in justice. . . . Society is an association for the protection of property as well as of life, and the individual who contributes only one cent to the common stock ought not to have the same power and influence in directing the property concerns of the partnership, as he who contributes his thousands. He will not have the same inducements to care and diligence and fidelity. His inducements and his temptations would be to divide the whole capital upon the principle of an agrarian law." [87]

Kent, with all his prophesying, failed to impress the majority of the convention. Their views were expressed by Tompkins when he declared that property as compared to other essential rights was insignificant and trifling, and that it was life, liberty and the pursuit of happiness, not of property, which according to the Declaration of Independence, were to be regarded as the objects of civil society.[88] This was the sentiment, regarded by Kent as wholly heterodox, that prevailed in the convention. The freehold qualifications were abolished. The cult of democracy had won the day; and Kent, withdrawing from the convention before its deliberations ended,[89] departed too late to save his offended eyes from the spectacle of members bowing down to the seductive idol. The new constitution received the approval of a great majority, and upon being submitted to the voters of the state, was adopted with but little dissent.

For the exertions that he had made to stem the democratic tide, the chancellor received the rewards that he might have anticipated. The people liked him even less than before: men of eminence praised and commiserated him in the same breath.

[87] Carter's *Convention of 1821*, 221.

[88] *Ibid.*, 235.

[89] *Ibid.*, 605.

"We rejoice," wrote Judge Van Ness, "at the noble and gallant manner in which you have conducted the cause of truth, morality and religion. . . . We mourn over the portentous state of things which your letters portray." [90] In the same vein, his kinsman, Jonas Platt, another judge discomfited, wrote to commend the chancellor for the "able, patriotic and dignified stand which [he] had maintained in resisting the torrent of the volcano. I rejoice," said Platt, "on your own account as well as for the honor of the state that you have been stationed in the straights of Thermopylae. . . . You have erected there a noble monument, my dear friend, and even our ungrateful republic will one day do justice to your merits and character." As he proceeded, the worthy Platt became excited, and lapsed into Latin: "You have never before," wrote he, "been exposed to the buffeting of Jacobin factions—*gaudet tentamine virtus, indignante invidia florebat justus, post nubila Phoebus.*" [91] From this classical eloquence, Kent extracted what comfort he could. But in truth, he was filled with misgiving.

The constitutional convention had voted down the proposal of Erastus Root to abolish an independent chancery, and had signified its desire that Kent stay in office until he should become sixty. But the legislature, falling even more than had the convention under the influence of radical Democrats, was apparently attempting to get rid of him sooner. A bill to do away with his court had been introduced before the convention met, and though it had failed, the attack, assuming other forms, continued. Kent's stipend, which in 1816 had been raised to $4500 a year was now reduced several times in succession. In the spring of 1820, it had been cut by a thousand. Before the convention, in the spring of 1821, it was cut again,

[90] William W. Van Ness to James Kent, October 22, 1821. *Kent Papers*, Vol. V.

[91] Jonas Platt to James Kent, October 29, 1821. *Ibid.*

and two years later, on the very eve of his retirement, it was still further reduced to a paltry $2000 a year.[92] It was not strange that the chancellor, as he informed his friend Johnson, was gloomy from the spirit of misrule which he found prevalent within the walls of the capitol. "You can hardly imagine," he wrote, "how rapid the progress of things is to the decay and ruin of our pride and hopes as republicans and jurists." [93]

Indeed, with Peter Livingston in the chair as speaker of the assembly and with Erastus Root presiding as Lieutenant-governor over the deliberations of the senate,[94] democracy was triumphant in New York as it had never been before. In this changed scene, Kent began to be uncomfortable and lonely; [95] the Court of Errors furnished less and less congenial company; [96] and the chancellor declared that he "was sincerely happy [that he was] to withdraw so soon from any future concern in the government of the state." [97] Nevertheless, he was disposed to remain on the bench to the limit of his tenure; and in spite of reductions in stipend and of even stronger hints that he should go, he refused to budge.

Some six months before his birthday he was mortified by the nomination of a successor. The new constitution furnished a pretext for this act by providing that the commissions of the judges should expire with the expiration of the year 1822. Governor Yates lost no time in making appointments, and before the end of January, 1823, sent the nomination of a new chancellor to the senate, where it was unanimously confirmed. But Kent, taking the view that the appointing process was

[92] James Kent to William Johnson, March, 1821. *Ibid.; Laws of New York*, Ses. 39, ch. ccxxxvi, April 17, 1816; Ses. 43, ch. cxxiv, April 1, 1820; Ses. 44, ch. ccxl, April 3, 1821; Ses. 46, ch. cclxix, April 24, 1823.

[93] James Kent to William Johnson, April 13, 1822. *Kent Papers*, Vol. V.

[94] Jabez D. Hammond, *History of Political Parties in New York*, II, 106.

[95] James Kent to William Johnson, February 7, 1823; April 22, 1823. *Kent Papers*, Vol. V.

[96] James Kent to William Johnson, February 7, 1823. *Ibid.*

[97] James Kent to William Johnson, April 22, 1823. *Ibid.*

incomplete until a commission had issued,[98] informed Yates that pending the accomplishment of that formality he intended to remain in office "until the thirty-first day of July next when I shall have arrived (if my life be spared) to the age of sixty. Indeed," he continued, with a suggestion of irony, "I think I should be wanting in respect to you from whom I have already received constant marks of friendship and good will, and in duty to the government and people of this state, to whom I have been placed under so many obligations, to retire before I was sixty without just cause." [99]

The old chancellor prevailing, tarried in office through the remaining months of the winter of 1823. The spring came on apace, and with chancery business rapidly accumulating, the midsummer drew near. Though troubled with a slight rheumatism,[100] Kent applied himself as diligently as ever to his labors. "I retire from office the last of July," he wrote to Joseph Story, "and I am now very busy in disposing of the cases that were argued at the last chancery term in New York. The business thrown on me for the last five months has been overwhelming, but I shall dispatch it all, and leave nothing unfinished." [101] As the final day approached, the chancellor sent off a sheaf of opinions to his old friend Johnson, and in the letter that accompanied it, spoke affectionately of their many years of collaboration and of the agreeable memories that arose within him at the severing of official ties. Modestly he alluded to the opinions which he was sending. They will form, he said, "a proper conclusion to the second decade of a great body of valuable and accurate law learning." [102] This communication

[98] James Kent to Joseph Yates, January 28, 1823. Kent MSS., New York Public Library.

[99] *Loc. cit.*

[100] William Kent to Isaac Hone, June 12, 1823. *Kent Papers,* Vol. V.

[101] James Kent to Joseph Story, June 30, 1823. *Story Papers,* Massachusetts Historical Society.

[102] James Kent to William Johnson, July 29, 1823. *Kent Papers,* Vol. V.

Johnson received with unfeigned regret to which he gave official utterance in his reports. "This day," he recorded of July 31, 1823, "the chancellor terminated his judicial labors, having heard and decided every case and motion brought before him." [103] He added that people outside the state were astonished that the age limit of sixty years had been retained at the cost of losing the services of a jurist so celebrated.[104]

To those familiar with the course of politics in New York, this gave no surprise whatever, though here and there, and in other bosoms than that of William Johnson, it occasioned regret. Meeting in the chancery court room in the city hall, the members of the New York bar, headed by the now venerable Richard Harison, drew up their resolutions in honor of the retiring chancellor. Addressing themselves to him directly, they expressed grave doubts concerning the wisdom of that provision which compelled him, though in the full enjoyment of his intellectual faculties, to relinquish the station which he had filled with such honor and advantage to the state.[105] Observing that by his decisions in law and equity, he had contributed "to establish the fabric of our jurisprudence," they concluded their address with an eloquent prophecy: "Your labors on this magnificent structure will forever remain eminently conspicuous, commanding the applause of the present generation and exciting the admiration and gratitude of future ages." [106]

Thus, amidst the polite but cordial plaudits of the bar over

[103] 7 *Johns. Ch.* 346.
[104] *Ibid.*, 347.
[105] 7 *Johns. Ch.* 347–356.
[106] *Loc. cit.* The resolutions were signed by Richard Harison, Thomas A. Emmet, John Wells, Josiah O. Hoffmann, Samuel Jones, Samuel Boyd and William Johnson. At Albany and Utica the bar associations presented resolutions, to which were appended the names of eminent up-state lawyers like Van Vechten and Elisha Williams. The resolutions compare Kent in law to Mansfield, and in equity to Sir Heneage Finch. The authors were of course predisposed in Kent's favor. They were all old Federalists or, at least, partisans of De Witt Clinton.

whose learned disputations he had now for many years presided, Chancellor Kent descended from the bench, and with a gracious response to the resolutions, retired from the public scene.

VII

The American Blackstone

Hac ratione studiorum cognitio legum nostrarum nunc elicienda est; donec postea genius magnus quidam juralis extiterit, quidam sive Bractonus, sive Fleta, Baconus, Cokeus Seldenusve e nobismet exoriturus sit . . . extiteruntque ii sive i'. consulti, sive iudices caeterive eruditi juris atque periti, qui narratas actiones forenses dictaque judicia libris commentariisve mandata tradiderint.

Ezra Stiles *Oratio Inauguralis*

It is with the immortal commentaries on the laws of England that those on American Law are now classed, and the names of Blackstone and Kent are fated never to be disjoined.

Law Reporter, VI, 294

* * *

THWARTED in his ambition to grow old in the service of the state, Kent ruefully contrasted his own with the happier lot of those British judges who, like Mansfield,[1] still wore the ermine at the age of eighty. The ex-chancellor, however, was a man of too much sense to waste his time in brooding over the ingratitude of republics; and upon the morrow of his retirement, he decided to forget his injuries in the pleasures of travel.

The month of August, 1823, found him in Boston and Cambridge [2] rejoicing in the society of distinguished men who

[1] *Kent Journal*, 1821–1824. He says that Mansfield continued as Lord Chief Justice for twenty-three years after he was sixty; Sir Robert Graham, a Baron of the Exchequer, still on the bench at eighty; Lord Eldon and Lord Stowell on the bench at eighty-one.

[2] *Ibid.* (No. 7), Tour of New England, August, 1823.

vied with one another to do him honor. Chief Justice Parker accompanied him to the Athenaeum; Daniel Webster invited him to dinner. Christopher Gore and Mr. Justice Story received him with open arms and flattered him with every attention. Josiah Quincy took him to hear a sermon by Dr. Channing. At Cambridge, President Kirkland not only showed him the college, but entertained him in his own house over night. Mrs. Winthrop, on his return to Boston, invited him to a brilliant party. He was dined by George Ticknor who, moreover, accompanied him to Quincy where he paid his respects to the venerable John Adams, now bowed with the weight of almost ninety years.[3]

A more opportune time for his visit to the east, Kent could not have chosen. It was the season when the sons of Harvard foregathered to celebrate commencement. Yale men too were present in goodly numbers, and on the eve of the festivities in Cambridge, they assembled to hold a feast in honor of their own Alma Mater, and to drink a toast to "*The James Kent*—with better machinery, greater force and greater safety than any other boat, yet constitutionally forbidden to take another trip." [4] The Yale banquet was followed next day by the commencement ceremonies at Cambridge, after which the chancellor dined in the college hall in a great company of some five hundred persons among whom, as he was careful to note in his journal, were all the leading men of Boston. But the climax of the celebration occurred on the twenty-eighth at the brilliant Phi Beta Kappa banquet presided over by Mr.

[3] *Ibid.*, August 24, 26, 28 and 30, 1823.

[4] Other toasts drunk at this banquet:

"The Constitution of New York,—we hear that it diverts the operations, but we see that it neither abates the force nor obscures the splendor of intellectual light."

"Our distinguished guest, Chancellor Kent,—we had hoped that the 'gladsome light of jurisprudence' which had been barred out of New York might have been permitted to shine at Washington." *Kent Journal* (No. 7), August 28, 1823.

Justice Story. With this affair Kent was delighted, and with good reason.

It was the chancellor whom above all others that learned society delighted to honor. "The Athenians banished Aristides for excess of virtue," said one proposer of a toast. "It was reserved for an American state to banish a great man for the excess of learning. *Infelix! qui potuit rerum cognoscere causas.*" Amidst acclamations the assembly drank to "the happy climate of New York whose citizens enjoy their physical vigor and intellectual preeminence after they are constitutionally superannuated." To this the chancellor responded with a toast to Harvard, bespeaking "Perpetual gratitude to its wise and benevolent founders," and though the sentiment was neither imaginative nor witty, it won applause and furnished occasion for another bumper in his honor. "The combatants of the forum," went the new proposal, "may they be ever governed by the notes of the Kent bugle." When Story rose with uplifted glass, anticipation was at its keenest; and he drank, as had been expected, to his friend from New York, "Our distinguished guest, who so administered the law of the land, as to make New York the land of the law." Almost immediately, as the applause died down, Kent was upon his feet, proposing amidst great enthusiasm, "Massachusetts, the land of Story as well as of song." [5]

If the chancellor had been ruffled by the Jacobinical winds blowing in his own state, his visit to Massachusetts soothed him again into his habitual good humor. Upon returning home, he participated in another celebration which enhanced the beneficial effect of his journey. In the convention he had noted the progress of the state's efforts in "connecting the Great Lakes with the ocean by stupendous canals." The autumn of 1823 saw the first passage of vessels through the lock

[5] *Boston Evening Gazette,* August 30, 1823, *Kent Journal* (No. 7), 1821–1824.

and dam at Troy; and Kent, in company with De Witt Clinton, witnessed the event, and shared with him the plaudits of the multitude,[6] a pleasure rare for the jurist, yet not undeserved. For Kent, in his last decision as chancellor,[7] had not only explained the scope and purpose of the injunction, but also, by dissolving an injunction that forbade the contractors from taking necessary materials from a neighboring hillside, had hastened the completion of the very lock through which, amid shouts and the peal of bells and the boom of cannon, he was now being borne in triumph with De Witt Clinton.[8]

Such demonstrations were gratifying. At the same time they could not banish the anxiety which Kent felt for his future. By means of unostentatious living and prudent investments, he had contrived to amass a small capital which he feared to exhaust by spending his retirement in leisure.[9] Had he desired it, he might have had the headship of a college, for as early as 1821, Daniel Webster had approached one of Kent's friends with the inquiry whether the presidency of Dartmouth "were not altogether beneath his acceptance." [10] Of this proposal, however, nothing came. Nor was Webster's suggestion to Story that the chancellor might well be appointed to the Federal Supreme Court any more fruitful.[11] As for Kent himself, he pondered the notion of founding at Albany a law school after the model of Judge Reeve's famous institution at Litchfield.[12] But this project never developed beyond a mere idea. Another scheme began to take shape. With his learning, his experience and his reputation, Kent was convinced that he could reestablish his practice in New

[6] *Kent Journal* (No. 7), September 10, 1823.

[7] Jerome v. Ross, *supra cit.*

[8] Dorothie Bobbé, *De Witt Clinton,* 257.

[9] James Kent to Moss Kent, Jr., January 4, 1824. *Kent Papers,* Vol. V.

[10] Daniel Webster to Samuel Boyd, January 3, 1821. *Ibid.*

[11] Frederick C. Hicks, *Men and Books Famous in the Law,* 148.

[12] James Kent to William Johnson, September 27, 1823. *Kent Papers,* Vol. V.

York City, whither he removed in October, 1823, to open an office as chamber counsel.[13]

The venture was fortunate beyond his expectations. Becoming a lawyer's lawyer, he numbered among his clients the most eminent members of the bar; and questions of infinite variety were submitted to him, not only from all parts of the United States, but also from England and the British provinces.[14] Nor was it only great lawyers like William Wirt and Daniel Webster that consulted him.[15] Judges themselves did not hold it beneath their dignity to do the same.[16] If Kent was a prophet without honor in official New York and there considered as superannuated, his mail, coming to his office in Pine Street,[17] pleased him with the proof that official opinion in New York was extremely fallible. Elsewhere he was regarded as an oracle.

[13] James Kent to Moss Kent, Jr., January 4, 1824. *Ibid.*

[14] William Kent, *Memoirs and Letters of James Kent*, 273; *Law Reporter*, I, 57, publishes an elaborate opinion of Kent on a question of corporation law. If a corporation, in one state, make a contract in another, which would have been lawful in their own, and not prohibited by the other state, would the corporation be entitled to enforce performance of that contract in courts of that other state? Kent said "yes."

[15] James Kent to Daniel Webster, January 21, 1830. *Kent Papers*, Vol. VI. The subject is on the President's power of removal, whether the consent of the senate be necessary. Kent thought that theoretically it ought to be, and was intended to be; but that usage made it inconvenient to require it after the exercise of the power by the President exclusively had long been acquiesced in. Cf. Myers v. United States. William Wirt to James Kent, October 1, 1830; October 8, 1830; October 28, 1830. *Kent Papers*, Vol. VI, for opinions on various questions raised by Cherokee Nation v. Georgia. *Vide et* George McDuffie to James Kent, December 10, 1826, *Kent Papers*, Vol. V. Sir Charles Vaughan to James Kent, March 3, 1837, *Kent Papers*, Vol. VIII. Thomas Handley to James Kent, November 30, 1837. *Ibid.*, praising him for the "luminous ability" of his opinion on the title of Lords Arthur and George Hill to certain lands in America.

[16] Chief Justice Hornblower (of New Jersey) to James Kent, January 12, 1836. *Kent Papers*, Vol. VIII. James Kent to David Daggett, August 30, 1827. *Daggett Papers*, Vol. I.

[17] William Kent to Moss Kent, Jr., November 21, 1825. *Kent Papers*, Vol. V. His office was later in Cedar Street and St. Mark's place. James Kent to Moss Kent, Jr., October 7, 1833. *Ibid.*, Vol. VII.

Even within the state, there were a chosen few who held him in equal veneration. Among these the trustees of Columbia College were conspicuous. That corporation Kent had already served as a professor, but more especially as a judge when, sitting in the Council of Revision, he had defended its charter against legislative assault. Of all the colleges, Columbia had been the first to recognize his attainments with a doctorate of laws; and if at the time when that distinction was bestowed, he had already done the college much honor, as Brockholst Livingston observed, he was now about to do it an honor greater still by assuming his professorship again [18] and proceeding to deliver that series of lectures from which grew his plan for the celebrated commentaries on the law.[19]

Kent had no American model for his undertaking; [20] nor did Sir William Blackstone serve him as a pattern unless perhaps in felicity of style. There had been American writers who had published special treatises on legal subjects of considerable variety though none of these had dealt with jurisprudence as a comprehensive system.[21] The ex-chancellor was more ambitious. His project, as carried out, embraced a discourse on

[18] Formal notice of his appointment, November 3, 1823. *Ibid.*, Vol. V.

[19] The series of lectures at Columbia extend from the fall of 1824 to the spring of 1826 when Kent began to think seriously of publication. William Kent, *Memoirs and Letters of James Kent,* 193. The volumes appeared in the following sequence: Vol. I in 1826; II in 1827; III in 1828 and Vol. IV in 1830. *Law Reporter,* I, 1–3.

[20] Frederick C. Hicks, "Kent's Commentaries," *Columbia Alumni News,* XIV, 369.

[21] Frederick C. Hicks, "Kent's Commentaries," *Columbia Alumni News,* XIV, 369. St. George Tucker had treated of American constitutional law in his edition of Blackstone (1803). There were, besides, Wilson's lectures (1804), Sergeant's *Constitutional Law* (1822) and the works of Taylor and Rawle (1823 and 1825). Another work that should be cited, the first American law text, is Zephaniah Swift's *A System of the Laws of the State of Connecticut* (1795–1796) in two volumes; see also Nathan Dane's *General Abridgement and Digest of American Law,* 1823–1824 and 1829. But Dane only summarized statutes and decisions. The following references are to the 12th edition of the *Commentaries* edited by Oliver W. Holmes, Jr., and will be cited simply as *Commentaries.*

the law of nations, a treatise on the constitutional jurisprudence of the American Union, an investigation of the sources, both English and Roman, of the municipal law of the several states; and of the chief divisions of that law, the rights of persons and the rights of property, personal and real, it comprehended a discussion even more searching and elaborate than the others.[22] Yet even here, where technicalities the most abounded, the language continued to be lucid and urbane. As the commentator's old friend, John Cotton Smith, was pleased to observe, it amused and instructed at the same time, and through what he called its *curiosa felicitas* made even such matters as executory devises and contingent remainders not only clear but captivating.[23]

This admirable work the author dedicated to the man who had reported his decisions in the Supreme Court and in the Court of Chancery.[24] As he perused it, Johnson had no difficulty in recognizing the old familiar features of Kent's juridical thought; for though the commentator dealt not alone with the municipal law of New York as the judge had usually done, yet the tendency of both his literary and judicial labors was the same. The same strong, conservative doctrine that had appeared in the *Reports* emerged also from the *Commentaries*.

Kent held the antiquity of a legal system to be in itself some evidence of its soundness. "In the just language of Sir Matthew Hale," as he said in discussing the sources of the municipal jurisprudence of the American states, "the common law of England is 'not the product of the vision of some one man or

[22] *Commentaries*, Parts i, ii, iii, iv, v and vi respectively.

[23] John Cotton Smith to James Kent, September 14, 1830. *Kent Papers*, Vol. VI. Smith was the Governor of Connecticut, 1813–1817. *D. A. B.*, XVII, 300. A modern authority agrees with Smith that Kent, "has a precision and a charm seldom found in expository writing for students of law." Thomas R. Powell, "Kent's Contributions to Constitutional Law," *Columbia Alumni News*, XIV, 373.

[24] Preface to *Commentaries*. Johnson had dedicated his chancery reports to Kent.

society of men in any one age; but of the wisdom, counsel, experience and observation of many ages of wise and observing men.' "[25] Revealing his own distrust of systems created by sudden fiat, Kent further observed that Sir Matthew's other remarks upon the subject "would be well worthy the consideration of those bold projectors who can think of striking off a perfect code of law at a single essay."[26] With approval, then, he quoted that famous oracle as declaring: "Where the subject of any law is single the prudence of one age may go far at one essay to provide a fit law; and yet, even in the wisest provisions of that kind, experience shows us that new and unthought of emergencies often happen that necessarily require new supplements, abatements or explanations. But the body of laws that concern the common justice applicable to a great kingdom is vast and comprehensive, consists of infinite particulars and must meet with various emergencies, and therefore requires much time and much experience as well as much wisdom and prudence successively to discover defects and inconveniences, and to apply apt supplements and remedies for them; and such are the common laws of England, namely the production of much wisdom, time and experience."[27]

[25] *Commentaries,* Part iii, Lect. xxi, 471–472. In the 1830's and '40's codification was being widely advocated. Kent was opposed to it. See his criticism of Edward Livingston's penal code for Louisiana in a letter from himself to Livingston, undated, but published in *American Jurist,* XVI, 370. This shows Kent's conservatism admirably. "I have no doubt you will . . . wonder at my lagging so far behind the spirit of the age. My apology is to be found . . . in the fact that I have spent the best years of my life in administering the old common law of the land . . . *with all its imperfections on its head.* I have likewise imbibed from the stupendous events of the French Revolution . . . an aversion to innovation, except by cautious steps. These are some of the reasons . . . why you will find me standing so firmly upon the old ground—*super antiquas vias.*" He criticizes Livingston's code for its leniency to criminals, its want of liberal discretion in the judges—and generally, because it is a code. He says, "I think Lord Hardwicke or Lord Mansfield or Burke or Pitt possessed ten times as much practical good sense and sound wisdom as William Godwin or Jeremy Bentham."

[26] *Commentaries,* Part iii, Lect. xxi, 471–473.

[27] *Loc. cit.*

This ancient system which he thus praised in the words of Sir Matthew Hale, Kent was happy to proclaim the common jurisprudence of the United States brought by the colonists from England and "established here *so far* as it was adapted to our institutions and circumstances.[28] . . . It fills up," said he, "every interstice and occupies every wide space which the statute law cannot occupy. Its principles may be compared to the influence of the liberal arts and sciences; *adversis perfugium ac solacium praebent, delectant domi, non impediunt foris, pernoctant nobiscum, peregrinantur, rusticantur,*—we live in the midst of the common law; we inhale it at every breath, imbibe it at every pore; we meet with it when we wake and when we lie down to sleep, when we travel and when we stay at home; and it is interwoven with the very idiom that we speak and we cannot learn another system of laws, without at the same time, another language." [29]

Of other systems, Kent was partial to the Roman which he admitted had exerted a profound influence upon the development of the common law of England. He had himself when sitting as a judge hearkened with benefit to the civilians, had stated from the bench that in the absence of English decisions he was willing to be guided by the wisdom of the "foreign jurists"; and he had gone so far upon occasion as to concede the superior justice of a civil maxim, although, following what he considered the path of his duty, he had adopted the English rule.[30] As a commentator, he enjoyed a larger freedom to praise the Roman jurisprudence, of which he observed that "upon subjects relating to private rights and personal contracts and the duties which flow from them there is no system of law in which principles are investigated with more good sense, or

[28] *Commentaries,* Part ii, Lect. xvi, 343–344.

[29] *Loc. cit.* The paraphrase was Duponceau's from his treatise on jurisdictions.

[30] Thorne and Thorne v. Deas, 4 *Johns. Rep.* 97.

declared and enforced with more accurate and impartial justice." [31] But though the system lacked uniform excellence, Kent recommended it in its entirety to the consideration of the student. "The whole body of the civil law," he said, "will excite never failing curiosity and receive the homage of scholars as a singular monument of wisdom. It fills such a large space in the eye of human wisdom; it regulates so many interests of man as a social and civilized being; it embodies so much thought, reflection, experience and labor; it leads us so far into the recesses of antiquity and it has stood so long 'against the waves and weathers of time' that it is impossible while engaged in the contemplation of the system not to be struck with some portion of the awe and veneration which are felt in the midst of the solitude of a majestic ruin." [32]

In one very important aspect, however, Kent held the civil law far inferior to that which Americans had inherited from their English ancestors. "The value of the civil law," said he, "is not to be found in questions which relate to the connection between the government and the people, or in provisions for personal security in criminal cases. In everything which concerns civil and political liberty it cannot be compared with the free spirit of the English and American common law." [33] This peculiar superiority of Anglo-American jurisprudence Kent had alluded to as a judge; in doing the same as a commentator he examined one by one and approved the barriers which that law had thrown about the rights of the individual to protect them from the abuse of power by government; [34] but no rights thus protected moved him to such eloquence as did the rights of property.

To this intricate subject he devoted the greater part of his

[31] *Commentaries,* Part iii, Lect. xxiii, 547–548.
[32] *Ibid.,* 548 *et seq.*
[33] *Ibid.,* 547.
[34] *Ibid.,* Part iv *passim.*

treatise. How far he would go in the justification of property he had already indicated when dealing with the rights of persons, not as toward government, but as toward one another in their private relations. He had at that time taken occasion, in discussing the subject of master and servant, to express his sentiments upon the institution of chattel-slavery in the south. As a man who prided himself upon having been throughout his life an "intrepid guardian of good old English common law liberty" Kent might well have been expected to offer no excuse whatever for property in human beings. He knew that the common law, since the case of Sommersett, had rejected that institution. He remarked that the presence of slavery in the republics of antiquity "cannot but diminish very considerably our sympathy with their spirit and our reverence for their institutions." [35] Nevertheless, he refused to be carried away by the tide of indignation rising against slavery in his own country. There the slaves were of a distinct race, and Kent could not bring himself to believe that they deserved a much better status. "The African race," he noted, "even when free are essentially a degraded caste. . . ." [36] Conformably with that view he couched his criticism of slavery in moderate terms. After summarizing the slave codes of the South, he concluded that they were "doubtless as just and mild as is deemed by those governments to be compatible with the public safety or with the existence and preservation of that species of property. . . . The great principle of self-preservation doubtless demands, on the part of the white population dwelling in the midst of such combustible materials, unceasing vigilance and firmness. . . ." [37] Kent granted that slavery was an evil,[38] cleared the contemporary generation of responsibility for it,[39]

[35] *Commentaries*, Part iv, Lect. xxxii, 250.
[36] *Ibid.*, 258 note (a).
[37] *Ibid.*, 253–254.
[38] *Loc. cit.*
[39] *Loc. cit.*

criticized the activities of the abolitionists [40] and believed that the South "ought to be let alone, and [that] time, self-interest and reflection will gradually undermine domestic slavery in these states, as it has done in New York. . . ." [41]

If Kent could thus tolerate property in persons, what his attitude would be toward property in things can be readily conceived. Upon this theme he waxed eloquent. "There have been modern theorists," he wrote, "who have considered separate and exclusive property and inequalities of property as the cause of injustice and the unhappy result of government and artificial institutions." This heresy he mentioned but to reject, for said he, "human society would be in a most unnatural and miserable condition if it were possible to be instituted or reorganized upon the basis of such speculations." Denying the possibility of such a thing, he proceeded to sing the praises of the institution. "The sense of property," he declared, "is graciously bestowed on mankind for the purpose of rousing them from sloth, and stimulating them to action; and so long as the right of acquisition is exercised in conformity to the social relations and the moral obligations which spring from them, it ought to be sacredly protected. The natural and active sense of property pervades the foundations of social improvement. It leads to the cultivation of the earth, the institution of government, the establishment of justice, the acquisition of the comforts of life, the growth of the useful arts, the spirit of commerce, the productions of taste, the erections of charity and the display of the benevolent affections." [42]

[40] James Kent to Moss Kent, Jr., October 7, 1833. *Kent Papers,* Vol. VII.

[41] James Kent to William E. Channing, April 18, 1842. *American Historical Review,* XXXVII, 520–521. Kent further says, "I do not believe that a sudden and general abolition would be expedient or wise." He was for tolerating slavery in the states where it was "and not a foot beyond except so far as we are bound by the Constitution of the United States to surrender fugitives." *Loc. cit.*

[42] *Commentaries,* Part v, Lect. xxxiv, 319. Of the modern theorists whom Kent had in mind as believing property to be the source of social injustice,

Lest these benefits be abridged, the commentator was careful to prescribe narrow bounds to the government's power of regulating the use of property in the hands of owners.[43] He did not deny that such a power was necessary but the exercise of it he reserved for extraordinary occasions, and the limitations he placed upon it were entirely conventional [44] as though the new era in transportation and in industry which was already beginning to dawn required nothing more drastic or novel.[45] To be sure, Kent recognized the power of the state to promote the comfort and convenience of its citizens; but it was a power which he was reluctant to interpret liberally, lest it be used by faction to invade the sacrosanct domain of chartered rights and vested interests.[46]

For the rights of labor Kent showed little concern. Perhaps his somewhat cavalier treatment of the subject may be pardoned on the ground that industrial laborers, as a class, were still comparatively few and that their problems did not as yet loom large in the life of the nation. Those problems, however, were already in the shaping, as Kent himself had had the opportunity to observe in the summer of 1823 when visiting

---

Rousseau was one of the most conspicuous. J. J. Rousseau "Discours de l'inégalité parmi les hommes," p. 66 of *Contrat Social* (Classiques Garnier).

[43] *Ibid.*, 339–340.

[44] Public authority could destroy houses near a conflagration to check the spreading of the flames; could abate a nuisance, permit a passenger without trespass to go through a private close when the highway was out of repair, could take property by eminent domain, etc. See *Commentaries*, Part v, Lect. xxxiv, 339–340. For cases in which Kent as judge protected the rights of property see Gardner v. Newburgh, 2 *Johns. Ch.* 161, Croton Turnpike Road Company v. Ryder, 1 *Johns. Ch.* 101. Gardner v. Newburgh is noticed with approval in "Restrictions upon the State Power in Relation to Private Property," *United States Law Intelligencer and Review*, I, 94 *et seq.*

[45] A letter from Henry Pirtle of Louisville, Kentucky to Kent, December 11, 1838, refers to the problem to which technical improvements were already giving rise: "The landmarks between the private rights of the citizen and the powers of the state are fast sweeping away by the rush of new modes of internal improvement—very useful to be sure, but how favorable to the spirit of liberty waits to be proved." *Kent Papers*, Vol. IX.

[46] See below, his comments on the Charles River Bridge Case.

the commonwealth of Massachusetts. He had seen there other sights than academic processions and had heard other sounds than the speeches and applause at academic banquets. He had visited not only Cambridge but also Waltham where he had heard the whirring of machinery in a cotton mill and had seen some three hundred persons, "mostly females," as he said, at work.[47] If it ever occurred to him that their situation, or the situation of laborers in general, rendered them liable to be exploited, his *Commentaries* offer no evidence of the fact. In his treatment of the conditions of free labor there was nothing that suggested his mild and temperate criticism of chattel slavery. That women and children would be required to work long hours in factories he seems to have taken for granted; and the harsh statutes which dealt with the indenturing of infants he reviewed complacently.[48] Upon the fellow servant rule he touched briefly without taking cognizance of the injustices it was capable of inflicting.[49] So far as the regulation of wages by public authority was concerned, he condemned it as pernicious and relegated it to the same category as sumptuary measures which "if, of any efficacy, are calculated to destroy the stimulus to exertion." [50] Such views may strike the modern reader as antiquated, if not, worse. They seem, however, to have been the conventional views of the time; and as Professor Commons has pointed out, the judges in those days were generally indifferent to the claims of labor, if not actually hostile.[51] Kent would have been out of character had he advocated reforms here or elsewhere.

Needless to say, he would have viewed with extreme distaste

[47] *Kent Journal*, August 30, 1823.

[48] *Commentaries*, Part iv, Lect. xxxii. "Of Master and Servant" *passim*. The law sometimes made the infant liable to imprisonment if he refused to work. *Ibid.*, 263 *et seq.*

[49] *Ibid.*, 260 and note (b) at end of note.

[50] *Ibid.*, Part v, Lect. xxxiv, 330 note (b).

[51] John R. Commons, *History of Labour in the United States*, I, 405–407.

those modern refinements of policy whereby the rich are taxed to subsidize the poor. His attitude in the Council of Revision foreshadowed that which as commentator he was to adopt upon the subject of taxation. "Every person," said he, "is entitled to be protected from all unequal and undue assessments on the part of government"; [52] and, in language reminiscent of his experience in the council, he went on to complain of measures, which in the name of promoting the equality of citizens, discriminated by means of taxation against the lands of non-resident proprietors.[53] Indeed, as he insisted again and again, the ideal of economic equality is delusive. "A state of equality as to property is impossible to be maintained," he repeated, "for it is against the laws of our nature, and if it could be reduced to practice, it would place the human race in a state of tasteless enjoyment and stupid inactivity which would degrade the mind and destroy the happiness of social life." [54] It might be objected that if the inequalities of property were to be allowed to accentuate themselves unceasingly, the liberty of citizens in general would be exposed to the caprice of a small but opulent aristocracy, which possessing a preponderance of economic power would be in a strategic position to bend political institutions to its will. This danger was apprehended by Democrats. Kent, on the other hand, chose to consider it negligible. "Liberty," he said, "depends essentially upon the structure of the government, the administration of justice and the intelligence of the people, and it has very little concern with equality of property. . . ." [55]

This doctrine is somewhat surprising when viewed in relation to the author's comments upon the English land law as it had been modified to conform to American desires. In no

[52] *Commentaries,* Part v, Lect. xxxiv, 331.
[53] *Ibid.,* 332.
[54] *Ibid.,* Part v, Lect. xxxiv, 328–329.
[55] *Ibid.,* 330

branch of municipal jurisprudence had the departure from English usage been so radical as here; and though Kent professed to stand *super antiquas vias,* upon the whole he approved the transformation.[56] The law of America, as described by him, was favorable to a wide diffusion of ownership; and in furtherance of that policy, regarded land as a less dignified species of property than did the law of England. In some respects it assimilated land to chattels. It made it liable equally with the personal estate for the debts of an ancestor.[57] While at common law, a creditor might only hold his debtor's lands in trust until the debts should be discharged from the rents and profits, the American law gave him satisfaction by rendering the land liable to the same execution as the personal estate.[58] These alterations, though significant, yet indicate but slightly the direction which the divergence of the land law in America was taking from its parent stock.

The simpler methods of conveying and alienating real property which were prevalent in America, evinced more strikingly the disposition to stimulate its rapid circulation. The seisin of land could pass with the mere delivery of a deed;[59] nor was it necessary in every state that the deed should bear a seal.[60] As for restraints upon alienation, the commentator

[56] Though he regretted the passing of the rule in Shelley's case, which, observed in the Supreme Court during his tenure (Brant v. Gelston, 2 *Johns. Cases* 384), had been abolished by the revised statutes. Kent's objection was in part, that abrogating the rule increased, contrary to the usual American policy, "the fetters on alienation." He was ". . . scarce able to withhold an involuntary sigh . . ." at the passing of the rule. *Ibid.*, Part vi, Lect. lix, 233, note (a).

[57] *Ibid.*, Part vi, Lect. lxv, 429.

[58] *Commentaries,* Part vi, Lect. lxvi, 429. "Of title by execution." However, as Kent had said in chancery, personal property was, by American law, still the primary fund as a rule, for the payment of debts.

[59] *Ibid.*, Part vi, Lect. lxvii, 461–462, 490.

[60] *Ibid.*, 453. Kent did not approve the use of a scrawl for a seal. A complete account of the changes made in the old common law as to land would require a treatise in itself. Only a few of the more significant ones can be indicated here. The changes are summarized by the *London Law Magazine,*

observed that it was the general policy to discourage them,[61] a policy which had in large measure been effectuated by the device of turning estates tail into estates in fee simple which the owners, as a matter of course, could alien freely.[62] Entailed estates, said Kent, could be recommended as the means of

---

VI, 153 *et seq.* (1831), and they are approved there with the exception of the abolition of tithes, of primogeniture, of the preference of males, and of male stocks in descents. These are the notable changes summarized by that journal:

a. Feudal tenures (including socage) abolished. Cf. *Commentaries,* Part vi, Lect. liii, 488.
b. Primogeniture and preference of males abolished. Cf. *Ibid.,* Part vi, Lect. lxv, 382–384.
c. Preference of male stocks in descents abolished. Cf. *Ibid.,* 406.
d. The making in America of all estates descend in the same course, whether got by purchase or by descent from paternal or maternal ancestors. Cf. *Ibid.,* 405–406. This was not universally done, however. *Loc. cit.*
e. Taking by the rule *per capita* rather than that *per stirpes.* Cf. *Ibid.,* 390–391.
f. Exclusion of the half-blood abolished. Cf. *Ibid.,* 412.
g. Enabling parents in America to become heirs of their children. Cf. *Ibid.,* 393 *et seq.* See general summary as to inheritance laws *ibid.,* 412.
h. Making seisin of land pass by the delivery of a deed. Cf. *Ibid.,* Part vi, Lect. lxvii, 461–462.
i. Enabling tenants in tail to convey in fee-simple without fine or recovery. Cf. *Ibid.,* Part vi, Lect. liv, 17–20.
j. Abolition of doctrine of tacking in mortgages. Cf. *Ibid.,* Part vi, Lect. lviii, 176–178.
k. General registry of deeds in America. Cf. *Ibid.,* Part vi, Lect. lxvii, 456–460.
l. Making all real estate liable to execution for debt, and having it sold on execution, like personal property. Cf. *Ibid.,* Part vi, Lect. lxvi, 429.
m. Rendering real estate assets for payments of all debts without preference. Cf. *Ibid.,* Part vi, Lect. lxvii, 430 *et seq.*
n. Changing of joint tenancies into tenancies in common. Cf. *Ibid.,* Part vi, Lect. lxiv, 360–361, 368.
o. Enabling married women to convey estates and bar their dower without a fine. Cf. *Ibid.,* Part vi, Lect. lv, 60.
p. Abolition of tithes.

[61] *Commentaries,* Part vi, Lect. liv, 17.

[62] *Ibid.,* 14–17.

protecting the power and influence of a landed aristocracy, "but such a policy," he added, "has no application to republican establishments where wealth does not form a distinction [and] every family, stripped of artificial supports is obliged . . . to repose upon the virtues of its descendants for the perpetuity of its fame." [63]

The observation was equally apposite as applied to the rule of primogeniture, a rule, in the author's opinion, "incompatible with that equality of right . . . which it is the constitutional policy of this country to preserve and inculcate." [64] It was a rule, which, like the law of tenures, derived from the Middle Ages; and like that law, it had wisely been done away as a result of the Revolution.[65] There were other provisions concerning inheritance which had been no more acceptable to Americans than primogeniture. Indeed, as Kent remarked, the distinguishing rules of the common-law doctrine of descents were the converse of those prevailing in the United States.[66] Here the preference of males, and of male stocks no longer obtained.[67] Here the half-blood was not excluded [68] and here the inheritance was no longer strictly *per stirpes*.[69] All these changes Kent applauded and that despite the fact that he considered beneficial the general principle of transmission through hereditary descent.[70] The faults with the old common law refinements upon that principle were that they limited inheritances excessively, kept property tied up, and

[63] *Ibid.*, 20.

[64] *Ibid.*, Part vi, Lect. lxv, 382.

[65] *Loc. cit.* For the author's notice of the abolition of feudal tenures *ibid.*, Part vi, Lect. liii, 488.

[66] *Ibid.*, Part vi, Lect. lxv, 412.

[67] *Loc. cit.*

[68] *Loc. cit.*

[69] *Loc. cit.*

[70] *Ibid.*, 376. Hereditary descent, he says, is "the dictate of the natural affections . . . which encourages paternal improvements, cherishes filial loyalty, cements domestic society. . . ."

were repugnant to the free institutions of a republic.[71] This view, while no doubt commendable in itself, would hardly seem to be logically deduced from the proposition that "liberty . . . has very little concern with equality of property." Apparently a subtle but significant relation did exist between them, and republican institutions throve or languished according to the manner in which property, at least in land, was permitted to circulate in a given society and to be distributed among many families or concentrated in a few.

Kent's frank approval of the peculiar principles of the land law in the United States shows that, regardless of his deference to English authority, he had retained certain characteristically American habits of thought. He would have been reluctant to concede that he harbored any ideas which resembled those of Thomas Jefferson; notwithstanding, the land law which he praised was such a law as Jefferson himself could not but have pronounced suitable for the basis of democracy.

If democracy was favored by the American doctrines of

[71] *Commentaries,* Part vi, Lect. lxv *passim.* How primogeniture, the preference of males and of male stocks operates to retain the mass of real estate in one family, or a few at most, is obvious. Less obvious is inheritance *per stirpes* followed in England but departed from, generally, in America. This can be more easily explained by diagram than otherwise:

A, dies leaving property to his heirs, thus

B—a son who has died C—another son who has died

X—sole child of B L M N O—four surviving children of C.

Thus, if A's heirs, here his five grandchildren, take *per stirpes,* they take according to the shares that their respective fathers would have taken, if surviving, *i.e.,* the children of B take one half, and the children of C take one half. But B has only one child X, who takes one half, whereas C has four children, L, M, N and O who take each one eighth only. The device keeps the property from being broken up into such small parcels as the rule *per capita,* which would have been applied in a similar situation in the United States. Thus, here, the five grandchildren, each being in an equal degree of kindred, would have inherited each one fifth. *Per stirpes* would have been followed here only where the heirs were in an unequal degree of kindred. *Ibid.,* Part vi, Lect. lxv, 390.

real property on the axiom that political influence proceeds from economic power, Kent should have handled them more cautiously, since the tendency which they encouraged he condemned. It is plausible to explain away this inconsistency by assuming it to have been his idea that ownership of property gives men a stake in the traditional social order; that hence, the more numerous the owners, the less their disposition to democratic change. Kent had implied a notion of that sort as a justice-in-eyre when contrasting to their advantage the substantial freeholders in the vicinity of Canandaigua with the squatters and demagogues in other places.[72] He had made observations in the same vein during the convention: "The great body of the people are now the owners . . . of the soil. . . . Their habits inspire them with a correct spirit of freedom and justice; they are the safest guardians of property and the laws. . . ." [73] That was an engaging theory; and if Kent was sincere in holding it, then the people should have given him no apprehension over their increasing political power. The theory, however, did not accord with all the facts. Freehold farmers had once supported Jefferson and were now supporting Jackson. Ownership, therefore, was no guarantee of orthodox principles; and Kent in lauding the policy of diffusing ownership contributed somewhat to the confirmation of principles which, from his point of view, were heretical.

But while owners of the soil, especially small freeholders, tended to be more democratic in politics than Kent could have wished, they were also more moderately democratic than they would have likely been had the policy of the law tied up real property and bound them to till the fields as tenants of a landed aristocracy. Class conflicts resulting from that situation would have been more bitter than they were, and the

[72] *Vide supra,* Ch. iv.

[73] *Reports of the Proceedings and Debates in the Convention of 1821,* 220.

democracy that Jackson led would have been more turbulent. To Kent it seemed turbulent enough; in an unprejudiced view, it indicated that his theory of the sobering effect of ownership was not entirely unsound. That the wealth of America consisted chiefly in land and that land through operation of law was widely distributed were factors in sparing the country, if not from democracy, then at least from the vindictive behavior which democracy had exhibited in Europe. They were factors also in saving it from the cruel retaliations which that behavior had inspired.

In spite of these favorable circumstances in its social situation, the country was only comparatively free from the political antagonism that grows out of economic cleavage. Kent as a student of the *Federalist* had long been aware of that antagonism; [74] he had remarked upon it as a judge,[75] prophesied about it as a member of the convention; as an author he alluded to it in the *Commentaries:* ". . . In the constant struggles," he wrote, "and jealous collisions between men of property and men of no property, the one to acquire and the other to preserve; and between debtor and creditor, the one to exact and the other to evade or postpone payment; it is to be expected, especially in popular governments and under the influence which the poor and unfortunate naturally excite that the impartial course of justice and the severe duties of the law-giver should in some degree be disturbed." [76] This danger, according to Kent, became the more formidable, as the tide of democracy, rising steadily through the several states, carried away one by one the checks which an older generation had devised to restrain the capricious will of the multitude.

That will made itself first felt in the legislative assemblies, and of these bodies the commentator evinced the same distrust

[74] Cf. *The Federalist,* No. X.

[75] Bayard v. Hoffman.

[76] *Commentaries,* Part v, Lect. xxxiv, 333, where the author is speaking of the Federal Constitution as a protection to the rights of property.

that he had shown in the Council of Revision. "They are presumed," he said, "to partake with a quicker sensibility of the prevailing temper and irritable disposition of the times and to be in much more danger of adopting measures with precipitation and of changing them with levity. A mutable legislation," he continued, "is attended with a formidable train of mischiefs to the community. It weakens the force and increases the intricacy of the laws, hurts credit, lessens the value of property and it is an infirmity very incident to republican establishments and has been a constant source of anxiety and concern to their most enlightened admirers. A disposition to multiply and change laws, upon the spur of the occasion, and to make constant and restless experiments with the statute code, seems to be the natural disease of popular assemblies." [77]

In writing these words Kent had in mind the national House of Representatives to membership in which he had once aspired. It had been that house which in company with Alexander Hamilton he had seen in its first session at the very beginning of the republic; and it may be imagined that the ghost of Hamilton haunted the commentator's study as he wrote. Be that as it may, it was good old-fashioned Federalist doctrine that he here set forth, and it was good old-fashioned Federalist faith in the strength and stability of the Senate that prompted him to conclude that after all the representatives could do but little harm. Unfortunately, in the state legislatures the senates, having been reconstituted upon more democratic principles, were less effective in resisting the democratic contagion. This change, and all the other constitutional changes which had resulted in the increase of the people's power Kent viewed with forebodings. "Such a rapid course of destruction of the former constitutional checks is matter for grave reflection," was his warning, and he made it clear that such reflection was

[77] *Commentaries,* Part ii. Lect. xi, 227.

disquieting: "To counteract the dangerous tendency of such combined forces as universal suffrage, frequent elections, all offices for short periods, all offices elective . . . and to prevent them from racking and destroying our political machines, the people must have a larger share than usual of that wisdom which is *first pure, then peaceable, gentle and easy to be entreated*." [78] In private Kent bluntly denied that the people possessed this larger share of wisdom, and as the Jacksonian democracy waxed in strength, he confided to Daniel Webster, "All theories of government that suppose the mass of the people virtuous and able, and willing to act virtuously are plainly Utopian and *will remain* so until the return of the Saturnian age." [79]

From the perversity of the populace communicating itself to the legislature, Kent sought his surest refuge in the courts of justice. To safeguard their independence had been one of his chief concerns while he occupied the New York bench. Since then, however, the state courts had been affected by the general democratic change in consequence of which he regarded them as no longer fully capable of the role that he thought it their highest duty to sustain. That role he defined in his characteristic fashion. It consisted in nothing less arduous than resistance to tyranny; and though the tyranny to be dreaded in America was something different from that which Sir Edward Coke had once withstood, yet it was equally oppressive. It was that same tyranny of the multitude which Kent had reflected upon when, during the days of the revolutionary disturbances in France, he had delivered his first series of lectures at Columbia College. Now, as then, now perhaps more certainly than then, he held fast to the conviction that majorities are fierce and pitiless, that they are prone to destroy, not only chartered rights, but the freedom of discussion and the independence of

[78] *Commentaries*, Part ii, Lect. xi, 229 note (a) at end of note.

[79] James Kent to Daniel Webster, January 21, 1830. *Kent Papers*, Vol. VI.

the mind.[80] Against these dangers of majority rule Kent interposed "an independent judiciary, venerable by its gravity, its dignity, and its wisdom"; [81] and for an example of such a judiciary he pointed to the Supreme Court of the United States under Chief Justice Marshall.[82]

In discussing the contributions with which that tribunal had enriched the constitutional law of the Union, Kent was gratified to find that the checks imposed by the federal instrument upon the legislatures both state and national had not only been preserved "with great steadiness and skill," but been increased in efficacy, and made thereby to furnish added protection to the rights of minorities, and especially to those of the propertied classes.[83] As an illustration of this he cited the case of Marbury v. Madison, and summarizing it with utmost satisfaction, he hailed the doctrine of judicial review there elaborated as "one of the most interesting points in favor of constitutional liberty and the security of property in this country that has ever been judicially determined." [84] But it was the power of Congress which that decision served to circumscribe; and from the acts of Congress, deliberated as they were by a senate removed from direct popular influence, less harm was to be expected than from those of legislatures in the several states. Here too, however, the Supreme Court through Marshall had established a strong safeguard in the doctrine of the Dartmouth College case, that "celebrated case," as the commentator called it, which "contains one of the most full and elaborate expositions of the constitutional sanctity of contracts to be met with in any of the reports. The decision in that case," he continued, "did more than any other single act proceeding from the authority of the United States, to throw

[80] *Commentaries,* Part ii, Lect. xiv, 294; Lect. xx, 450, note (a).
[81] *Ibid.,* Part iii, Lect. xx, 450.
[82] *Ibid.,* Part ii, *passim.*
[83] *Ibid.,* Part iii, Lect. xx, 454.
[84] *Loc. cit.*

an impregnable barrier around all the rights and franchises derived from the grant of government." [85]

But there was one great case which Marshall had decided that, contrary to his usual tendency, had resulted in the annulling of rights and franchises so derived. The long-protracted litigation over the New York steamboat monopoly was at last brought to an end just as Kent was weighing the project of the *Commentaries;* and as one might have predicted, he devoted much space in that work to a critical consideration of Gibbons v. Ogden, firmly defending the soundness of his view [86] that the issue of a mere coasting license fell short of that exertion of the paramount power of Congress in interstate commerce before which New York was bound to retire from the support of her own law.[87] At the same time he made it clear that it was only concerning the interpretation and effect of the license that he and Marshall differed, that so far as the fundamental theory of congressional powers was concerned they had seen eye to eye.[88] In spite, then, of their difference of opinion on the effect of the license, in spite of the consequence of Marshall's decision in terminating a franchise which the New York chancellor had long contended for, Kent announced his acquiescence in the Chief Justice's course, recognizing no doubt that it had been pursued in the general interests of that Union to which both were devoted.

Kent's praise of Marshall was the more impressive inasmuch as it was far from indiscriminate. But though he was critical, he could declare with perfect truth ". . . it has been my invariable disposition to inculcate a strong sentiment of defer-

[85] *Ibid.*, Part ii, Lect. xix, 418.

[86] Thomas R. Powell thinks Kent's view was the more reasonable and lawyer-like of the two. *Vide* "Kent's Contributions to Constitutional Law" *Columbia Alumni News*, XIV, 373.

[87] *Commentaries*, Part ii, Lect. xix, 432–438.

[88] *Ibid.*, 438.

ence and respect for the judicial authorities of the Union." [89] Having completed his review of the progress of our constitutional law as recorded in the pages of Cranch and Wheaton, he observed, "There are several important constitutional questions which remain yet to be settled; but if we recur back to the judicial annals of the United States since the year 1800, we shall find that many of the most interesting discussions which had arisen and which were of a nature to affect deeply the tranquillity of the nation have auspiciously terminated. The national jurisprudence has been growing and improving ever since, and it has now become a solid and magnificent structure, and seems destined, at no very distant period of time, to cast a shade over the less elevated and perhaps we must add the less attractive and ambitious system of justice in the several states." [90] At this prospect Kent was not disturbed. "I cannot," said he, "conceive of anything more grand and imposing in the whole administration of human justice than the spectacle of the Supreme Court sitting in solemn judgement upon the conflicting claims of the national and state sovereignties and tranquillizing all jealous and angry passions, and binding together this great confederacy of states in peace and harmony, by the ability, the moderation and the equity of its decisions." [91]

The generation that first read these memorable words may well have admired the author's eloquence, and like the author, they may have been able to conceive nothing more sublime than the spectacle to which he alluded. But to many that spectacle must have appeared like the dissolving fabric of a dream. For at the time when Kent completed the first edition of his *Commentaries*,[92] state pride was already preparing to bid de-

[89] *Ibid.*, 440.
[90] *Commentaries*, Part ii, Lect. xix, 444.
[91] *Loc.* cit.
[92] *I.e.*, 1830, James Kent to Moss Kent, Jr., September 11, 1829. *Kent*

fiance to that same judicial authority for which he had striven to inculcate strong sentiments of deference and respect. To overawe that defiance, the Supreme Court relied principally upon the power of logic and persuasion; but as Chief Justice Marshall's unfortunate experience with Georgia in the Cherokee cases was soon to prove, such a power operated without effect upon a state inflexibly determined to have its own way.[93] In the still more resolute opposition to the national government offered by the commonwealth of South Carolina, even less encouraging was the possibility of the court's sitting in judgement on the conflicting claims of the state and national sovereignties, and by the wisdom of its decisions, tranquillizing all jealous and angry passions and binding together the confederacy in harmony and peace. As Kent's contemporaries read his discourse on John Marshall, they must have more than once closed up the book to listen in anxiety to the deep and ominous rumblings of thunder from the south.

Those rumblings were neither unheard nor unheeded by Kent himself. He had friends and admirers as well in South Carolina as in Massachusettes; and among them was Chancellor De Saussure, who informing him of the state of opinion at Charleston, expressed the general abhorrence of the protective tariff and admitted that secession was preferred to a continued suffering of injustice and tyranny.[94] Though the chancellor, like other Carolinians, declared his attachment to the Union,[95] and made much of the Federal Constitution, it was clear that he had his own views concerning the nature of that instrument and that those views did not precisely correspond with the views of Kent who held that the ultimate arbiter of

---

Papers, Vol. VI, the author says he is preparing his fourth volume for the press.

[93] Albert J. Beveridge, *The Life of John Marshall*, IV, Ch. x *passim*.

[94] Henry DeSaussure to James Kent, August 4, 1831. *Kent Papers*, Vol VI.

[95] Henry DeSaussure to James Kent, November 4, 1830. *Ibid.*

constitutional questions was the federal government itself speaking through the Supreme Court.[96] This doctrine beginning to be regarded as heresy in South Carolina hardly recommended the *Commentaries* to the unqualified admiration of men in that state. Doctor Thomas Cooper wrote to inform the author that he would use his work as a college textbook, but that in his lectures he would take occasion to differ from him on the subject of constitutional law.[97] In that field of jurisprudence, the Carolinians had a native authority in John C. Calhoun who proposed to make the states themselves the ultimate arbiters of their constitutional rights. He had favored Kent with one of his pamphlets on the subject; [98] and Kent had read it with close attention. "It is ingeniously written," he remarked to Webster, "but such a construction of the constitution and such principles as he deduces are visionary and most unsound and sophistical. His repugnance to all solid constitutional principles would fix a deadly power of destruction in the very vitals of the government." [99]

However it appeared to a lawyer of Kent's principles, the doctrine of Calhoun was destined to become popular through the south. The situation was not without its irony. The power and the primacy of the Federal Union, which Kent steadily upheld as the surest means of protecting the interests of the

[96] This is implied throughout Part ii of the *Commentaries*. Kent, in one of his last judicial utterances, had stated the same view with great emphasis. *Vide* Hicks v. Hotchkiss, 7 *Johns. Ch.* 313–314.

[97] Thomas Cooper to James Kent, December 1, 1833. *Kent Papers*, Vol. VII.

[98] James Kent to Daniel Webster, October 31, 1832. *Ibid.*, Vol. VI. The pamphlet is Calhoun's letter to Governor Hamilton in defense of nullification. Webster proposed to reply to Calhoun in the form of a letter addressed to Kent, and he gained Kent's permission for it. *Vide supra,* and also Daniel Webster to James Kent, October 29, 1832. *Ibid.*, Vol. VI. Kent in his letter granting permission speaks of the nullification crisis as "portentous and frightful."

[99] James Kent to Daniel Webster, October 31, 1832. *Kent Papers*, Vol. VI.

propertied classes against assault by the states, were through the teachings of Calhoun now challenged by a class whose sense of property was the keenest to be met with anywhere upon the continent and whose vast possessions in lands and slaves furnished them the base whereon to build that edifice of aristocracy for which their pride of stock and lineage gave them a natural predilection. By them the Union itself was regarded as dangerous to the rights of property. It levied duties upon them which they sincerely believed discriminating and hurtful; and if it had the power of depriving them of their property thus indirectly, well might they question how long it would be ere the self-same Union would resort to methods more direct, and under the pretense of a moral crusade and with the support of an aggressive democracy seek to strip them of that peculiar form of property upon which they conceived the foundations of their social order to rest. Thus were they impelled to calculate the value of the Union; nor could they be blamed too harshly if they found Kent's calculations false. To them it was becoming more clear each day that the Union in no single department of its government was affording them that protection of property interest in which Kent had proclaimed that its principal usefulness consisted. Indeed, while the ink of the *Commentaries* was still fresh, Kent expressed his own doubts concerning that very advantage. Radical democracy which once had operated for the most part within the limits of the states, had now become national; and it had elevated to the presidency a man whom Kent described "as a detestable, ignorant, reckless, vain and malignant tyrant." [100] Toward chartered privileges this tyrant displayed an inveterate hostility. Disregarding the famous decision of McCulloch v. Maryland on the constitutionality of the United States Bank, a decision which the *Commentaries* highly praised, he had presumed to set himself up as an authority on jurisprudence

[100] James Kent to Joseph Story, April 11, 1834. *Story Papers.*

and to declare, in vetoing the bill for the rechartering of that bank, that such an institution was not countenanced by the fundamental law. Not satisfied with that, he had gone further, and before the old charter had yet expired, had sought to destroy the bank by ordering the removal of the federal funds from its vaults. Worst crime of all, that secretary of the treasury who had been his agent in the act, was raised to the bench of the Supreme Court to succeed Chief Justice Marshall.

For Taney, the new Chief Justice, James Kent had only scorn. "I can never think well of a man who consented to do what his predecessor thought it dishonest to do," he wrote to Story, "that is, remove the United States Bank deposits to gratify the malignant persecutions of a savage despot and in palpable violation of contract." [101] From Kent's point of view, Taney's judicial career was even more calamitous than he had expected. It seemed to him that Taney was trying to undo the work of Marshall by throwing down those barriers which the Dartmouth College case and Craig v. Missouri had raised against attacks on property. There was no doubt that constitutional law was undergoing a change, that it was being modified to conform more closely to the wishes of the people, and the evidence of this was the liberality with which the new court was interpreting the clauses that forbade the states to emit bills of credit and to impair the obligations of contracts.[102] Those changes Kent deplored, and to Story, now in a minority in the court, he expressed his resentment freely, "I have just now finished a careful and studied perusal of the second volume of Peters's reports," wrote he, "and I cannot avoid venting my grief and mortification *in confidence* to you. It appears to me that the court has fallen from its high station

[101] James Kent to Joseph Story, June 17, 1845. *Ibid.*

[102] Briscoe v. Bank of Kentucky and the Charles River Bridge case are referred to. For the Bridge Case in the Massachusetts Courts, *vide* 7 Pickering 396 *et seq.*

and commanding dignity, and has lost its energy and spirit, and independence and accuracy, and surrendered up to the tempter of the day the true principles of the constitution." [103] Continuing, he paid his respects especially to the Charles River Bridge case which he said he had reperused "and with increased disgust." [104] The decision there which had generously construed the power of the state to promote the comfort and convenience of its citizens albeit at the expense of vested rights, Kent roundly criticized as ignoring "the moral scruple of the community" and destroying "the sanctity of contracts." [105] He went on to observe, "if the legislature can quibble away or whittle away its contracts with impunity the people will be free to follow. *Quicquid delirant reges plectuntur Achivi.* I abhor the doctrine that the legislature is not bound by anything that is necessarily implied in a contract in order to give it effect and value, and by nothing that is not expressed *in hoc verbo.* Not one rule of interpretation is to be applied to their engagements and another rule to the contracts of individuals." [106]

The decision in which Taney had held that a state successfully evaded the prohibition to emit bills of credit, if it had taken the precaution to emit them, not directly by its own authority, but by the intermediation of a bank, Kent considered to be quite as distressing as the decision in the bridge case.[107] "It absolutely overwhelms me in despair," he said, "I think that decision is monstrous. It is a collision with the case of Craig in the state of Missouri. If the bills of the Bank of Kentucky formed as that bank was, and with these bills a tender on execution in payment under a penalty for refusing to take them, [if these] be not *bills of credit* emitted by and

[103] James Kent to Joseph Story, June 23, 1837. *Story Papers.*
[104] *Loc. cit.*
[105] *Loc. cit.*
[106] *Loc. cit.*
[107] Briscoe v. Bank of Kentucky.

under the authority of the state and within the intendment of the constitution I don't know what would be." [108] Neither, no doubt, in their hearts did the Jacksonian Democrats, but they rejoiced nevertheless in having gained their desire for cheaper money and preserved the decent constitutional forms at the same time. With such casuistry Kent was impatient. "I have lost my confidence and hopes in the constitutional guardianship and protection of the Supreme Court. *I respect it no longer,*" [109] he declared, and a few years later, when Story in despair descended from the bench, he wrote in even stronger terms of condemnation: "I would not sit on that bench for all the world! I do not regard their decisions with much reverence, and for a number of the associates I feel habitual scorn and contempt." [110] The great days of Marshall were gone forever. "Now," cried Kent in tones of lamentation, "now we feel with a pang the loss of Marshall. Now we sadly realize that we are to be under the reign of little men—a pigmy race and that the sages of the last age are extinguished." [111]

It was small wonder that Kent was discouraged at the course which politics and law were taking. That course appeared opposite to all that he had stood and striven for throughout his life. And now as he brought forth in his *Commentaries* the ripe counsels of his experience, events seemed to conspire to deprive those counsels of their influence. He had advocated the cause of federal Union and the Union had all but dissolved before his eyes. He had identified that Union with the interests of the propertied class by whom it had been established. A rival faction, however, had risen to power, a faction which devoted its energies to perverting the institutions that he had most extolled. Dominated by democracy, even the Union lost somewhat of its wonted charm.

[108] James Kent to Joseph Story, June 23, 1837. *Story Papers.*
[109] *Loc. cit.*
[110] James Kent to Joseph Story, June 17, 1845. *Ibid.*
[111] James Kent to Joseph Story, June 23, 1837. *Ibid.*

Nor was it only in the large social and political aspects that the tendency of the time seemed to go counter to Kent's teaching. Innovations not only in the law itself but in the methods of administering it made him apprehensive over the future of the legal system which he had contributed to establish in his own state. In the year 1846, a convention met at Albany to propose further changes in the constitution. Its programme, summarized by Kent,[112] aimed to codify the common law,[113] abolish the independent chancery, facilitate admission to the bar and make the bench elective. Generally successful in accomplishing its purposes, the convention reflected the age in nothing more clearly than in its attitude toward equity and the common law. To the old chancellor it appeared bent on damaging, if not ruining, both. It seemed determined to impair thereby the value of his own judicial labors.

Moreover, Kent believed there was cause for further anxiety in the condition of the bar. If his opinion on this matter was exaggerated, it was at least held by others who were as well qualified as he to know.[114] It probably is true that the quality of the profession had not kept pace with its increasing numbers. Considering many of the more recent practitioners inferior, Kent was convinced that their presence in the forum diminished its dignity; and anything which might encourage their ambition he refused to countenance. When one of his proof-readers asked why it would not be better for both lawyer and client if all Latin phrases were in English, he replied, "It's all right; we don't want every man to be his own lawyer, and he could not be, even if all the Latin was in the plainest possible English. What kind of legal protection would you have if every man could be a lawyer? All things are changing, it is true, but when you find law made easy to the meanest compre-

[112] James Kent to William Kent, July 16, 1846. *Kent Papers*, Vol. X.
[113] *Loc. cit.*
[114] *Law Reporter*, VI, 286–287.

hension, look out for countless volunteers in our noble profession, to whom good Latin and correct English are alike inaccessible." [115] Against the influence of such volunteers Kent warned his legal brethren to be vigilant. Addressing the Law Association of New York City in the autumn of 1836,[116] he contrasted the conditions of the day with the better state of affairs that prevailed when men of distinguished talents, like Alexander Hamilton, had led the bar; held up Hamilton and his colleagues as examples of what barristers should be, exhorted his hearers to emulate them and to have a care for "the honor of the professional reputation." That this advice bore fruit Kent had reason to doubt. The kind of lawyer whom he wished to see copied was apparently not in favor, at least for the time being. A revised edition of the *Commentaries* had hardly left the press, when Story, writing to acknowledge receipt of it, informed the author that President Tyler had declared "he never would appoint a Judge of the school of Kent." [117]

Notwithstanding the chagrin which that announcement doubtless caused him, Kent must have perceived that the situation was not wholly comfortless. Strong as the winds of adverse doctrine might blow, they could not beat down the legal tradition which he stood for. Against some of its external bulwarks they might indeed prevail. That happened in New York with the abolition of a separate court of equity. In his calmer moments, however, Kent was well aware that chancery could not be done away merely by doing away with the post of chancellor. The doctrines of the court were indispensable, though the court itself was not. "They must exist somewhere. It is impossible to do without them in a civilized community and if equity be not assigned to a distinct tribunal it will

[115] William Kent, *Letters and Memoirs of James Kent*, 199–200.

[116] James Kent, *Address to the Law Association of New York City*, October 21, 1836.

[117] Joseph Story to James Kent, April 25, 1844. *Story Papers*.

shoot out and intwine on a common law stock." [118] This was Kent's considered opinion. He could be confident therefore, that the essential principles of equity would be perpetuated and that the courts, despite the blending of jurisdictions, would continue to rely on his own equity decisions for guidance.

Nor were his decisions at law likely to be ignored simply because the law was to be codified. An indispensable ingredient of the future code would be the principles laid down in Johnson's *Reports*. Though in theory the judges would no longer have the broad discretion of the common law judge, the device of a code would hardly nullify the common law influence in a state which a jurist like Kent had taught to cherish the legacy of Sir Matthew Hale. Experience would show in the future as it had done in the past "that new and unthought of emergencies often happen that necessarily require new supplements, abatements or explanations," and that "the body of laws that concern the common justice applicable to a great [commonwealth] is vast and comprehensive, consists of infinite particulars and must meet with various emergencies, and therefore requires much time and much experience as well as much wisdom and prudence successively to discover defects and inconveniences, and to supply apt supplements and remedies for them. . . ." This task of discovering defects and of applying remedies would remain committed to the courts, and in performing it, they could be counted upon to refine the code itself with numerous interpretations elaborated in the light of the learning of the bench where Kent had presided as Chief Justice.

If that jurist's fears to the contrary persisted, they should

[118] James Kent to Peter L. Duponceau, April 19, 1826. *Washburn Papers*. In the *Commentaries*, Kent treated law and equity side by side. In Roman law, equity was thought of as requiring no distinct court for its administration. Frederick C. Hicks, "Kent's Commentaries," *Columbia Alumni News*, XIV, 370.

have been at least compensated by his growing fame as an expounder of the common law tradition; albeit fame in foreign countries could contribute little to the defense of that tradition in his own. Nevertheless it was a source of satisfaction that, regardless of what the President of the United States might think of him, he was recognized in British America as a jurist whose doctrines deserved to be followed. The Recorder of Halifax in Nova Scotia informed him that the *Commentaries* were widely used as a textbook in that province.[119] Abroad he was favorably known in France and Germany; [120] in Great Britain he was admired. Upon returning from that country in 1845, Edward Everett wrote to Kent, "I was led to think that an estimate of your authority . . . had been formed in the House of Lords and in Westminster Hall, which might be called generous if it were not so entirely just"; and he admitted that he had often had recourse to the *Commentaries* to answer the questions which English public men had asked him concerning the law of the American states.[121] Everett's report was confirmed by those of others. "Yesterday," wrote George Bancroft, the American minister, "I passed the morning in the Queen's Bench. I sat by the side of Mr. Justice Coleridge. Lord Denman [122] paused in the business of the day and said to Sir J. Coleridge, 'Ask Mr. Bancroft after Chancellor Kent.' They were very particular and warm in their inquiries about you," continued the minister, "[and] I answered according to the best of my knowledge, and at once resolved to tell you of the interest felt in you by the eminent lawyers of England. Be very sure that that lucid mind which has gained for you such a name in America has also won

[119] Alexander Stewart to James Kent, September 27, 1847. *Kent Papers*, Vol. XI.

[120] Mittermeier of Heidelberg to James Kent, June 15, 1841. *Ibid.*, Vol. X. Charles Sumner to James Kent, September 24, 1838. *Ibid.*, Vol. IX.

[121] Edward Everett to James Kent, October 31, 1845. *Ibid.*, Vol. X.

[122] Thomas Denman, Lord Chief Justice of the Queen's Bench.

for you friends and authority on this side of the Atlantic." [123] Years before, when Kent was still on the bench, Story had spoken of him as another Hardwicke; and Story's opinion was confirmed by the man who in all the English speaking world was best qualified to know. "For learning and ability," declared Lord Campbell, "[I consider] Kent equal to any of those [Chancellors] whose lives I have written." [124]

Nor was Kent without honor in his own country. His address to the New York Law Association on the superior talents of an earlier bar was published in *The American Jurist* with the editorial comment, "We feel disposed to regard all that falls from [Kent's lips] as the speaking voice of the law." [125] Whatever professional decline the jurist implied in that address, he neither incurred the profession's resentment nor forfeited its respect. The bar of the state observed the twentieth anniversary of his retirement by tendering him a public dinner and adopting eloquent resolutions in his honor. His judicial services were admiringly reviewed and his decisions compared in ability to those of the highest courts in England.[126] On the same occasion the Philadelphia bar offered its felicitations through John Sergeant, who, inviting Kent to a banquet in that city, wrote, "Should you accede to our wishes, you will find yourself surrounded by those who feel proud to admit that a large portion of the sound legal principles which they possess can be traced to your judgements and writings; and indeed there is no doubt that there is scarcely a doctrine acknowledged by our cisatlantic jurisprudence which you have not had some part in illustrating or establishing." [127]

[123] George Bancroft to James Kent, November 25, 1846. *Ibid.*, Vol. XI.

[124] Lord Campbell to George Bancroft, February 8, 1847. *Kent Papers*, Vol. XI.

[125] *American Jurist*, XVI, 471.

[126] Resolutions of the New York Bar at the July Term of the Supreme Court at Utica, July 18, 1843; John Duer and others to James Kent, July 31, 1843, *Kent Papers*, Vol. X.

[127] John Sergeant to James Kent, June 7, 1843. *Ibid.*

If these professions of respect for the former Chancellor and Chief Justice were insufficient to convince contemporaries that the court of equity should be kept distinct or that the common law should be handed down uncodified, they at least indicated the spirit in which the bar, and the judges to be recruited from it, would go about their task of administering the legal system when codification should have been completed and the court of chancery should be no more. The eagerness with which those lawyers and judges greeted the publication of the *Commentaries* indicated the same thing.

In demand throughout the remainder of the author's life, the work continued in demand beyond the period of the Civil War. The successive editions which Kent personally supervised were rapidly exhausted.[128] There were five of these in all, and the author contemplated a sixth.[129] As the editions severally appeared, the most eminent jurists hastened to offer their congratulations. "Your *Commentaries*," wrote Chief Justice Savage of New York, "will remain a living testimonial of your learning and industry to future generations." [130] The praise was reechoed by the judges of New England. Chief Justice Parker referred from the bench to "that recent work which does its author so much honor and the public so much good." [131] Mellen of Maine declared that the volumes constituted "a Law Bible"; [132] while Shaw, the famous Chief Justice of Massachusetts, predicted that they would give stability and

[128] James Kent to Moss Kent, Jr., December 22, 1830. He states that the first edition is almost sold out. *Kent Papers,* Vol. VI.

[129] *Law Reporter,* I, 1–3. The first edition, 1826–1830; second, 1832; third, 1836; the fourth is reviewed, *ibid.*, III, 402; the fifth, *ibid.*, VII, 60, mentioned; the fourth is reviewed *American Jurist,* XXV, 102–117 (April, 1841); the fifth came in 1844, James Kent to Joseph Story, April 18, 1844, *Story Papers.* Kent finished the sixth edition but did not live to publish it.

[130] James Savage to James Kent, May 6, 1830. *Kent Papers,* Vol. VI.

[131] Blake v. Williams, 6 Pickering 309. Cf. Holmes v. Remsen, 4 *Johns Ch.* 460.

[132] Frederick C. Hicks, *Men and Books Famous in the Law,* 155.

unity to the jurisprudence of all the states.[133] Story was of course among the first to proclaim the merit of the work; and ere it was completed, began to prophesy: "When we cease to read your works I think we shall cease to read anything." [134] In a tone less menacing to the future of poetry and the novel, he added "[The *Commentaries*] will become an American textbook and range on the same shelf with the classical work of Blackstone in all our libraries." [135] Nor did the chorus of approval resound only in New England. It was heard in the West and in the South. Judges of North Carolina and of Alabama made pilgrimages to New York that they might consult the oracle personally.[136] One of the progressive educators of the day, Philip Lindsley, the President of the University of Nashville, wrote to request that the first volume be separately edited for academic use.[137]

Kent decided to do this, and thus the volume which contained his exposition of the constitutional law of the American Union passed into the hands of boys at college and became a textbook at the University of Nashville, at West Point, at Harvard and at the author's Alma Mater in New Haven.[138] Though the work was everywhere admired, its doctrines sometimes incurred criticism, in the North occasionally,[139] more

[133] Lemuel Shaw to James Kent, August 9, 1837. *Kent Papers,* Vol. VIII.

[134] Joseph Story to James Kent, December 26, 1826. *Story Papers.*

[135] Joseph Story to James Kent, December 15, 1827. *Ibid.*

[136] James Kent to Moss Kent, Jr., August 22, 1836. *Kent Papers,* Vol. VIII; see also Isaac Blackford (of Indiana) to James Kent, December 24, 1831, *Ibid.*, Vol. VI; Thomas Ewing (of Ohio) to James Kent, March 13, 1834. *Ibid.*, Vol. VII; and *passim.*

[137] Philip Lindsley to James Kent, January 14, 1833. *Ibid.*, Vol. VII. *Vide et American Historical Review,* XLII, 57–58.

[138] Little and Company to James Kent, April 12, 1838, with appended note by Kent in *Kent Papers,* Vol. IX.

[139] In 1840 the Democratic majority of the Board of Visitors to West Point protested the use of Kent as a textbook. Douglas S. Freeman, *R. E. Lee,* I, 79, note 79.

often in the South.[140] In the New England colleges the book was received with entire approval. Story, writing from the Law School at Cambridge, said that the students there universally read it; [141] that they also admired it was proved by the portrait of the author which they caused to be painted at their own expense.[142] One day the author showed himself among them in the flesh, whereupon they rose and cheered him as he slowly entered Dane Hall leaning on the arm of his son.[143] He was seen too, and in a more official capacity, at that academy where the future generals of the Civil War were being trained. In 1828, Kent was named to the Board of Visitors to West Point; and going thither to perform his duties, he attended an examination of the cadets in constitutional law. "They appeared," he said, "to be masters of the first volume of my Commentaries." [144]

Into how many other hands than those of college youths the *Commentaries* must have come, is a question that cannot be answered with certainty; but if one considers how rapidly the work went through its several editions, if he accepts the contemporary opinion that no American work had ever earned so

[140] Thomas Cooper to James Kent, December 1, 1833, *Kent Papers*, Vol. VII.

[141] Joseph Story to James Kent, July 18, 1831. *Story Papers*.

[142] James Kent to Moss Kent, Jr., December 26, 1836. *Kent Papers*, Vol. VIII.

[143] *Kent Journal*, October 15, 1846. His son, William Kent, was Royall Professor of Law.

[144] *Kent Journal*, April 23, June 3, 1828. Curiously enough, the cadets whom he singled out as most proficient were Lee and Davis. Davis himself states that he was taught Kent's *Commentaries*. Douglas S. Freeman, *R. E. Lee*, I, 78–79. Dr. Freeman appears to be less certain about Lee, whether he was taught Kent or Rawle's *On the Constitution* which defends the right of secession. *Loc. cit.* The above entry in Kent's journal may dispose of that doubt. Perhaps the Davis to whom Kent refers was not Jefferson Davis. ". . . John P. Davis and Robert E. Lee were classmates, and they are probably the ones Chancellor Kent had in mind." Lt. Col. T. Hughes to the author, June 13, 1937.

much money,[145] the conclusion suggested by Sergeant is inescapable. Kent had become the favorite preceptor of the legal profession.

That fact made him significant in more than a professional way and assured him a hearing beyond the bounds of the forum. He therefore had added reason to hope that despite adverse influences his counsels would not pass unheeded. Subsequent events justified that hope. The Union, though threatened, was ultimately to prevail, and in prevailing, was to rally again to its support a class more closely akin than the southern planters to the one that under Hamilton's leadership had established it.[146] To that class and to the spirit of the age it dominated the doctrines of Kent were to prove congenial.[147] Thus his labors were not in vain. If they contributed little to humanitarian progress, to social stability they contributed much; and along with the opinions of Marshall which the *Commentaries* expound in clearer language than Marshall's own,[148] along with the speeches of Webster they may justly be accounted among those intellectual forces which moulded sentiment in favor of an indivisible Union perpetuated according to the interests and principles of the Federalist fathers.

[145] According to Philip Hone, $5000 a year since the first edition. This he states on the authority of Kent. Philip Hone *Diary,* II, 645–646. The fifth edition consisted of 3000 sets at $10 a set to the trade. Within the week, Kent says, 535 sets had been sold, and no sale under 25 sets. James Kent to Joseph Story, April 18, 1844. *Story Papers.*

[146] Charles and Mary Beard, *Rise of American Civilization,* "The Second American Revolution," *passim.*

[147] Cf. the *Commentaries* as discussed above; also Dash v. Van Kleeck and Gardner v. Newburgh. Kent perceived the possibilities latent in due process. Kent had edited, but not published the sixth edition of the *Commentaries.* This edition came out after his death. There were eight subsequent editions, fourteen in all. Frederick C. Hicks, "Kent's Commentaries," *Columbia Alumni News,* XIV, 370.

[148] "Marshall's ideas stand forth [in Kent's *Commentaries*] more clearly and more succinctly than in his own less tightly articulated pronouncements." Thomas R. Powell, "Kent's Contributions to Constitutional Law," *Columbia Alumni News,* XIV, 373.

That a work primarily intended for the profession should have influenced the public as it did, was possible only because of the place which lawyers had finally made for themselves in American life. Unpopular in the years following the Revolution, and never popular in the common meaning of the word, they had nevertheless contrived to win enough public esteem to exercise power out of all proportion to their numbers. Their dominant position struck that acute foreign observer, De Tocqueville, as one of the peculiar features of our society; and he had much to say about it in his study of democracy in America.

Without nobles or men of letters, and distrustful of mere wealth as such, the people, according to De Tocqueville, look to the lawyers for direction, "and . . . lawyers . . . ," he says, "form the highest political class, and the most cultivated circle of society. . . ." He added, "If I were asked where I place the American aristocracy, I should reply without hesitation that . . . it occupies the judicial bench and the bar." Like all other aristocracies, the legal caste in the America of Kent's time contributed to create the tone and temper of the common people. The habits of the profession were imitated by the laity. "As most public men are, or have been legal practitioners," De Tocqueville continues, "they introduce the customs and the technicalities of their profession into the affairs of the country. The jury extends this habitude to all classes. The language of the law thus becomes, in some measure, a vulgar tongue; the spirit of the law, which is produced in the schools and courts of justice, gradually penetrates beyond their walls into the bosom of society, where it descends to the lowest classes, so that the whole people contracts the habits and tastes of the magistrate. . . . The lawyers of the United States form a party [which] extends over the whole community . . . it acts upon the country imperceptibly, but it finally fashions it to suit its purposes. . . . When the American people are intoxicated by passion, or carried away by the impetuosity of their ideas, they are checked and stopped by the almost invisible influence of their legal counsellors. These secretly oppose their aristocratic propensities to the nation's democratic instincts . . . their habitual procrastination to its ardent impatience."[149]

In the light of these observations one may say, without going beyond the bounds, that a jurist who has left his mark on the profession, has left it upon the country. So it was with Kent who, laying aside the robe of a local judge, became doctor of laws to the whole republic.

[149] Alexis De Tocqueville, *Democracy in America* (Reeve's translation, as revised by Francis Bowen, 1898), I, 348–358.

VIII

Senectus

Quid juris consulti, quid pontifices, quid augures, quid philosophi senes? Quam multa meminerunt! Manent ingenia senibus, modo permaneat studium et industria, neque ea solum claris et honoratis viris, sed in vita etiam privata et quieta.

de Senectute

Ita enim senectus honesta est, si se ipsa defendit, si ius suum retinet, si nemini emancipata est, si usque ad extremum spiritum dominatur in suos.

Ibid.[1]

* * *

WHILE in New England during the summer of 1823, Kent, it will be recalled, made a pilgrimage to Quincy to see John Adams. He found him faint of voice, dim of eye and feeble of limb; yet admirable in spite of his infirmities. The old statesman's son, soon to be President himself, was in Quincy at the time; and the chancellor may well have fancied that no man, having such a son, was to be pitied. But the elder Adams commanded respect in his own right and that for what he was as well as for what he once had been. His person still had dignity; and as his guest observed, his countenance still kept its freshness, and his mind its powers.[2] There was another patriot surviving from the same epoch whom Kent visited some time after the death of Adams. With his brother Moss and with a son

[1] The second observation of Cicero is quoted in the address of the bar of the State of New York to Chancellor Kent on the occasion of his eightieth birthday, July 31, 1843. William Kent, *Memoirs and Letters of James Kent*, 270.

[2] *Kent Journal* (No. 7), 1821–1824, August 30, 1823.

of Alexander Hamilton he went to Jamaica on Long Island to pay his respects to Egbert Benson, who, cheerful and sprightly at eighty-seven, invited his guests to remain to dinner and entertained them with reminiscences of the Revolution.[3] Nor was Benson the only sage of whom New York could boast. John Jay lived likewise to attain a patriarchal fullness of years; and Kent on a tour through Westchester in the late July of 1826, tarried for a while at Bedford where he "found Governor Jay on his stoop with a long pipe by his side." He was thin as a shadow, noted the chancellor, and his face was shrunken so that his chin and nose were nearly touching; but for all his frailty, his mind was clear, and as he drew occasionally on his long pipe and gazed out across the broad rich acres of his farm,[4] he looked the very image of serenity. He lived surrounded with descendants; and over his numerous and devout household his son, William Jay, presided, relieving him of cares to enjoy his pipe in undisturbed contentment.[5]

These examples of men grown old with dignity James Kent followed almost as if by conscious imitation. His last years, it is true, were not entirely tranquil, but if they were disturbed, it was by vexations without immediate personal concern. Though he professed to be losing interest in politics,[6] he never tired of complaining on the subject, and he sometimes aired his complaint with originality.[7]

[3] *Ibid.* (No. 10), 1829–1833, April 30, 1833.

[4] Kent says his farm contained a thousand acres.

[5] *Kent Journal* (No. 8), 1825–1828, July 25, 1826.

[6] James Kent to Moss Kent, Jr., August 10, 1836. *Kent Papers,* Vol. VIII.

[7] Usually he gave way to rather tiresome abuse. He called President Tyler a ". . . weak, vain, perfidious wretch. . . ." Polk was "an unprincipled demagogue." See James Kent to Joseph Story, April 18, 1844. *Story Papers;* James Kent to William Kent, February 15, 1847, *Kent Papers,* Vol. XI. Kent objected to Polk as an expansionist;—James Kent to Robert Winthrop, February 21, 1845. *Winthrop Papers:*—"I acknowledge the favor of your speeches in the House of Representatives on the *Texas* & on the *Oregon* questions. . . . I need hardly add . . . that my whole soul goes with you on both questions."

One spring day in 1844, he came suddenly into the insurance office of his friend, Philip Hone, and, taking a chair beside the desk, inquired:

"Do you write marine risks?"

"Certainly, sir," answered Hone, "it is our business."

"I want some insurance," said Kent.

"You?" asked the surprised underwriter, "what can you possibly have to do with marine insurance?"

"I have an interest in a vessel which I wish insured for nine months," was the answer.

"Very well, sir, what vessel is it?"

"I suppose I must disclose everything?"

"Certainly," said the underwriter in a serious tone.

"Well," his customer continued, "she is as good a vessel as ever floated, staunch and sound, but I have no confidence in the captain, and am afraid of barratry, which I would insure against."

"Well, sir, what is her name?"

"The good ship Constitution; John Tyler, master; will you write her?"

Hone, rising to the occasion, replied, "Change the captain, stop up her leaks with *Clay*, and we will write her upon the most favorable terms." Pleased with the suggestion, Kent departed as suddenly as he had come.[8]

It was not only affairs of government, however, that were the source of his disquiet. He was annoyed by the rise of zealots, and whether they expressed themselves in religious revivals or in the cause of temperance or of abolition made slight difference in his attitude. Revivals he called crazy;[9] and if possible, he was more contemptuous of the temperance movement than of abolitionism.[10] "Our religionists are fanatics," he said,

[8] Philip Hone, *Diary,* II, 704.

[9] James Kent to Moss Kent, Jr., April 3, 1835. *Kent Papers,* Vol. VII.

[10] Kent's opinion of abolitionism has been indicated in connection with the *Commentaries*. *Vide* James Kent to Moss Kent, Jr., October 7, 1833.

"our temperance societies are pushing to disgusting excess and become intemperate in temperance." [11] When a committee called upon him to urge that he sign a prohibitionist pledge, he stoutly refused to grant their request. "Gentlemen," he said, "I refuse to sign any pledge. I never have been drunk, and by the blessing of God I never will get drunk, but I have a constitutional privilege to get drunk and that privilege I will not sign away." [12] Both temperance and abolitionist agitation proceeded, in his analysis, from those extremes of opinion which he branded with the name of ultraism and regarded as dangerous to the public taste and tranquillity. In an age harassed with such agitations, Kent yearned for the classic repose of a generation that was gone. "Give me Addison and Locke," sighed he, "and the Presbyterianism of Dr. Styles." [13]

Unfortunate that his predilections were not more widely shared, Kent ought nevertheless to have thanked his star that he had no other cause for murmuring. He was blest with all the felicity which should accompany old age; and honor and love and troops of friends made the last of life almost the pleasantest of all. Few ailments troubled him. A twinge of rheumatism at sixty left him hardly less agile than before; and at sixty-nine, spending an August holiday at Stratford in Connecticut, he went swimming three times every week.[14] The burden of eighty years he bore so lightly that men marvelled. He became a little deaf; [15] but in outward appearance, except perhaps for a greater whiteness of his locks, he had scarcely changed. Swift of step and upright in his bearing, he

Kent Papers, Vol. VII. He there doubts whether he will even trouble to attend a meeting of the African Colonization Society, though he has lent his name in support of it.

[11] James Kent to Moss Kent, Jr., April 3, 1835. *Ibid.,* Vol. VII.

[12] William Kent, *Memoirs and Letters of James Kent,* 165.

[13] James Kent to Moss Kent, Jr., April 3, 1835. *Kent Papers,* Vol. VII.

[14] James Kent to Moss Kent, Jr., August 6, 1832. *Ibid.,* Vol. VI.

[15] Philip Hone, *Diary,* II, 665.

walked the Battery each day; [16] in the country he would sometimes quicken his gait and break into a brisk run.[17] "I should be sorry to run a race with him of a mile if I had money to bet upon it," remarked Philip Hone; and somewhat later he added, referring to the chancellor in his eighty-third year, "I begin to think there is no such thing as old age." [18] James Kent, it seemed, had somewhat of that tough resistance which his *Commentaries* lauded in the laws of Rome that had stood so long against the waves and weathers of time.

Free from disease and feebleness, he escaped penury too, that other common evil of old age; and, in spite of panic and depression, he escaped it with a kind of flourish. The crash of 1837 and the lean years that had followed it, left him fairly secure in his estate,[19] where folk far richer had been ruined. "Here we see some fifty or a hundred men who have rolled in carriages and lived in boundless luxury in a week dragged down to absolute poverty," [20] wrote William Kent to his uncle at the time of the crisis; but of his father's losses he mentioned little, except that the chancellor thought it wise to forego a journey which he had planned to the westward.[21] Kent's affairs had been prudently managed, and his fortune, while not great, continued to be substantial. The cause of this affluence was the *Commentaries,* from which he had made a

[16] This seems to have been his favorite walk in the city.

[17] Philip Hone, *op. cit.,* II, 665. *Vide et* "The Eightieth Birthday of Chancellor Kent," *Law Reporter,* VI, 289: "His venerable years are another illustration of the saying of one of the early masters of the law (it is Littleton who speaks, or his commentator, Lord Coke) that there is something in the cultivation of jurisprudence favorable to a protracted life and that grave judges, by the benign regard of Providence, are sure to be crowned by a green old age."

[18] Philip Hone, *op. cit.,* II, 757.

[19] William Kent—notes on the close of his father's life—*Kent Papers,* Vol. XI.

[20] William Kent to Moss Kent, Jr., April 10, 1837. *Ibid.,* Vol. VIII.

[21] William Kent to Moss Kent, Jr., April 23, 1837. *Ibid.*

profit of $5000 every year since their appearance,[22]—an annual income which, more than double what he was getting when he left the bench, enabled him to spend his closing years in a fine house on fashionable Union Square.[23]

Here, with the wife of his youth, he lived in gracious style, paying and receiving the visits of the quality of New York; [24] going to the dinners of Peter Jay [25] and Philip Hone,[26] attending the theatre to see the Kembles,[27] presiding at public banquets given to celebrities like Washington Irving and Daniel Webster.[28] As in the days of his first sojourn in the city he delighted in conviviality, drawing around him a congenial and distinguished company which came to be known as the Kent Club.[29] "Until ten o'clock," said Hone, "they talk law and science and philosophy, and then the scene changes to the supper table where Blackstone gives place to Heidsick, reports of champagne bottles are preferred to law reports, and the merits of oyster pâtés and charlotte russe are alone summed up." [30]

Among the members of this sprightly band was the chancellor's son. He had now for a number of years been sustaining an honorable reputation at the bar,[31] and to his father's satisfaction, he would one day ascend the bench.[32] William Kent, like

[22] Philip Hone, *Diary,* II, 645–646.

[23] At No. 26. His residence prior to this was 68 Greenwich Street. *Vide New York Genealogical and Biographical Record,* IV, 89.

[24] *Kent Papers,* Vols. VII, VIII, IX, X, XI *passim.*

[25] Son of John Jay, another leader of New York society.

[26] Philip Hone, *op. cit.,* I, 143.

[27] William Kent, *Memoirs and Letters of James Kent,* 261. As Miss Kemble called on him, this is a fair inference.

[28] Philip Hone, *op. cit.,* I, 38–39, 63–64.

[29] *Ibid.,* I, 300. Hone was a member, also President Duer and Albert Gallatin.

[30] Philip Hone, *Diary,* I, 396.

[31] William Kent passed his bar examination in 1824; Moss Kent, Jr., to James Kent, March 4, 1824. *Kent Papers,* Vol. V. He got his start in the profession in the office of Josiah Ogden Hoffman: William Kent to Moss Kent, Jr., May 20, 1824. *Ibid.,* Vol. V.

[32] William Kent, *Letters and Memoirs of James Kent,* 262.

the chancellor himself, opened his doors to the club who found his entertainment all that could be desired. "We had a handsome supper with oceans of champagne," recorded Hone in his diary, "I was right in calling it 'high jinks,' for a more jovial, noisy, roystering set I never met with. They seemed to condemn all law but that of passing the bottle, and the counsel on both sides summed up together without regarding the admonitions of the court." [33]

Fond as he was of clubs and supper parties, Kent was never happier than when at home, where he lived somewhat as the dominie, his grandfather, had been wont to live in the vale of Croton, with his descendants [34] settled not far away. Over this circle he reigned benignly with his wife, who resisting the encroachments of age with as much gallantry as he, made her house the rendezvous of all the Kents. Of a Sunday evening her tea table was often merry with the presence of children and grandchildren; [35]—Isaac and Eliza Hone with their comely daughter Elizabeth; William Kent and his wife with their little son, the namesake of the chancellor; Mary Kent and her successful suitor, Dr. John Stone, an Episcopal divine who, after a brief residence in Boston, was to become rector of Christ Church in Brooklyn. Thus the family circle was to be broken but temporarily, and even then the situation had its redeeming advantages. Mary Stone dwelling in Boston made that city more attractive than ever to her father who visited her there twice in a single year, on the second occasion seeing James Kent Stone, her infant son, baptized.[36] The same year he rejoiced in the birth of a great-grandchild in Philadelphia whither his granddaughter Elizabeth Hone had gone as a bride and where,

[33] Philip Hone, *op. cit.*, I, 300.

[34] *Nati natorum et qui nascentur ab illis* as Kent called them.

[35] Note on Sunday evening at tea-time, December 17, 1837. *Kent Papers*, Vol. VIII.

[36] *Kent Journal* (No. 14), 1836–1840—trips to Boston in March and December, 1840—entry in Journal for baptism of James Kent Stone. *Ibid.*,

as he proudly recorded,[37] "she lives a lady." The Chancellor and Mrs. Kent, taking the cars, lost little time in hastening to see their small descendant. "He is my *great-grandson,*" exulted the venerable man, "and it is quite an interesting fact that his great maternal grandparents should be so well and active as to visit him in a rapid journey from New York of ninety-six miles in six and a half hours! My dear wife and I went on purpose and for no other purpose than to see our granddaughter and her son." [38]

Thus James and Elizabeth Kent, surviving among their posterity to the third generation, found their interest in life increasing as the years went by. The joys of their own comradeship remained as keen as ever, whether in travelling or in tarrying at home. Alone together of an evening, the chancellor would be sitting in the library at work upon revision of the *Commentaries,* when Mrs. Kent would enter with her "little round black" spy glass to pore over the papers and new books lying about in profusion. Of her presence Kent was no less aware than he had been in the bygone times when as Elizabeth Bailey she had come stealing into Benson's office at Poughkeepsie to find him bent over a volume of Blackstone. Times had not greatly altered, except that now the *Commentaries* were by an author more familiar and present in the flesh, who would lay down his pen, read aloud a chapter from his manu-

December 20, 1840. *Vide et New York Genealogical and Biographical Record,* XVI, 11–13 for descendants referred to:

James Kent, the Chancellor

Elizabeth m. Isaac Hone | William m. Helen Riggs | Mary m. John S. Stone, D.D.

Elizabeth Hone m. Wm. H. Ashhurst (of Philadelphia) | James Kent | James Kent Stone

Henry Ashhurst, Kent's first great-grandchild

[37] *Kent Journal* (No. 14), 1836–1840, February 25, 1840.

[38] *Loc. cit.*

script,[39] and as he had done formerly when on the bench, perhaps talk over some problem of the law with his sensible and understanding spouse.[40] Less weighty themes would presently ensue, the gaiety of old Poughkeepsie days, the reminiscences of interesting journeys, the pleasures of a Sabine farm.

Such a retreat the Kents had always longed to possess; and they had at length gratified their desire with the purchase of a modest but attractive country place in Jersey.[41] A farmhouse made over to their own taste stood on the sloping side of a breezy hill looking out across the valley of the Passaic rich with its variegated patterns of woodland interspersed with besteepled villages and well-tilled fields.[42] Hither they came to spend several weeks of every summer, passing the days in great contentment. Astir at five in the morning, they sallied forth to delve in their garden and to rejoice in their shrubs and flowers hardy and gay from much careful tending. Kent resolving to play the farmer in authentic style, had bought a team and wagon, and he would occasionally ride out to his fields and orchard to busy himself like Cato with scythe and pruning-hook, returning at noonday to see his chimney lazily asmoke in the summer air and to find his aged Thyrsis setting out a savory dinner. The afternoon would be less arduous, for Kent oftentimes stretched himself out upon the floor in slumber. Refreshed by his nap, he might decide to do a little writing or while away the hours with Tully or with Horace or with Vergil's verses that sing the delights of dwelling in the country.[43] Ere ten o'clock had struck, the evening was over, and the cot-

[39] For this scene James Kent to William Kent, December 23, 1846. *Kent Papers,* Vol. X.

[40] Irving Browne, *Short Studies of Great Lawyers,* 234.

[41] In 1837, William Kent's notes. *Kent Papers,* Vol. XI.

[42] *Loc. cit.*

[43] James Kent to Moss Kent, Jr., February, 1833. *Kent Papers,* Vol. VII. He speaks of literature as the solace of old age. James Kent to Moss Kent, Jr., November 23, 1837. *Ibid.,* Vol. VIII.

tage was surrendered to the summer darkness and to sleep.[44]

The days upon the Sabine farm, though all spent tranquilly, were not all spent in solitude. Visitors crossed over from the city to admire the place and hear the old chancellor pronounce his low opinion of life in town.[45] The younger Kents came frequently.[46] The voices of children rang out upon the breezy hillside; and with the simplicity of children, Kent and his wife welcomed all their callers and entertained them with a zest that would have done credit to folk of half their years. Sometimes the visitors arriving unexpectedly witnessed rather startling feats of youthful vigor and agility in old age; and Kent's own son upon occasion was astonished. Finding one day his venerable sire sitting aloft in the branches of a cherry tree, he admonished him to come down and to be careful lest he come too suddenly. The chancellor replied calmly, though perhaps in a tone that sounded like rebuke: "My son, I am used to elevated stations and know how and when to descend with dignity." [47]

There were other diversions than those of country life from which the Chancellor and Mrs. Kent derived great pleasure. They were fond of travel, although their journeys, judged even by the standard of the time, were not extensive. They never carried them beyond the seas, as Moss Kent's journeys carried him.[48] Quebec and Portland in the north and east, the Niagara frontier upon the west, and to the south, Richmond in Virginia were their limits. Yet within these bounds the Kents passed to and fro with curiosity and admiration, and with adventure too, if it could be called adventure to change as they did, in their means of transit, from the sloop to the steamboat and from the stage-coach to the locomotive. But however interesting their

[44] Philip Hone, *Diary*, II, 665.

[45] Philip Hone, *ibid.*, I, 420.

[46] William Kent, *Memoirs and Letters of James Kent*, 258.

[47] Irving Browne, *Short Studies of Great Lawyers*, 232.

[48] Moss Kent, Jr., his niece Elizabeth Hone and William Kent went to Europe.

expeditions were, the Kents invariably returned with gladness to their own region, the country that Irving had made famous, the borders of the Hudson, the blue mountains, the deep mountain glens of the Catskills and the Sleepy Hollow with its twilight superstitions.[49]

Here James Kent and Elizabeth Bailey trod their native ground, making pilgrimage to old familiar places and bringing to life again the days of their youth. Urged by an impulse of ancient piety, the chancellor turned his steps toward the Croton Valley where Elisha Kent had once held patriarchal sway, where many kinsmen had once lived as neighbors and the holidays had sped as if on wings. "I passed gently along by the very house in which I was born," [50] the chancellor jotted in his journal; and though a few years later that house had been demolished, other and more conspicuous landmarks remained. The manse withstood the weathers of time.[51] The meetinghouse was still in use, and there Kent tarried one Sabbath morning to worship with the home-spun congregation.[52] Among the inhabitants of the parish he was happy to find an aged woman who remembered his grandsire and was able to reminisce upon the olden time.[53] Before departing, Kent sought the church yard, visited his mother's grave, and lingering pensively among the mossy stones and myrtle-covered mounds, bethought him of the forefathers of the hamlet, how jocund they once drove their teams afield.[54]

As a rule, the chancellor's journeys were more light-hearted and they often brought him into fashionable as well as distinguished society. At Saratoga he was a well-known figure,

[49] Cf. Kent's speech at the Irving banquet in May, 1832. William Kent, *Memoirs and Letters of James Kent,* 233.

[50] *Kent Journal* (No. 6), 1803–1816. This in August, 1813.

[51] *Ibid.* (No. 8), 1825–1828, July 29, 1827.

[52] *Loc. cit.*

[53] *Ibid.* (No. 9), 1828–1830, July 4, 1828.

[54] *Loc. cit.,* and see *ibid.* (No. 14), July, 1844. Grey's *Elegy* occurred to him. He quotes it:—*Journal,* July 4, 1828.

pointed out to strangers,[55] greeted on every hand by admirers and friends; [56] who, pausing as they drank the waters, joined him in damning Democrats.[57] He in turn joined them in other pleasures; and was a favorite everywhere. None was more welcome to company than he; and in Richmond, in Boston and in Philadelphia, gentlemen counted it a signal favor when he paid a visit, and they made his coming the occasion for elaborate banquets.[58] Nowhere was he more hospitably received than in Virginia whither he went in the spring of 1835 to see John Marshall. The Chief Justice, though failing rapidly, had greeted him with warmth and exacted a promise that the chancellor come again to see him in the winter at Washington. The Richmond Bar were delighted with their guest, and the famous Barbecue Club took him immediately into their charmed circle, feted him with a celebration in the country, proved his skill at quoits and regaled him with a great feast on barbecued pork and mutton washed down with copious draughts of mint-julep, porter and grog.[59]

Delights like these furnished relief to the more reposeful

[55] *Kent Journal* (No. 12), clipping from *New York Commercial Advertiser,* August 25, 1834.

[56] *Loc. cit.*

[57] *Ibid.* (No. 13), August 20, 1837. "All our conversations with intelligent men [at Saratoga] are on the sad hopes of self-governing democracies. We are going to destruction—all checks and balances and institutions in this country are threatened with destruction from the ascendancy of the democracy of numbers and radicalism and the horrible doctrines and influence of Jacksonism."

[58] In June and July, 1836, Kent was in Boston where Story, when he saw him in court, stopped proceedings and came down from the bench, *cir.* July 2, 1836. Jeremiah Mason gave a party in his honor, *ibid.* (No. 13), 1835–1838. September 3, 1836, Kent was entertained by Nicholas Biddle. *Ibid.* March 11, 1839, Mr. Ashhurst of Philadelphia entertained him with Binney, Chauncey, Biddle, *et al. Ibid* (No. 14), 1838–1846. May 15, 1829, *Ibid.* (No. 10), 1829–1832, a great lawyers' dinner at Andrew Bayard's in Philadelphia.

[59] *Ibid.* (No. 12), May 16, 1835. On this trip Kent was introduced to Jackson whom he describes:—(May 14, 1835) ". . . to see President Jackson. We found him a plain, respectable, affable, old, tall, thin, emaciated gentleman, with flowing grey hair."

pleasures of the Sabine farm, and of pilgrimages to the valley of the Croton. They made a happy contrast to the delights of literature which Kent after the fashion of Cicero was wont to proclaim the chief solace of old age.[60] He held the opinion without pose or affectation; and spent much of his leisure among his books, especially those of the classic authors. Their yellowing pages awakened memories of college-halls, of the yard and the green, of the bell bidding to chapel and of the friends and companions of his college days; again and again those memories drew him to the academic scene. It was much the same whether at Princeton, Cambridge or New Haven, and Kent visited them all to witness their solemnities.[61] With Cambridge he was enchanted. There the law was cultivated with as much diligence as were the arts themselves. His friend, Judge Story, lectured there; [62] his son, Judge Kent, in the course of time did the same; there the chancellor himself was often seen, a venerable doctor of laws walking with congenial companions under the shade of academic elms.[63]

But Kent, after all, was a loyal son of Yale, and thither he repeatedly returned. His friend, Judge Simeon Baldwin, dwelt near the college, and he seems to have kept open house for the elderly alumni who, like the chancellor, were pleased to visit their Alma Mater and note the changes wrought upon her by the passing years.[64] On the fiftieth anniversary of the class of 1781, eight of the twelve surviving members sat down to Baldwin's dinner table and revived the days of Doctor Stiles.[65]

[60] James Kent to Moss Kent, Jr., February, 1833—November 23, 1837. *Kent Papers,* Vols. VII, VIII.

[61] At Princeton September 29, 1835. *Kent Journal* (No. 13), 1835–1838.

[62] *Ibid.* (No. 13), July 5, 1837.

[63] It was rumored Kent would remove thither. But see his letter to William Kent, November 10, 1846. *Kent Papers,* Vol. X. He was satisfied to live in New York City. William Kent became Royall Professor of Law.

[64] *Kent Journal,* September 8, 1824; *et passim.*

[65] *Ibid.,* September 14, 1831; William Kent to James Kent, September 20, 1831. *Kent Papers,* Vol. VI.

Having just attended the Commencement ceremonies, they no doubt reverted to those ceremonies half a century before, when hostile fleets were gliding ominously along the Sound and the descent of Arnold was feared from hour to hour. They no doubt discussed the transformation which not only the college and the commonwealth but the entire country had undergone since that exciting day.

In the developments of that half century, Kent and his classmates, together with the other Yale men of their generation, had played impressive parts; and if the aim of liberal education is to form leaders, then in their careers, they had amply justified their college. Of the class of 1781, there had been twenty-seven members; of that number added to other classes in part contemporaneous, some twenty-five had attained high public honors, among them several Congressmen, a minister to Europe, a Chief Justice of Vermont, a Chief Justice of Connecticut, a Governor of Vermont, three Governors of Connecticut and two Senators of the United States.[66] These men had helped lay firm the foundations of the republic; nor is it an unlikely conjecture that in part at least they owed the distinction of their services to the fact that they had been disciples of Ezra Stiles. Whatever else he had done, he had kindled their imaginations and inspired them with the ambition for leadership. The classical learning which he had advocated, with its stress upon the deeds of antique statesmen and upon the policies and principles of antique states, had proved relevant to the lives of these now aging leaders foregathered to live over again the days they had spent as Stiles's pupils.[67]

[66] James Kent, *Phi Beta Kappa Address,* 45–47. The most eminent men here mentioned are Joel Barlow, Zephaniah Swift, Uriah Tracy, Roger Griswold, Oliver Wolcott. Distinguished in intellectual pursuits were Jedediah Morse, Abiel Holmes and Noah Webster.

[67] Cf. Alfred N. Whitehead, "The Education of an Englishman," *Atlantic Monthly,* CXXXVIII, 195–198 ". . . I will disclose one private conviction . . . that, as a training in political imagination, the Harvard

Nor did they show any inclination to see that president's programme materially altered. On the contrary, as Kent, their spokesman made it clear, they were gratified to find in President Jeremiah Day a faithful adherent to the Stiles tradition. Kent, who held decided opinions upon educational matters, was proud to sit with Day upon the Commencement stage; [68] and as a more substantial sign of his esteem, to preside over a meeting of the alumni and to contribute, as a result of that meeting, four hundred dollars to the college.[69] Furthermore, he spoke in defense of Day's conservative policy. Mounting the pulpit in the Chapel he delivered a long address to the Phi Beta Kappa Society,[70] in the course of his remarks dwelling upon the condition of Yale at the period when the Society was introduced. The excitements of that far-off time he described in telling phrases, he glorified its spirit, lauded his tutor, Ebenezer Baldwin, as the very embodiment of that spirit and as the true pattern of Yale chivalry and learning.[71] He acknowledged

---

School of Politics and Government cannot hold a candle to the old-fashioned English classical education. . . ."

[68] *Kent Journal*, September 14, 1831.

[69] *Ibid.*, September 13, 1831.

[70] James Kent, *An Address Delivered at New Haven before the Phi Beta Kappa Society,* September 13, 1831. Hereafter cited as *Address.*

[71] *Address,* 31 *et seq.*

In relation to Kent's views on education his correspondence some years later with Townsend Harris is interesting. Harris observed that classical education is for the few, and for them but an adjunct. He praised the aim of the New York System of public instruction which was to educate for the productive pursuits of life. He found in Kent no sympathy with his ideas; nor does Kent seem to have given him the advice he sought concerning a curriculum for the New York City Schools. Instead Kent criticized the recent education law, expressed his fear that the task of free public instruction would be overwhelming. As for practical education for the masses, he asserted that it would "only enlarge their capacity for mischief and add a fresh stimulus to delinquencies and to novelties, to change and revolution and contempt for the ordinary restraints of law, morality and religion." *Vide* Townsend Harris to James Kent, July 16, 1847; Townsend Harris to James Kent, July 23, 1847; James Kent to Townsend Harris, July 22, 1847; and the letter quoted above, undated, presumably to Harris;—all in *Kent Papers,* Vol. XI.

himself indebted to the young hero for his own love of learning; nor did he omit the praises due to Doctor Stiles whose emphasis on the classical curriculum he proceeded to defend against the innovators.

"The tendency of some modern theories of education," he said, "is to depress the study of ancient languages and literature, and to raise up, in their stead, a more exclusive devotion to the exact sciences and mechanical philosophy." As for himself he had no prejudice against scientific education, was glad that Yale was giving more attention to it than formerly; [72] he resented the intrusion of the new subjects only if they crowded out the old. "My only wish," said Kent, "is that science and literature may flourish in concert; and that one is not to regard the other as a useless or dangerous rival." [73] But the innovators did regard the traditional studies as such; and they did seek to crowd them out. It was this which Kent deplored; for this, said he, "would be to prefer the study of the laws of matter, to the study of man as an intellectual, moral and accountable being." [74]

But could not this study be as advantageously pursued by other means than the ancient languages? Kent doubted that it could. Stiles had once remarked that the great body of European learning had been transmitted in Latin; and though that was less true in the nineteenth than it had been in the eighteenth century, still, as Kent insisted, "Classical literature is the established standard throughout Europe of high intellectual and liberal attainments." [75] That the bare facts could be had from translations, he admitted; but in his view, the mere amassing of factual knowledge was not education; education was something more, and it had to do with the training of the mind and the cultivation of the taste. In promoting both ob-

[72] *Address*, 21–22.
[73] *Ibid.*, 22.
[74] *Ibid.*, 21.
[75] *Ibid.*, 25.

jects at once and in yielding factual information at the same time, Kent pronounced the traditional studies preeminent.[76] It was as patterns of taste, however, that he presented them in their most appealing light, observing that in this respect the very persons most heeded in discrediting them were nevertheless the beneficiaries of the classical tradition. "It is easy to perceive," said the chancellor, "that the weapons which are sometimes most dexterously employed to explode the study of the ancient classics, have been polished by Attic wit, and sharpened by the hand that once 'tun'd the Ausonian lyre.' "[77]

Kent rejoiced that these weapons had not prevailed in New Haven. "The founders of this college," he said, "I consider . . . as having acted most wisely, in making the study of the ancient languages, and with them a familiarity with the ancient classics, one of the professed objects of the institution. And I am happy in having it in my power to observe, that the faculty of this college and a committee of the corporation, have recently vindicated the use and value of these languages, as a branch of academical learning, by reports which have exhausted the subject, and are masterly both in point of argument and style."[78]

Kent's own address was likewise considered masterly,[79] and what was more to the point, the advice which it contained, while perhaps not needed in New Haven, was followed there with fidelity as long as Kent was interested in the place. Some ten years later, again attending a Commencement, the venerable jurist once more presided over a meeting of the alumni; and it must have been with the heartiest approval that he joined his aged voice with theirs in singing the praises of the college. Many years before, he had heard President Stiles exhort the

[76] *Ibid.*, 23.
[77] *Ibid.*, 24.
[78] *Loc. cit.*
[79] Joseph Story to James Kent, October 25, 1831; Edward Everett to James Kent, November 6, 1831. *Kent Papers*, Vol. VI.

students, as beloved Sons of the Muses, so to excell in humane learning as to make Yale shine forth among the other colleges even as the moon among the stars.[80] That exhortation had by no means been in vain. As Kent and his companions proceeded with their singing, Alma Mater began presently to transcend even Stiles's aspirations. She began indeed to imitate the brightness of the sun, and the classics still remained her chiefest glory:

Yet still within
With mild control
The classics keep
The Seat of Soul.

Honor to Mother Yale!
She must forever stand
Though other lights shall fail
The sunlight of our land.

Sons of that Light!
With zeal conspire,
As one unite
To raise her higher! [81]

As the voices of the old and young mingled in the measure, the echoes, wafted toward the Elysian Fields, fell, it is hoped, upon the ears of Stiles who may well have lifted his hand, very gently, for Orpheus to pause at his lyre and listen too.

The reunions at New Haven were among the principal pleasures of Chancellor Kent's last years; yet there was a tinge of sadness in them as familiar faces became gradually more infrequent with the passing seasons. It was good to visit the ancient haunts, to ascend into Connecticut Hall and view again the low beamed room [82] where the brethren of Linonia had once been entertained; it was good to sit with President Day

[80] *Address*, 39.
[81] *Kent Journal*, August 17, 1842.
[82] *Ibid.*, *cir.* Sept. 14 or 15, 1831.

upon the Commencement stage and see the "Young Sirs" coming up to receive their diplomas and degrees. All such occasions stimulated the flow of reminiscences of a joyful past growing with each year more distant and elusive. But the reminiscences of old age, though they may be happy, blend easily with the premonition of the time when remembering itself shall cease.

Nor did James Kent escape the gloom of that foreboding. He had lived to mourn his contemporaries. His friends were dying.[83] His brother and his sister were no more; [84] and he himself, weary at last, was ready to be gathered to his fathers, full of years and honors and humbly "mindful of the One Thing needful" as the elder Moss Kent had admonished him to be.[85] The end of life came slowly; though the infirmities of age, repelled long and gallantly, accumulated as the summer of 1847 began to wane.[86] In November the chancellor laid aside his books and papers, and with the sixth edition of the *Commentaries* ready for the press, admitted that his days of studying were over.[87] From his house in Union Square the rumor went abroad that he was dying. "The accounts are unfavorable," said Hone, "the lamp burns dimly, the sun is nearly set." [88]

In his library where reposed the many stately tomes of the sages of the law, James Kent lay in a deep slumber, heeding no more the subtleties of Coke, oblivious to the elegance of Blackstone, breathing fainter as the twilight of a winter Sabbath

[83] Simeon Baldwin to James Kent, August 25, 1846. *Kent Papers,* Vol. X. Baldwin observes that he and Kent are the only survivors of the class of 1781.

[84] Kent's sister, Hannah Platt, died in 1846. James Kent to William Kent, December 23, 1846, *ibid.* Moss Kent, Jr., died June 1, 1838. *Kent Journal* (No. 13). Kent settled his brother's estate, *loc. cit.* Tour to Plattsburgh, 1838.

[85] Kent died in full communion with the Episcopal Church: James Kent to Rev. Mr. Samuel Miller, September 6, 1847 and to Simeon Baldwin, September 18, 1847. *Kent Papers,* Vol. XI.

[86] James Kent to William Kent, February 28, 1847 and May 21, 1847. *Ibid.* Philip Hone, *Diary,* II, 818.

[87] *Op. cit.,* II, 827.

[88] *Loc. cit.*

slowly deepened into evening. His wife was with him; his children waited by his side. Ere the evening was far advanced, the faint breathing ceased quietly [89] and the great chancellor had gone forth to join the company of the sages whose tomes were ranged around him on the lofty shelves.

[89] Sunday, December 12, 1847, at half-past eight o'clock in the evening, in the eighty-fifth year of his age. *Vide* Hone's *Diary,* II, 828–829. Kent was buried with pomp, *ibid.,* 830 in New York City. His body was subsequently taken up and removed to St. Luke's churchyard at Matteawan (now Beacon) in Dutchess County where his wife was laid beside him. Here on a marble slab the following inscription:

In
Memory of
James Kent
Chief Justice of the Supreme Court
Chancellor of the State of New York
Born July 31, 1763
Died Dec. 12, 1847

---

and
Elizabeth Bailey
his wife
Born Sept. 10, 1768
Died June 19, 1851

Bibliography

I. *Manuscript Sources*

A. Collections of Private Papers

Daggett Papers, Vol. I:—Yale University Library

Everett Papers, Letter Books—Vols. 13–16, 57–82 (extending from 1825–1847):—Massachusetts Historical Society

Herrick Papers:—Yale University Library

Kent Papers, Vols. I–XI:—Library of Congress

(These consist mostly of letters written between 1777 and 1847 and they constitute with the Law Reports and Kent Journals the principal source for Kent's affairs.)

Kent Journals, Vols. I–XIV:—Library of Congress

(These consist mostly of accounts of circuits, tours and excursions. They extend from 1797 to 1847.)

Livingston Papers: (Gilbert Livingston) 7 Packets (extending from 1745–1801):—New York Public Library

Pickering Papers: Memoranda, Vol. I:—
Massachusetts Historical Society

———: *Letters,* 1825–1829:—Massachusetts Historical Society

Story Papers; 1808–1845:—Massachusetts Historical Society

Sumner Papers; Boxes 57, 59, 60, 61:—Harvard College Library

Washburn Papers, Vol. VI:—Massachusetts Historical Society

Winthrop Papers, Vol. XXXIII:—Massachusetts Historical Society

B. Miscellaneous Manuscripts

Kent MSS. There are scattered fragments of these in the New York Public Library, the Library of Kent Hall, Columbia University, the Yale University Library and the Library of Congress. Here and there among them is an interesting and valuable item:

1. The New York Public Library has the MS. book in which is written in Kent's own hand his opinion in the Croswell case, together with an account of the circumstances and outcome of that litigation. The letters of Kent and Radcliffe to the legislature on

the subject of their task in revising the New York statutes are here, as is also Kent's letter to Governor Yates, expressing his intention of remaining chancellor until his sixtieth birthday. There are a few other items; but they are of negligible interest.

2. Kent Hall, Columbia University has a few letters of minor importance, a photostat copy of an opinion in a trust case, and two MS. lectures dealing with the real actions. Here, too, is a large part of Kent's law library.

3. The Yale University Library contains a few items, but these are mostly included in the *Herrick* and *Daggett* Papers. Aside from these are the original of Kent's notes on his Yale classmates, and the *Records of the Linonian Society,* 1768–1790, which illustrate his connection with that society by numerous entries in his own hand.

4. The Library of Congress, besides the *Kent Papers* and the *Kent Journals* has several diplomas of Kent, and also the *Account Book of Livingston and Kent* which is valuable as illustrating his early professional practice.

II. *Printed Sources Other than Newspapers and Law Journals*

Bond, C. T. Proceedings of the Maryland Court of Appeals, 1695–1729. Washington, D.C., 1933.

Broadhead, J. R., and E. B. O'Callaghan. Documents Relative to the Colonial History of the State of New York, Vol. VIII. Albany, 1857.

Caines, George. New York Term Reports of Cases Argued and Determined in the Supreme Court of that State. 3 vols. New York, 1804.

Carter, N. H., W. L. Stone, and M. T. C. Gould. Reports of the Proceedings and Debates of the Convention of 1821. Albany, 1821.

Chase, E. P. Our Revolutionary Forefathers: the Letters of François, Marquis de Barbé-Marbois During His Residence in the United States, 1779–1785. New York, 1929.

Clap, Thomas. Annals or History of Yale College in New Haven in the Colony of Connecticut from the First Founding Thereof in the Year 1700 to the Year 1766. New Haven, 1766.

Clarke, John. Corderii Colloquiorum Centuria Selecta. 20th edition. Boston, 1720.

Clarke, L. H. Reports of the Debates and Proceedings of the Convention of the State of New York. New York, 1821.

Collegii Yalensis Statuta—Novo-Portu MDCCLIX.

Dexter, F. B. The Literary Diary of Ezra Stiles. 3 vols. New York, 1901.

Duer, John. A Discourse on the Life, Character and Public Services of James Kent, Late Chancellor of the State of New York, delivered before the bench and bar of the City and State of New York (April 12, 1848). New York, 1848.

Fitzpatrick, J. C. Autobiography of Martin Van Buren. Washington, 1920.

Hastings, H. The Public Papers of Daniel D. Tompkins (Military). 3 vols. New York and Albany, 1898.

Hawley, Joseph (to Ephraim Wright, April 16, 1782). *American Historical Review*, XXXVI, 776–778.

Johnson, William. Reports of Cases Adjudged in the Supreme Court of Judicature of the State of New York, January, 1799–January, 1803. 3 vols. (with Shepard's notes). New York, 1895.

———. Reports of Cases Argued and Determined in the Supreme Court of Judicature and in the Court for the Trial of Impeachments and the Correction of Errors in the State of New York, 1806–1823. 20 vols. Philadelphia, 1807 (Vol. I in 1807).

———. Reports of Cases Adjudged in the Court of Chancery of New York. 7 vols., S. Rapalje. Albany, 1904 (1st vol. published 1816), 2nd edition.

Kent, James. An Address Delivered to the Law Association of New York City, October 21, 1836, *vide et* 16 American Jurist 471.

———. An Address Delivered at New Haven before the Phi Beta Kappa Society, September 13, 1831. New Haven, 1831.

———. An Anniversary Discourse Delivered before the New York Historical Society, December 6, 1828.
Collections of New York Historical Society Series, Series II, Vol. I.

———. A Course of Reading Presented to the Mercantile Library Association of New York City, March 10, 1840.

Kent, James. An Introductory Lecture to a Course of Law Lectures Delivered at Columbia College, *Columbia Law Review*, III, 1.

———. Commentaries on American Law, 4 vols., 11th edition. George F. Comstock, Boston, 1867.

———. Commentaries on American Law, 4 vols., 12th edition. Oliver W. Holmes. Boston, 1873.

———. Commentaries on American Law, 4 vols., 14th edition. John M. Gould. Boston, 1896.

——— (to William E. Channing, April 18, 1842, *American Historical Review*, XXXVII, 520–521).

———. Vindication of the Treaty of Amity, Commerce and Navigation with Great Britain—with Noah Webster—Nos. 6 and 7 by Kent—New York, 1795.

Kent, William. Memoirs and Letters of James Kent. Boston, 1898.

Lodge, H. C. The Federalist, 2 vols. New York, 1888.

Morris, R. B. Select Cases of the Mayor's Court of New York City, 1674–1784. Washington, D.C., 1935.

Nevins, Allen. The Diary of John Quincy Adams, 1794–1845. New York, 1928.

———. The Diary of Philip Hone, 1828–1851, 2 vols. New York, 1927.

New York. Constitutions of the State of New York, 1777 and 1821, printed in Carter's Convention.

———. Journal of the Assembly of the State of New York, January, 1791 to March, 1791 and November, 1796.

———. Laws of the State of New York, Vols. I–III. Albany, 1886.

New York Historical Society. The Diary of William Dunlap, 1766–1839. Collections of New York Historical Society. New York, 1930.

Schneider, H. and C., Samuel Johnson, His Career and Writings, 4 vols. New York, 1929.

Stiles, Ezra. Oratio Inauguralis. Hartford, 1778.

Story, W. W. Life and Letters of Joseph Story, 2 vols. Boston, 1851.

Street, A. B. The Council of Revision of the State of New York. Albany, 1859.

Van Norden and Kent (publishers). Proceedings of the Bar of the

City of New York on the Occasion of the Death of Chancellor Kent, December 14, 1847. New York, 1847.
Van Tyne, C. H. The Letters of Daniel Webster, New York, 1902.

III. *Contemporary Law Journals*

Several law journals had a brief existence during the time of Chancellor Kent. One of the longer-lived was the *American Jurist* which was started in 1829. For a list of other contemporary law journals, *vide American Jurist,* XXIII, 135 *et seq.* The list, in chronological order, is as follows:

The Law Journal (sometimes called *Hall's American Law Journal,* published by Hall in Baltimore from 1808–1821, and then succeeded by the *Journal of Jurisprudence* which had but a very brief existence.)
The Carolina Law Repository, published in North Carolina, 1813.
The United States Law Journal, 1822–1826.
Griffith's Law Register, 1822 (only two volumes appeared).
The Law Intelligencer, J. K. Angell, Providence, Rhode Island, 1829–1832.
Journal of Law, published at Philadelphia, 1830.
The Jurisprudent, Boston, 1830.
The Carolina Law Journal, 1830.
The Law Reporter, published by Chandler of the Suffolk County Bar, Boston, Massachusetts, 1838, and sharing with *The American Jurist* the honors of longevity. *The American Jurist, loc. cit.,* says that in 1840 only two of these journals remained in existence, viz., the *American Jurist,* and the *Law Reporter.*

Other journals were started in the 1840's, and to the list above mentioned, *Law Reporter,* VII, 65 *et seq.* adds the following:

The American Themis. New York, 1844.
The South Western Law Journal and Reporter, ed. M. A. Haynes, Nashville, Tennessee.
The Western Law Journal, T. Walker. Cincinnati, Ohio.
The American Law Magazine, Philadelphia, 1845.
The New York Legal Observer, ed. Samuel Owen. New York, 1842.
The Pennsylvania Law Journal, ed. H. E. Wallace. Philadelphia. (*Cir.* the same time.)

Most of these also seem to have been ephemeral.

The Law Reporter, however, beginning at Boston in 1838, continued through twenty-seven volumes.

The American Jurist exceeded this record, in January, 1843, having attained its twenty-eighth volume, and it continued for some time thereafter, though it has not been consulted after that date.

Of English Law Journals, *The (London) Law Magazine or Quarterly Review of Jurisprudence* has been cursorily examined from volume I which appeared in London in 1828, through to Volume XXX.

The *Law Reporter*, the *American Jurist* and the *London Law Magazine* are to be found in the library of the Harvard Law School, as also are other journals listed in *American Jurist*, XXIII, 135 *et seq.*, *vide supra.*

The following citations in the law journals have been found pertinent:

American Jurist

"An Address Delivered Before the Members of the Suffolk Bar at their Anniversary," September 4, 1821. Joseph Story. *American Jurist*, I, 22 *et seq.*

"An Address Delivered Before the Law Association of the City of New York," October 21, 1836. James Kent. *American Jurist*, XVI, 471 *et seq.*

"American Reports and Reporters," a valuable account of the development of the reporting of law causes in the United States at the end of the eighteenth and the beginning of the nineteenth century. *American Jurist*, XXII, 108 *et seq.*

"English Equity in America," being a review of Story on equity pleading as printed in the *London Law Magazine*, *vide infra. American Jurist*, XXII, 232 *et seq.*

Law Reporter

A biographical sketch of Chancellor Kent, *Law Reporter*, I, 1 *et seq.* Opinions of Chancellor Kent after retirement on questions of marine insurance law and the law of corporations, *Law Reporter*, I, 57 and *Law Reporter*, II, 257.

"Address of the New York Bar to Chancellor Kent, on the occasion of his Eightieth Birthday," July 31, 1843. *Law Reporter*, VI, 293.

"The Spirit of Misrule," adopting the same desponding tone as Kent as to the decline of the country in the Jacksonian era. *Law Reporter* VII, 209.

For a note on the decline of the bar, *vide Law Reporter*, VI, 286 *et seq.*

An obituary notice of Chancellor Kent. *Law Reporter*, X, 429.

The London Law Magazine

"Law Reform in America," an article which praises Chancellor Kent and his contributions to American Law. *London Law Magazine*, VI, 130 *et seq.*

"On Changes Undergone by the Law of Real Property in America," *London Law Magazine*, VI, 153 *et seq.*

"English Equity in America," a review of Story on equity pleading, reprinted in the *American Jurist, vide supra. London Law Magazine*, XXI, 233 *et seq.*

"Commentaries on Equity Jurisprudence as Administered in England and America," a review of Story on equity jurisprudence. *London Law Magazine*, XXII, 61 *et seq.*

Other Journals

"Restrictions upon State Power in Relation to Private Property," citing with approbation Gardner v. Trustees of the Village of Newburgh, *United States Law Intelligencer and Review*, I, 7, 26, 59, 90.

"Equity Jurisprudence in the State of New York," a criticism of the radicals' attack on the New York judiciary, and a laudatory account of Kent's career as chancellor, *United States Law Journal and Civilian Magazine*, I, 35 *et seq.*

And *vide et, ibid.* for a laudatory account of Chancellor Sanford, and his repudiation in Donovan v. Finn of the doctrine in Bayard v. Hoffman, *ibid.*, II, 286 *et seq.*

IV. *Newspapers*

Newspapers have not proved valuable as a source for Chancellor Kent's career. The reason seems to be that the proceedings of the state judiciary were somewhat too prosaic and technical to excite the interest of journalists. The *Ebling Collection* in the Widener Library, Harvard University, has been examined, for the decade 1791 to 1801; and from *cir.* 1800 to 1821 the collections of the American Antiquarian Society have been examined. These years cover most of the period when Kent was in public life. The occasional references in the text to newspaper material are drawn from the collections above mentioned, and they include the following:

The Albany Centinel	August 2, 1799
	July 4, 1800
	June 30, 1801
	August 11, 1801
The Albany Gazette	October 28, 1796
	June 19, 1800
The Albany Register	April 29, 1796
	June 20, 1796
	November 7, 1821
The Boston Evening Gazette	August 30, 1823
The Boston Gazette and Country Journal	June 27, 1791
The Diary or Loudon's Register (New York)	April 2, 1792
The New York Daily Advertiser	March 10, 1791
	March 26, 1791
	October 12, 1791
	November 17, 1791
	January 3, 1793
	January 8, 1793
The New York Evening Post	February 26, 1814
The New York Gazette and General Advertiser	April 5, 1797
The New York Herald	November 2, 1814
The New York Mercantile Advertiser	March 29, 1797

V. *Secondary Works*

Adams, H. *History of the United States*, Vol. I. New York, 1889–1891.

Alden, C. (*cum al.*). *Legal and Judicial History of New York*, 3 Vols. New York, 1911.

Alexander, D. S. *A Political History of the State of New York*, 3 Vols. New York, 1906.

Bailey, J. M. *History of Danbury, Connecticut*, 1684–1896. New York, 1896.

Bassett, J. S. *A Short History of the United States*, 3 Vols. New York, 1929.

Beard, C. A. *An Economic Interpretation of the Constitution of the United States*. New York, 1913.

———. *The Economic Origins of the Jeffersonian Democracy*. New York, 1915.

———. *The Economic Basis of Politics*. New York, 1922.

Beveridge, A. J. *The Life of John Marshall*, 4 Vols. Boston, 1916.

Blackstone, Sir William. *Commentaries on the Laws of England* (with Christian's Notes), 4 Vols. Portland, 1807.

Bobbé, D. *De Witt Clinton*. New York, 1933.

Brooks, J. W. *History of the Common Pleas of the City and County of New York*. New York, 1896.

Browne, Irving. *Short Studies of Great Lawyers*. Albany, 1878.

Burdick, C. K. *Law of the American Constitution*. New York, 1922.

Carson, H. L. (*et al.*). *Lectures on Legal Topics*. New York, 1921–1922.

Channing, E. *History of the United States*, Vol. IV. New York, 1909–1925.

Commons, J. R. *History of Labor in the United States*, 2 Vols. New York, 1918.

Corwin, E. S. *John Marshall and the Constitution*. New Haven, 1919.

———. *The Twilight of the Supreme Court*. New Haven, 1934.

Dexter, F. B. *A Selection from the Miscellaneous Historical Papers of Fifty Years*. New Haven, 1918.

Dexter, F. B. *Biographical Sketches of the Graduates of Yale College*, 3 Vols. New York, 1885–1903.

———. *Sketch of the History of Yale University*. New York, 1887.

Fish, C. R. *The Rise of the Common Man*. New York, 1927.

Fiske, J. *The Critical Period of American History*. Boston, 1888.

Flick, A. C. (editor). *History of the State of New York*. Vol. III. Columbia University Press, 1933.

Fox, D. R. *The Decline of Aristocracy in the Politics of New York*. New York, 1919.

Gillett, E. H. *History of the Presbyterian Church in the United States*. 2 Vols. Philadelphia, 1864.

Goodwin, M. W. (*et al.*). *Historic New York*. New York, 1898.

Gunn, Alexander. *Memoirs of the Reverend John H. Livingstone*. New York, 1829.

Hammond, J. D. *History of Political Parties in the State of New York*, 2 Vols. Cooperstown, 1846.

Harding, S. B. *The Contest Over the Ratification of the Federal Constitution in the State of Massachusetts*. New York, 1896.

Hasbrouck, Frank. *The History of Dutchess County New York*. Poughkeepsie, 1909.

Hicks, F. C. *Men and Books Famous in the Law*. Rochester, 1921.

Higgins, R. L. *The Expansion of New York, with Especial Reference to the Eighteenth Century*. Columbus, 1931.

Janvier, T. A. *In Old New York*. New York, 1894.

Lincoln, C. Z. *The Constitutional History of New York*, 5 Vols. Rochester, 1906.

Matthews, B. (*cum al.*). *A History of Columbia University*, 1754–1904. New York, 1904.

McAdam, D. (editor *cum al.*). *History of the Bench and Bar of New York*, 2 Vols. New York, 1897.

Morris, R. B. *Studies in the History of American Law*. Columbia University Press, 1930.

Platt, E. *History of Poughkeepsie from the Earliest Settlements*, 1683–1905. Poughkeepsie, 1905.

Plucknett, T. F. T. *A Concise History of the Common Law*. Rochester, 1929.

Pollock, Sir F. and F. W. Maitland. *History of English Law Before the Time of Edward I*, 2 Vols. Cambridge, 1895.

Pound, R. *The Spirit of the Common Law*. Boston, 1921.

Russel, E. B. *The Review of American Colonial Legislation by the King in Council.* New York, 1915.

Spaulding, E. W. *New York in the Critical Period: 1783–1789.* New York, 1932.

Sprague, W. B. *Annals of the American Pulpit,* 9 Vols. New York, 1857.

Wallace, J. W. *An Old Philadelphian: Colonel William Bradford, the Patriot Printer.*

Warren, C. *The Supreme Court in United States History,* 3 Vols. Boston, 1922.

———. *History of the Harvard Law School.* New York, 1908.

———. *A History of the American Bar.* Boston, 1911.

VI. *Articles, Pamphlets, etc.*

Cassaday, J. B. "James Kent and Joseph Story" *Yale Law Journal,* XII, 196.

Cox, Macgrane "Chancellor Kent at Yale" *Yale Law Journal,* XVII, 311, 553.

Dillon, J. F. "Chancellor Kent: Concerning the Erection of a Monument to his Memory" *Columbia Law Review,* III, 256.

Elliott, C. B. "An American Chancellor" *American Law Review,* XXXVII, 231.

Fox, D. R. "James Kent in Politics" *Columbia Alumni News,* XIV, 367–368.

Goebel, J. "King's Law and Local Custom in Seventeenth Century New England" *Columbia Law Review,* XXXI, 416.

Genzmer, G. H. "Kunze, John C." *Dictionary of American Biography,* Vol. X, 512–513.

Hall, C. R. "Samuel Latham Mitchill, A Queen's County Polymath" *New York History,* Vol. XIV, No. 2.

Hicks, F. C. "A Man of Law as a Man of Letters" *New York Times Book Review,* May 27, 1923.

———. "James Kent" *Dictionary of American Biography,* Vol. X, 344–347.

———. "Kent's Commentaries" *Columbia Alumni News,* XIV, 369–370.

Hiscock, F. H. "Speech in Acceptance of the Kent Memorial Tablet in the Court of Appeals" *American Bar Association Journal,* X, 851.

Hughes, C. E. "James Kent: A Master Builder of Legal Institutions" *American Bar Association Journal,* IX, 353.

Latting, J. G. "Notes for a Memoir of Chancellor Kent" *New York Genealogical and Biographical Record,* Vol. IV, 83.

Morris, R. B. "Records of the Suffolk County Court, 1671–1680" (Review) *American Historical Review,* XL, 135–137.

Nelles, W. "Towards Legal Understanding" *Columbia Law Review,* XXXIV, 1050.

Pelletreau, W. S. "The Birth Place of Chancellor Kent" *Magazine of American History,* Vol. XVII.

Plucknett, T. F. T. "The Laws and Liberties of Massachusetts" (Review) *New England Quarterly,* III, 157.

Powell, T. R. "Kent's Contribution to Constitutional Law" *Columbia Alumni News,* XIV, 372–374.

Proctor, L. B. "The Trials and Triumphs of a Young Lawyer—Incidents in the Career of a Great American Jurist" Albany, 1888.

Reynolds, H. W. "James Kent Sometime of Poughkeepsie" *The Year Book of the Dutchess County Historical Society,* 1923.

———. "Bartholomew Crannel" *ibid.* 1922.

Sandifer, D. V. "William Johnson" *Dictionary of American Biography,* Vol. X, 128.

Schmidt, G. P. "Cross Currents in American Colleges," *American Historical Review,* XLII, 46.

Thomas, M. H. "John Kemp" *Dictionary of American Biography,* Vol. X., 319–320 (and numerous other articles in the same work).

Table of Cases Cited

i. *Caines's Reports*

Cortelyou v. Lansing 2 Caines' Cases in Error 200
Furman v. Haskin 2 Caines 369
Jackson v. Richards 2 Caines 343
Williams v. Smith 2 Caines 1

ii. *Johnson's Cases*

Abbot v. Sebor 3 Johns. Cases 39

Brant v. Gelston 2 Johns. Cases 384
Conroy v. Warren 3 Johns. Cases 259
Duguet v. Rhinelander 1 Johns. Cases 360
——————— 2 Johns. Cases 476
Goix v. Low 1 Johns. Cases 341
——————— 2 Johns. Cases 480
Holmes v. United Insurance Company 2 Johns. Cases 329
Jackson v. Lunn 3 Johns. Cases 109
Jackson v. New York Insurance Company 2 Johns. Cases 191
Jackson v. Rogers 1 Johns. Cases 34
Jackson v. Sisson 2 Johns. Cases 321
Johnson v. Bloodgood 1 Johns. Cases 51
Ludlow v. Dale 1 Johns. Cases 16
People v. Croswell 3 Johns. Cases 362

iii. *Johnson's Reports*

Anderson v. Roberts 18 Johns. Rep. 513
Consequa v. Fanning 17 Johns. Rep. 511
Craig v. United Insurance Company 6 Johns. Rep. 255
Dash v. Van Kleeck 7 Johns. Rep. 477
Dunnet v. Tomhagen 3 Johns. Rep. 156
Emans v. Turnbull 2 Johns. Rep. 314
Gibbons v. Ogden 17 Johns. Rep. 488
Lansing v. Gaine and Ten Eyck 2 Johns. Rep. 302
Livingston v. Van Ingen 9 Johns. Rep. 572
Ludlow v. Bowne and Eddy 1 Johns. Rep. 1
Methodist Episcopal Church v. Jaques 17 Johns. Rep. 548
Mumford v. Commercial Insurance Company 5 Johns. Rep. 266
Noble v. Smith 2 Johns. Rep. 52
People v. Ruggles 8 Johns. Rep. 290
Rhinelander v. Barrow 17 Johns. Rep. 538
Robinson v. Marine Insurance Company 2 Johns. Rep. 325
Snider and Van Vechten v. Croy 2 Johns. Rep. 228
Thorne and Thorne v. Deas 4 Johns. Rep. 97
Verplanck v. Sterry 12 Johns. Rep. 556
Wheelright v. Depeyster 1 Johns. Rep. 470
in re J. V. N. Yates 4 Johns. Rep. 314

Yates v. Lansing 5 Johns. Rep. 282
Yates v. People 6 Johns. Rep. 422

iv. *Johnson's Chancery Reports*

Attorney-General v. Utica Insurance Company 2 Johns. Ch. 388
in re James Barker 2 Johns. Ch. 232
Bayard v. Hoffman 4 Johns. Ch. 450
Belknap v. Belknap 2 Johns. Ch. 463
Berry v. Mutual Insurance Company 2 Johns. Ch. 608
Brasher v. Van Cortlandt 2 Johns. Ch. 246
Codd v. Codd 2 Johns. Ch. 143
Connecticut v. Jackson 1 Johns. Ch. 13
Consequa v. Fanning 3 Johns. Ch. 587
Croton Turnpike Road Company v. Ryder 1 Johns. Ch. 610
Cumberland v. Codrington 3 Johns. Ch. 229
Davoue v. Fanning 2 Johns. Ch. 252
Fanning v. Dunham 5 Johns. Ch. 122
Gardner v. Newburgh 2 Johns. Ch. 162
Green v. Winter 1 Johns. Ch. 27
Hart v. Ten Eyck 2 Johns. Ch. 62
Hicks v. Hotchkiss 7 Johns. Ch. 307
Hine v. Handy 1 Johns. Ch. 5
Holmes v. Remsen 2 Johns. Ch. 460
Jerome v. Ross 7 Johns. Ch. 315
Livingston v. Newkirk 3 Johns. Ch. 319
Livingston v. Ogden and Gibbons 4 Johns. Ch. 48
Malin v. Malin 2 Johns. Ch. 238
Manning v. Manning 1 Johns. Ch. 527
Methodist Episcopal Church v. Jaques 3 Johns. Ch. 77
Murray v. Ballou 1 Johns. Ch. 565
Newburgh Turnpike Company v. Miller 5 Johns. Ch. 101
North River Steamboat Company v. Hoffman 5 Johns. Ch. 299
Ogden v. Gibbons 4 Johns. Ch. 150
Prior v. Rhinelander 3 Johns. Ch. 120
Reade v. Livingston 3 Johns. Ch. 495
Riggs v. Murray 3 Johns. Ch. 163
Roberts & Boyd v. Anderson 3 Johns. Ch. 371

Schieffelin v. Stewart 1 Johns. Ch. 620
Smith v. Smith 4 Johns. Ch. 281
Sterry v. Arden 1 Johns. Ch. 266
Thompson v. Berry 3 Johns. Ch. 399
Titus v. Neilson 5 Johns. Ch. 453
in re Wendell 1 Johns. Ch. 599
Williamson v. Dale 3 Johns. Ch. 292

v. *Miscellaneous Reports*

(a) The Supreme Court of the United States

Briscoe v. Bank of Kentucky 11 Peters 257
Charles River Bridge Co. v. Warren Bridge Co. 11 Peters 420
Craig v. Missouri 4 Peters 410
Dartmouth College v. Woodward 4 Wheaton 518
Fletcher v. Peck 6 Cranch 87
Gibbons v. Ogden 9 Wheaton 1
Marbury v. Madison 1 Cranch 137
McCulloch v. Maryland 4 Wheaton 316
Sturges v. Crowninshield 4 Wheaton 122
Worcester v. Georgia 6 Peters 515

(b) Other State Reports

Auburn & Cato Plank Road Company v. Douglass 9 New York 444
Donavan v. Finn 1 Hopk. Ch. 59
Enfield Toll Bridge Co. v. Hartford, New Haven R.R. 17 Conn. 454
Harper v. Clayton 84 Maryland 346
Jackson v. Town 4 Cow. 599
Mohawk Bridge Co. v. Utica & Schenectady R.R. 6 Paige Ch. 554
Oswego Falls Bridge Co. v. Fish 1 Barber Ch. 547
Thompson v. N.Y. & Harlem R.R. 3 Sandford Ch. 625
Tuckahoe Canal Co. v. Tuckahoe R.R. 11 Leigh 42

Index

INDEX

(1)